American Inside Out Evolution

Student's Book | Advanced

SUE KAY
VAUGHAN JONES
AMANDA JEFFRIES
TANIA BASTOW
CERI JONES

macmillan education

Contents

Walkthrough

SPEAKING
You are encouraged to relate the topics to your own life, views, and feelings.

READING
Contemporary reading texts have been adapted and graded to suit the level. They have been selected not only for their language content but also for their interest and appropriacy. The texts are supported by recordings.

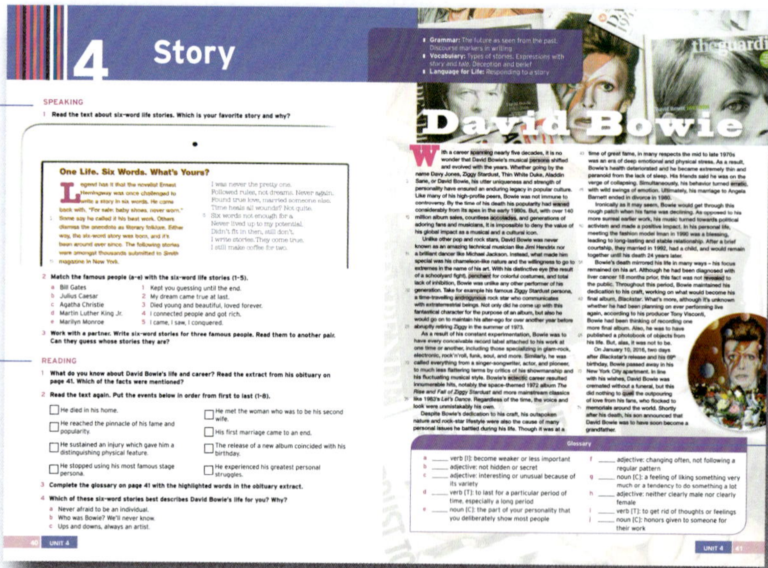

Glossaries give simple definitions for more challenging words. This minimizes interruptions and helps you read more fluently.

GRAMMAR
- Here you will explore new grammatical structures that have been contextualized in the reading / listening sections. You will focus on the way language works.
- A brief summary of the grammar point is provided in the box.
- Language is explored in realistic and meaningful practice exercises.
- You will use target language in controlled and personalized practice.

VOCABULARY
- Vocabulary is presented in context.
- Practice acitivities will help expand your knowledge of selective lexical items and will give you the opportunity to use vocabulary in meaningful exchanges.

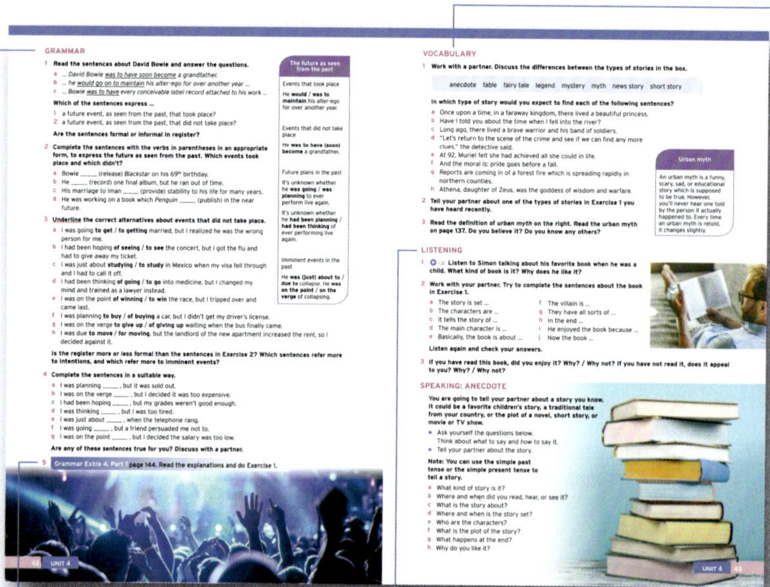

The Grammar Extra pages at the back of the Student's Book extend explanations and provide further practice.

LISTENING
The listenings include texts specially written for language learning – dialogues, conversations and monologues. They were carefully designed to develop real-life listening skills.

LANGUAGE FOR LIFE

The Language for Life section gives you a portable toolkit of functional language. Here, you notice how language is more than just form. You will see language in fun, engaging social situations.

VOCABULARY EXTRA

The Vocabulary Extra pages at the end of every unit recycle the key vocabulary items taught in the unit. This provides an activated wordlist and a useful bank of vocabulary.

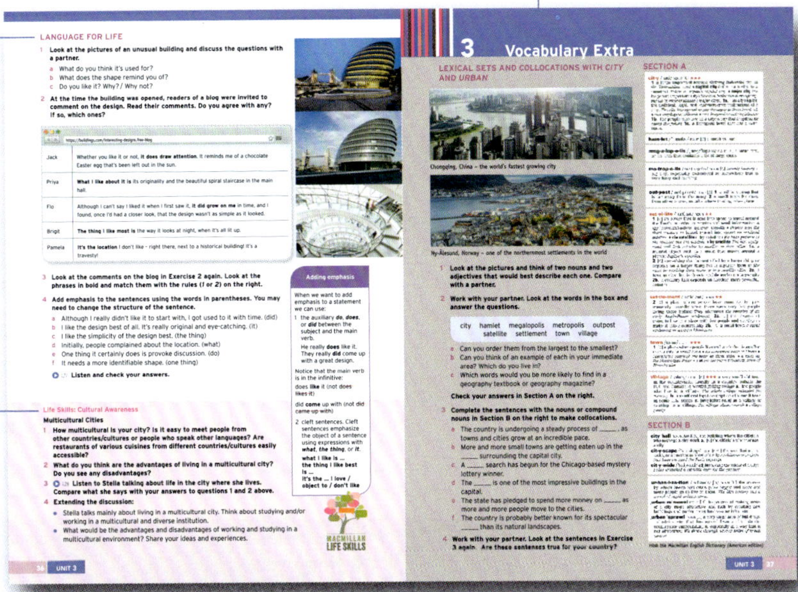

LIFE SKILLS

Developing life skills alongside language skills is an essential requirement to meet the demands of the contemporary world.

American Inside Out Evolution has a Life Skills section in every unit. Life Skills presents activities that require you to reflect on and discuss the skills necessary for social and work situations in today's world.

REVIEW

There are Review units in the Student's Book. They review the new structures and vocabulary taught in the previous teaching units.

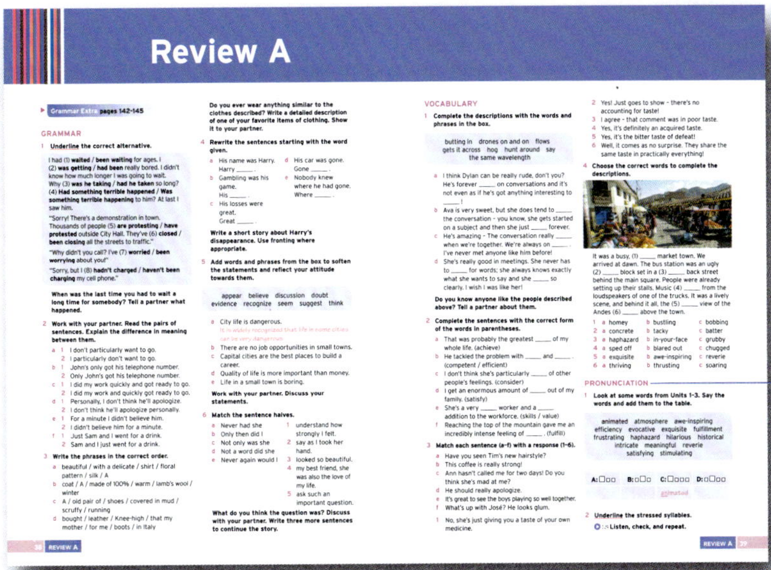

PRONUNCIATION

Pronunciation work on particular areas of sound, stress, and intonation is integrated into every unit.

3 Vocabulary Extra

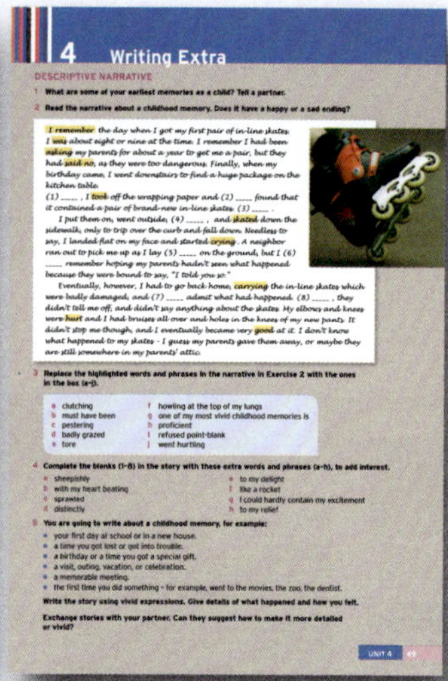

4 Writing Extra

The Vocabulary Extra pages alternate with the Writing Extra pages at the end of each unit. The Writing Extra pages develop important writing skills in a variety of genres.

The Vocabulary Extra pages explore key lexical areas such as collocations, metaphor, phrasal verbs, etc. They provide detailed practice activities and help promote useful dictionary skills.

GRAMMAR EXTRA

The Grammar Extra pages at the back of the Student's Book provide extended explanations and further practice.

Additional Material

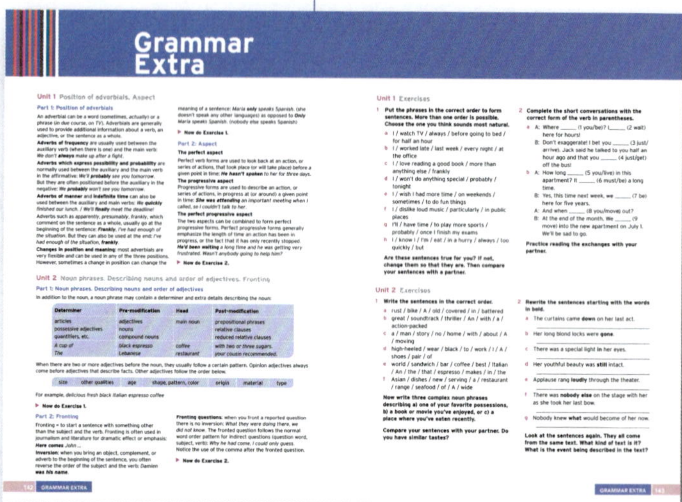

Grammar Extra

The section Additional Material includes pairwork activities as well as answers to quizzes and activities from the units.

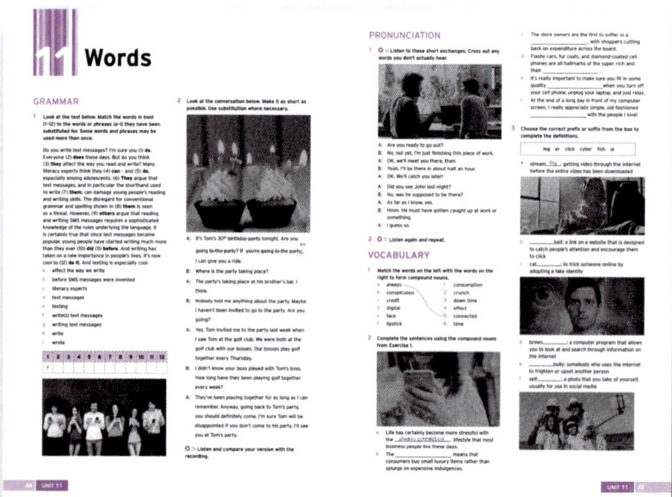

11 Words

The Workbook provides a review of all the main points in the Student's Book, plus extra listening practice, pronunciation work, and a writing program.

Student's Components

Student's Book with access code to Digital Student's Book

Workbook with access code to Digital Workbook

1 Conversation

SPEAKING & VOCABULARY

a

b

c

1 **Work with a partner. Look at the pictures (a–c) and discuss the questions.**

- a Who do you think the people in the pictures are? Where do you think they are? How do you think they know each other?
- b What do you think they're talking about?

2 **In the box there are some adjectives which are commonly used to describe conversations. Categorize the adjectives under the headings in the table. Use a dictionary if necessary.**

animated bizarre ~~boring~~ frustrating hilarious in-depth intense intimate lengthy meaningful one-sided pointless predictable stimulating

Positive	Negative	Neutral
	boring	

Add one or two more adjectives under each heading. Compare with your partner.

Look at the pictures in Exercise 1 again. Which adjectives would you use to describe each conversation?

3 **Work with your partner. Answer the questions.**

- a Which of the conversations below have you had recently in your own language?
  - a quick word in passing with a friend or co-worker
  - a brief exchange with a complete stranger
  - a long heart-to-heart with a close friend or family member
  - a hurried exchange of text messages
  - an online chat
- b What did you talk about? Choose an adjective from Exercise 2 to describe the conversations.

- **Grammar:** Position of adverbials. Aspect
- **Vocabulary:** Describing conversation styles. Conversation collocations. Word building
- **Language for Life:** Opening conversations

LISTENING & VOCABULARY

1 Work in small groups. Discuss the questions.

a What makes a conversation enjoyable?
b What makes a conversation frustrating?
c What's your definition of a good conversationalist?

Compare your answers with the rest of the class.

2 1.02-1.07 **Listen to six people, Joanna, Mike, Phil, Jessica, Brianna, and Rafael, answering one of the questions in Exercise 1. As you listen, decide which question (*a*, *b*, or *c*) each person is answering.**

Did the people interviewed have similar opinions to those expressed by your class?

3 Complete the extracts from the speakers' answers in Exercise 2. Use the words and collocations in the box.

butt in | drones on and on | flows | get across | hog | hunt around | on the same wavelength | something to say

a It helps if there aren't some people who _____ the conversation all the time.
b You need a conversation that _____ .
c It's somebody who has a point that they want to _____ during the conversation, somebody with _____ as opposed to somebody who just talks endlessly about various subjects.
d Some people don't care about whose turn it is to talk, so they just, you know, _____ when you're in the middle of a thought.
e I really hate it when I'm with somebody who just _____ in a conversation, and who doesn't give you a chance to speak at all.
f You're _____ and you can share the same tastes or experiences.
g That's really bad, when you're having to _____ for things to say.

Listen again and check.

4 Match the definitions (1-8) with the words and collocations in Exercise 3.

1 work hard to find
2 join a conversation without being asked
3 dominate
4 an interesting point to make
5 able to understand the way the other person thinks
6 explain or communicate
7 continues in an easy, natural way
8 talks for a long time in a very boring way

5 Work with a partner. Which words and collocations from Exercise 3 do you associate with ...

1 an uncomfortable silence?
2 a conversation where one person is dominating?
3 a successful conversation?

SPEAKING

Think about the last time you had a conversation in English outside the context of your English course. Work with your partner and discuss the questions.

a Who were you talking to? Did you know them well?
b What did you talk about? How long did the conversation last?
c Were you happy with your English? Why? / Why not?
d Who did most of the talking, you or the other person/people? Why?

READING & SPEAKING

1 **Work in small groups. Look at the statements. To what extent do you agree or disagree with them? Explain why.**

- a There are certain types of people that I will never get along with.
- b It is important to take into consideration other people's feelings before speaking.
- c When working in a team, everyone needs to have the same approach.
- d Breaking the ice in a work situation is essential for good teamwork.

2 **Work with a partner. Read the descriptions of the conversational styles and discuss the questions.**

Analytical – A person with this conversation style tends to be logical and data-driven, which can make them seem distant and cold.

Functional – The functional conversation style is characterized by an interest in detail and process, and by being extremely thorough, which can be tedious.

Personal – This is the conversation style of the diplomat. This person is a listener who looks to make connections. For some they can seem touchy-feely at times.

Intuitive – The intuitive style is built around seeing the big picture. These people are comfortable outside the box. Excessive detail can cause impatience for those with this conversation style.

- a Which of the conversational styles do you think best describes you?
- b Do you think that people have one fixed conversational style or can it change?
- c Which of the words in the box do you think goes with each of the conversational styles?

punctuality creativity focus technology flexibility productivity patience precision

3 **Work with your partner. You are going to read two extracts from co-workers talking about the resolution of a work conflict. Student A: read Testimonial A. Student B: read Testimonial B. As you read make notes about ...**

- a what the nature of the conflict was.
- b how the conflict was resolved.
- c the conversational styles of the workmates.

4 **Use your notes to tell your partner about your extract.**

Have you ever had a similar conflict with a workmate or classmate?

Testimonial A: Travis on working with June

"June used to drive me crazy. We'd be starting on the initial phase of a project, just brainstorming and checking the team's chemistry. I would throw around some ideas on our marketing approach and June would cling on to just one of them. June, I know now, has a tendency to look at fine details. She likes to probe, ask questions, and think about consequences in a very linear and logical way. Instead of hearing out the group, she was immediately asking questions for which nobody had answers yet. For June, everything had to be documented, annotated, and justified before we even got to thinking about the problem, and she was so dry about it that a number of the team members found it discouraging. The whole thing felt like putting the cart before the horse.

Over the course of the workshops, we were able to come up with strategies, and we became more aware of the purpose of the team meetings. So if a meeting was specifically for presenting proposals and brainstorming ideas, we wouldn't get caught up in analysis-paralysis or try to assess the specific strengths and weaknesses of a proposal. On the other hand, a planning meeting was not the time for introducing radically different ideas but rather ironing out the logistical problems of implementation.

In the end, I came to have a greater appreciation for June's way of communicating, even if it still isn't 100% comfortable or natural to me. I admire her persistence and attention to detail and her dedication. All of her questions can still distract me on occasion, but I recognize that it is crucial to have someone with her qualities, especially when it comes to the operationalization of projects. Nowadays, my initial impression of June being distant and cold has given way to an appreciation for her ability to identify inconsistencies and shortcomings."

VOCABULARY

1 **Complete the glossary with the highlighted words from the extracts.**

Glossary

a profitable adjective: beneficial, useful or giving financial gain
b ______ noun [U]: the effectiveness of productive effort
c ______ adverb [U]: in a way that is exact and clear
d ______ verb [T]: to evaluate or estimate the nature, ability, or quality of
e ______ noun [C]: a plan of action or policy designed to achieve a major or overall aim
f ______ adjective: favorable, helpful

2 **Complete the table with the noun, verb, adjective, and adverb forms for your answers in Exercise 1.**

Noun	Verb	Adjective	Adverb
profit / profitability	profit	profitable	profitably

3 **Complete the sentences with words from the table in Exercise 2.**

a We need to find a way to increase productivity at the company.
b To lead a better life, it is important to ______ one's diet and exercise regimen.
c One thing that gave me tremendous satisfaction was seeing my house built to my exact ______.
d One key to a ______ business is to have employees who share your vision.
e Unrelenting dedication to one's craft is a ______ advantage over competitors.

Testimonial B: June on working with Travis

When I first met Travis, he seemed confused, always jumping from one idea to another. He was never able to talk about any of his ideas in detail. It was completely impractical which led to wasting a lot of time on jabber without discussing assignments, actions, and deadlines. I also thought he often let his feelings get in the way. When I offered what I thought was feedback and constructive criticism, it almost felt like he took it as a personal attack, or that my suggestions were somehow off point.

When the company came up with the team communication workshops, it sounded like another waste of time to me. I'll admit that I initially resisted the idea, but I can now see how beneficial and profitable it was for the company. What we say, how and when we say things can have a huge impact on the atmosphere and productivity in the workplace.

It also allowed me to create a productive working relationship with Travis. I can now say that I enjoy working with him and appreciate the qualities that he brings to the team. What used to sound overly wordy and touch-feely, I now recognize was a way of sharing and building ideas and getting the whole team involved in the project. Also, Travis's ability to talk about the big picture allowed finding more comprehensive solutions.

SPEAKING & LISTENING

1 **Work in small groups. Brainstorm a list of common complaints girlfriends and boyfriends make about each other, for example:**

- He/She talks about himself/herself too much.
- He/She spends too much time with his/her friends.

2 **Work in two groups, Group A and Group B. You are going to act out a telephone conversation between a girlfriend (Suzi) and a boyfriend (Brian). Look at page 136. Read the information about your character and discuss what you are going to say.**

3 **Work with a partner. One student should be from Group A and one student from Group B. Act out the telephone conversation between the couple.**

4 1.08 **Listen to a similar conversation. Was it very different from yours?**

5 **Work with your partner. Here are some extracts from the telephone conversation in Exercise 4. Who said each line, the boyfriend (Brian) or the girlfriend (Suzi)?**

a ... a little stressed, had a hard day at work, you know, the usual.
b What's going on?
c I just don't feel like it tonight ...
d Have I done something wrong?
e But not tonight, huh? The football game is more interesting ...
f ... should I come and pick you up?
g Let's just drop it.
h Whatever. Do what you want.

Listen again and check your answers.

6 **What do you think Brian should do now?**

PRONUNCIATION

1 **Work with your partner. Look at these two extracts from the telephone conversation in Speaking & Listening, Exercise 4, and discuss the questions.**

a But not tonight, huh? The football game is more interesting, I guess.
b No, forget it! I wouldn't want you to go out of your way or anything!

Does the woman mean what she says? How does she convey her anger?

2 1.09 **Listen to the two extracts being repeated, first in a normal tone and then angrily. What's the difference?**

Look at the audioscript for track 1.08 on page 154. Find other phrases where the woman uses an angry tone of voice. Work with your partner and read the conversation aloud.

GRAMMAR

1 **Work with a partner. Suzi is talking to her sister about Brian. Look at the adverbials in bold and answer the questions.**

a He **never** used to want to spend so much time **by himself**.
b He said he wanted to do something **tomorrow**, but I don't believe him.
c He just sits **on the couch** and watches TV.
d I ended up shouting **dramatically** and slamming the phone down **like an overgrown teenager**.
e **Frankly**, I've had enough.

Which adverbial(s) ...

1 describe(s) how something is done?
2 describe(s) how often something is done?
3 describe(s) when something will happen?
4 describe(s) where something is done?
5 add(s) emphasis?

Position of adverbials

We stayed **home**.

I'm coming **tomorrow**.

He spoke **quickly**.

He came **to see us**.

We meet **every week**.

Frankly, I never believe a word he says **about Jane**.

Jeff has been working **late at the office every night this week**.

Jeff handed in the project **on time with a huge sigh of relief**.

2 **Look at this sentence and answer the questions below.**

(1) *Suzi* (2) *used to discuss her problems* (3) *with her twin sister* (4).

In which position (1–4) would you normally add these adverbials to the sentence?

a when she was younger
b always
c in secret
d only
e from time to time
f probably

What do you notice about the position of the one-word adverbials?

Make the sentence negative. How does this affect the position of the adverbials?

3 **Modify the sentence in Exercise 2 so that it is true for you. Add at least three adverbials.**

I (1) *never used to discuss my problems* (2) *in depth with my parents* (3) *when I was a teenager.*

Compare your sentence with your partner.

4 **Look at the pairs of sentences below. The underlined adverbials are in different positions. How does this change the meaning of the sentences?**

For example:

1 *Actually, he's performing in the play tomorrow.*
(and not doing something else)
2 *He's actually performing in the play tomorrow.*
(and not just sitting in the audience)

a 1 Honestly, I can't speak to her any more.
  2 I can't speak to her honestly any more.
b 1 Earlier, I wanted Rich to come to the meeting.
  2 I wanted Rich to come to the meeting earlier.
c 1 I get into fights when I'm particularly mad.
  2 I get into fights, particularly when I'm mad.

5 **Write answers to these questions. Use at least five adverbials in your answers. Compare your answers with your partner.**

a Who do you speak to most on a day-to-day basis?
b What do you talk about?

I usually work from home, so I talk to co-workers on the phone, and I always try to get in touch with my sister in the evening / for a long chat / on the phone or online.

6 **Grammar Extra 1, Part 1** page 142. Read the explanations and do Exercise 1.

SPEAKING

1 **Underline the correct alternative to complete the definitions.**

a Secretly listening to other people's conversations is called **eavesdropping / overhearing**.
b Accidentally hearing a conversation between other people is called **eavesdropping / overhearing**.

2 **Work in small groups. Discuss the questions.**

a In what kind of situation is it difficult not to overhear another person's private conversation? How do you feel when this happens?
b Describe the last time you overheard a conversation in a public place. Who was talking? Did they notice (or mind) that you were listening to them?
c Who would you like to eavesdrop on? What do you imagine them saying?

LISTENING

a

b

1 1.10–1.11 **You are going to listen to two conversations. Listen and match the conversations (*1* and *2*) with the pictures (*a* and *b*). For each conversation, answer these questions.**

a What is the relationship between the two people involved in the conversation?
b What are they talking about?

2 **Work with a partner. Look at the sentences. Which conversation from Exercise 1 do you think they refer to: *1*, *2*, or both?**

a They talk to each other often.
b There's some tension between them.
c One of them may not be being completely truthful.
d They're enjoying their conversation.

Listen again and check your answers.

3 **Work with your partner. Look at the audioscript for the second conversation on page 154. What do you think the other person was saying? Act out the complete conversation.**

GRAMMAR

1 **Work with a partner. Complete the extracts from the conversations in Listening, Exercise 1, using the past participle or *-ing* form of the verbs in the box.**

be begin come complete finish get
realize take talk wait (x2) work

a I'd been _____ and _____ ... and ... I was _____ to think ... he wasn't _____ .
b I thought he might have _____ caught up at work or something.
c There are two Italian restaurants named Casa Mia, and neither of us had _____ !
d We've been _____ on it all week.
e We've already _____ the initial plans.
f I'm sure we'll have _____ it by then.
g You must have been _____ to the wrong person.
h There must have _____ some kind of misunderstanding.
i I'll be _____ care of it personally. You can be sure of that.

Aspect

Perfect form
have + past participle

You'll **have received** it by then.

Progressive form
be + **ing**

He **was driving**.

Perfect progressive form
have + **been** + **ing**

He must **have been doing** something important.

2 **Work with your partner. Look at the sentences in Exercise 1. Find three examples of each of the verb forms (1–3).**

1 a perfect verb form
2 a progressive verb form
3 a perfect progressive verb form

3 **Work with your partner. Underline the correct form of the verb.**

a We **'d waited** / **were waiting** / **'d been waiting** for over half an hour by the time *it* finally arrived.
b We'll **have finished** / **be finishing** / **have been finishing** *it* by the end of the day.
c He must **have put** / **be putting** / **have been putting** some extra time in at work. *He*'s usually here by now.
d I **'ve already posted** / **'m already posting** / **'ve already been posting** *them* on my website.
e We **'ve seen** / **'re seeing** / **'ve been seeing** *each other* for about six months.
f Sorry, I can't find *it*. I think I might **have left** / **be leaving** / **have been leaving** *it* at home! Can you pay this time? Thanks!

Look at the words in italics. What do you think they refer to?

4 **Work with your partner. Look at the pictures. Complete the thought bubbles with an appropriate form of the verb, as in the example.**

5 **Work in small groups. Discuss the questions.**

a When was the last time you had to make an excuse because you were late or had forgotten to do something?
b What exactly did you say?
c Did the other person believe you?

6 **Grammar Extra 1, Part 2** page 142. Read the explanations and do Exercise 2.

LANGUAGE FOR LIFE

1 **Work with a partner. Read the tips on the right and answer the questions.**

Do you think it's good advice? Is there anything you'd like to change or add?

What would you say in these situations, if you wanted to ...

a start a conversation with a person you don't know at a party?
b introduce yourself to a new member of staff or a new student in your class?
c start a conversation with a friend you haven't seen for a long time?
d talk to the person standing next to you at the bus stop or at the check-out?

How to start a conversation

- Always approach the person you want to talk to with a smile.
- Use a question to start the conversation, but don't make it too direct.
- Better still, comment on something in your surroundings.
- Or pay the person you're talking to a genuine compliment (for example, "Where did you get your T-shirt? I love it!").
- To keep the conversation going, use follow-up questions or introduce a new topic.

2 1.12 **Listen to the conversations (1–4). Match them with the situations (a–d) in Exercise 1.**

3 **Look at the four conversation openers. Do they follow the advice in the tips in Exercise 1?**

a Fancy *meeting you here*! How are *things*?
b Excuse me. Do you know *what time it is*?
c Hi, you must be *Ruben*. I've *heard a lot about you*.
d Great *party*, isn't it?

Are the conversation openers similar to the ones you came up with in Exercise 1?

4 **Match the responses (1–4) with the conversation openers (a–d) in Exercise 3.**

1 Hi, you must be Steve. I've heard a lot about you, too!
2 Hi! How are you? You're looking great!
3 Yes, it really is. I haven't been to their house before. It's really nice!
4 No, I don't, sorry. But there's a clock over there.

Listen to the conversations again. Which responses do you prefer, the ones above or the ones in the audioscript?

Life Skills: Communication

Creating Rapport

What is rapport?

How can we improve the chances of creating rapport? Look at some hints below.

- remember names
- listen carefully
- be prepared
- ask open-ended questions and look for common ground

Work in pairs. You have been invited to take part in a very important project that could make or break your career. You will be meeting the team members for the first time and want to ensure that everything goes smoothly. Come up with three ice-breaker topics that would be safe and interesting, and three topics that you should avoid. Report back to the class and explain why you chose those topics.

MACMILLAN LIFE SKILLS

1 Vocabulary Extra

MULTIPLE MEANINGS AND USES OF *TALK*

1 **Work with a partner. Look at the proverbs and answer the questions.**

> One must talk little and listen much.
> (African proverb)

> Those who know do not talk, those who talk do not know.
> (Turkish proverb)

> It's not the same to talk of bulls as to be in the bullring.
> (Spanish proverb)

a What do they mean?
b Which do you like best?
c Do you know of any other proverbs about talking?

2 **Work with your partner. Look at the list below. It shows some of the most common uses and forms of the word *talk*. Which part of speech is used in each sentence: noun (countable or uncountable), verb, or adjective?**

A small man was **talking** intently to the woman on his left.
My mother has **talked** of little else since meeting you.
The next stage will be **talks** between US and Russian leaders.
I was already hearing **talk** about the merger of the two companies.
He's quite a smooth **talker**, don't you think?
Morris gave a fascinating **talk** on his visit to East Africa.
He's not very **talkative**, but you certainly feel his presence.
She has become the **talk** of the town since her very public affair.
In this brief **talk** I will ask three key questions.
We listened to Fred's hilarious **talk** about how to avoid becoming a millionaire.
After the meeting, the main **talking** point was the threat of layoffs.
You can **talk**! You never do any exercise!
All that **talk** of food made me feel extremely hungry.
There's fresh **talk** of a strike at the car factory.

3 **Work with your partner. Look at the sentences in Exercise 2 again and answer these questions.**

a What does *the talk of the town* mean? And *smooth talker*?
b In what situation would you say *You can talk!*?

Check your own dictionary. Look for other words formed with *talk*.

4 **Complete the sentences using one of the forms of *talk*.**

a Are there any international peace _____ taking place right now?
b Who's the most _____ person you know?
c What's the main _____ point among your friends these days?

5 **Work with your partner. Discuss the questions in Exercise 4.**

talk¹ /tɔk/ verb ★★★

1 communicate	**5** achieve sth by talking
2 discuss	**6** send information
3 give lecture	**7** have power to persuade
4 give secret information	+ PHRASES

talk² /tɔk/ noun ★★★
1 [C] a conversation with someone: **have a talk (with sb)** *We had a nice talk yesterday.* **1a. talks** [plural] discussions between important people from opposing sides designed to help them agree about an issue: **+with** *He visited Egypt in March for talks with the president.* ♦ **+between** *the outcome of talks between the government and the rebels* ♦ **+on** *preliminary talks on the future of the steel industry* ♦ **have/hold talks** *The management will be holding informal talks with union officials.* ♦ **a round/session of talks** *the need for a fresh round of peace talks* ♦ **talks break down/collapse** *Talks broke down last week over the issue of overtime pay.* ♦ **talks resume/reopen** *The trade talks will resume next month.*
2 [C] an informal lecture about a subject: **give/deliver a talk (on sth)** *Williams gave a series of talks on his travels in Nepal.*
3 [U] ordinary conversations between people: *I sat there listening to the sailors' talk.* ♦ **+of** *Talk of housework bored her.* ♦ **the talk turns to sth** (=the conversation begins to be about something) *Then the talk turned to the upcoming exam.* **3a.** conversations and discussions about what may happen: **+of** *There was no talk of any cuts in wages.* ♦ **+about** *There is a lot of talk about welfare reform.* ♦ **hear talk** *We hear talk about being good citizens.* **3b.** the activity of talking, especially when you think it does not achieve anything: *Most radio stations need less talk and more music.* ♦ **be all/just talk** *She appears to be an expert on men, but it's all talk!* ♦ **despite/for all sb's talk** *For all the government's talk, it does nothing to improve housing conditions.* **3c.** discussion of other people's private lives: *At first there was a lot of talk, but people soon lost interest.* **3d.** a style of talking used by a particular group of people: *girl/boy talk* ♦ *youngsters using up-to-the-minute street talk* (=a fashionable way of talking) **3e. the talk of sth** if something is the talk of a place, people there talk a lot about it: *a fashion display that was the talk of New York* ♦ **the talk of the town** *The couple had suddenly become the talk of the town.*
talk is cheap *informal* used for saying that you do not believe that someone will in fact do what they are saying they will do

talk·a·tive /ˈtɔkətɪv/ adj a talkative person talks a lot

talk·er /ˈtɔkər/ noun [C] *informal* someone who talks a lot or talks in a particular way: *She's quite a talker.* ♦ **a smooth talker** (=someone who is good at persuading people by saying nice things) *Your brother certainly is a smooth talker, isn't he?*

talk·ing point /ˈtɔkɪŋ ˌpɔɪnt/ noun [C] something interesting that people are likely to want to discuss

From the *Macmillan English Dictionary (American edition)*

2 Taste

Julia, art teacher

SPEAKING

1 **The people in the pictures (1–4) were asked "If you were a food, what food would you be?" Which of the four do you think gave each of the answers (a–d)? Why?**

a "Refried beans, because they're full of protein and good for you."
b "Cauliflower, because it's flowery and intricate."
c "A bar of dark chocolate, because it's smooth and velvety like me!"
d "Nuts, because they're tough but worth opening for what's inside!"

Check your answers on page 136.

Brad, US Marine

2 **If you were a food, what would you be? Why? Discuss your answer with a partner.**

LISTENING

1 **Work in small groups. What kind of food or drink would you associate with the following situations? Why?**

a falling in love
b waiting at a bus station
c rainy days
d summer
e the end of a long day
f your grandmother's house

Max, sailor

2 1.13 **Listen to six people giving their answers to Exercise 1. Answer the questions for each person (1–6).**

a Which situation (a–f) are they talking about?
b What food do they associate with that situation?

Janet, senior citizen

3 **Complete the descriptions of the foods you heard in Exercise 2.**

a b_____ coffee i_____ a p_____ c_____
b big bowls of f_____ salad w_____ h_____-m_____ d_____
c huge plates of t_____ s_____ w_____ m_____ p_____
d the b_____ gravy y_____ h_____ e_____ t_____
e c_____ c_____ - c_____ cookies d_____ i_____ m_____
f s_____, s_____ strawberries w_____ i_____ c_____
g some kind of m_____ convenience food t_____ d_____ n_____ a_____ c_____

Listen again and check your answers.

- **Grammar:** Noun phrases: describing noun phrases and order of adjectives. Fronting
- **Vocabulary:** Describing places to eat. Word building. Idioms with *taste*
- **Language for Life:** Agreeing and disagreeing

GRAMMAR

1 **Read the descriptions (a–d) and decide which best fits the picture.**

a bitter vending-machine coffee in a plastic cup
b the espresso coffee that you can get in a gas station
c a cup of strong, black coffee with two or three sugars
d hot, milky coffee steaming in a mug

Which of the descriptions above is most similar to the coffee served in your country?

2 **Look at the descriptions in Exercise 1 again. Find ...**

1 the head: the main noun (it is the same for all the descriptions).
2 an adjective.
3 a noun used as an adjective.
4 a prepositional phrase (preposition + noun phrase).
5 a relative clause.
6 a participle clause.

Answer the questions.

- Which parts of speech (2–6) are used before the head?
- Which are used after the head?

Noun phrases

some coffee
a cup of coffee

Describing noun phrases
a milky coffee served in an enormous mug

Order of adjectives
delicious, creamy, home-made, French onion soup

3 **Work with a partner. Put the words and phrases in the correct order.**

a tea / with a / green / slice of lemon / a cup of
b Greek / served / yogurt / creamy / with nuts and dried fruit
c freshly made / dripping with maple syrup / a pile of / pancakes
d two / of bacon / cooked to a crisp / rashers

Do you ever have any of these things for breakfast? Write a complex noun phrase describing your favorite breakfast food.

4 **Look at these descriptions. Which (if any) appeals most to you right now? Why?**

a a slice of delicious home-made apple pie
b a glass of refreshing, ice-cold lemon tea
c a strong wake-me-up Italian espresso

5 **Look at the adjectives in Exercise 4 and answer the questions.**

a Which adjectives describe ...
 1 the basic ingredients or qualities (for example, the country it comes from)?
 2 the ways it can be prepared or served (for example, *fresh*, *frozen*, *home-made*)?
 3 the speaker's personal opinion?
b What order are they used in?

6 **Complete the menu descriptions with the words and phrases given. Which dish would you most like to try?**

a a selection of ______ cheeses (French / local / delicious)
b a bowl of ______ chowder (piping-hot / clam / tasty)
c half a dozen ______ crayfish (freshwater / exquisite / grilled)
d a ______ pancake (buttery / mouth-watering / blueberry)

7 **Work in small groups. Expand the sentence below as much as possible. You have three minutes. The group with the longest and most coherent sentence wins.**

The restaurant served food.

8 **Grammar Extra 2, Part 1** page 142. Read the explanations and do Exercise 1.

READING

1 **Read the introduction to a restaurant review and answer the questions.**

a What type of restaurant is it? What words would you use to describe it?
b Why was the journey to the restaurant unusual?
c Why do you think the writer liked it so much?

https://visitingcuba.blog/la-estrella-del-mar

My first culinary tour of Cuba, nearly a decade ago, had not started very promisingly. Yes, there were lavish hotels catering to wealthy tourists, but by and large the fare was nothing spectacular. That is, until I stumbled upon *La Estrella del Mar*. After fortuitously running into a fellow writer, I learned of this diamond in the rough, tucked away just outside the city. Not knowing what lay in store for me, I set out on my own, trying to give directions to the taxi driver in my rudimentary Spanish. After a few wrong turns, winding roads, and one stop to get directions, the hand-carved wooden sign finally came into view.

It's a good thing too that the sign existed – otherwise one could easily have mistaken the restaurant for an old colonial house. With charming, Spanish-inspired architecture and a worn, weather-beaten look, I was instantly transported to a scene from a bygone era. Only the presence of a few outdoor tables gave any clue that there was a restaurant within. Immediately, I was greeted at the door by an elderly waiter, speaking impeccable, formal English.

From there, I was ushered inside where the interior matched the exterior perfectly, with old wooden furniture and elegant table cloths and settings. There were a few other patrons, but I was whisked to my own private table on the balcony. From the balcony was an amazing view of the ocean, and the sound of crickets was the perfect accompaniment.

Although somewhat limited in scope, the menu captured the essential local flavors. Starting with an incredibly fresh shrimp ceviche, I moved on to a delicious risotto made with local cheese, peppers, and cilantro. Finally, I found room for a Cuban coffee and unbelievable 'tres leches', a sponge cake topped with almonds. The rest of the menu looked equally appetizing, and my one regret was that I could not try more, especially considering the very reasonable price. It was truly a meal I would not soon forget.

Years later, I was closely following the news about the devastation of Hurricane Irma, and I decided to revisit the country where I had made so many fond memories. I thought, if I could help, even in a small way, to bring back tourism, then it was the least I could do. Of course, a return to *Estrella del Mar* was high on my list of priorities.

2 **Work with a partner. Answer the questions.**

a Is this the type of restaurant you would enjoy eating at? Why / Why not?
b What three changes would you make to the restaurant to make it better known?

3 **You are going to read the rest of the review. Divide into two groups. Group A: read text A on page 21 and make notes about what changed in terms of ...**

a how well-known the restaurant is.
b the journey to the restaurant.
c the exterior of the restaurant.

Group B: look at page 136 and read the instructions.

Compare your answers with a member of your group.

4 **Work with a partner from the other group. Close your book and use your notes to tell your partner about the changes that had been made.**

5 Work with your partner. Discuss the questions.

a Were any of the changes made similar to the ones you thought of?

b What was the writer's attitude towards the changes? Do you think the review was fair?

c Do you know of anywhere, not necessarily a restaurant, that has changed its style significantly? Were the changes for the better or the worse?

TEXT A

https://visitingcuba.blog/la-estrella-del-mar

Upon return, my first impression was that, considering the hurricane, the city had made a remarkably swift recovery. The infrastructure didn't seem markedly changed and everyone was in good spirits – all of this gave me great joy and also hope for what lay in store at my favorite restaurant. Although I had worried that it might have closed, a quick check of travel sites showed that no, *La Estrella del Mar* was still in business and had a mountain of reviews. (Thankfully the internet had been restored in my hotel!) There was no relying on word of mouth this time, but to maintain an element of surprise, I deliberately avoided reading any reviews.

While the internet was now readily accessible, Cuba still doesn't allow for ridesharing apps, so back in a cab I went. I'm sure my Spanish had only gotten worse in the intervening years, so I was surprised to find that the driver knew exactly where I was heading. Within a few miles of the destination, on telephone poles and trees appeared crudely made signs, with arrows and distances to the restaurant. I figured, with the hard times, they must have decided to boost their visibility somewhat, and who could blame them?

Rounding the final corner to the restaurant, I nearly told the driver to just continue on – I couldn't believe it was the same house. I had been mentally prepared for signs of damage from the storm, and yes this was apparent in the flattened vegetation, water-stained walls, and sagging roof. But what I had not anticipated was the barrage of color and noise which assaulted my senses; cheap plastic chairs and tables outside, a gift shop stand overflowing with tacky merchandise, and gone was the beloved hand-carved sign. In its place, a huge neon monstrosity hung over the entrance. It was quite unnerving and gave off the impression of an old antique decorated by a child. To be fair, the original architecture had remained intact but little else as far as I could tell.

Needless to say, there was no stately older gentleman to greet me at the door. Instead, the rhythmic pounding of *reggaeton* indicated they were open for business. Having made the trek, I decided there was no turning back now.

VOCABULARY

1 Work with a partner who read the same text as you and follow the instructions.

Students from Group A: prepare to teach four of the words and expressions in the box from your part of the review to a student from Group B.

swift	markedly	in good spirits	word of mouth	sagging	barrage	monstrosity	unnerving

a Read text A again and find the words.

b Discuss their meanings with your partner. Think about the best way to explain them.

Students from Group B: look at page 137.

2 Work with a partner from the other group and follow the instructions.

- Teach your partner the words.
- Ask your partner to write sentences using the new words.
- Check that the words have been used correctly in the sentences.

GRAMMAR

Fronting

Used for changing emphasis and adding dramatic effect.

Gone were the days when one could sit and enjoy a quiet meal.

Through the silence came the noise of crickets.

Why it had changed, I couldn't say.

1 **Look at the sentences (a-e), which have been taken from the restaurant review. Write the words in the correct order without looking back.**

a from / was / an / the / balcony / of / amazing / there / view / the / ocean (page 20)
b electrical / made / signs / on / poles / and / trees / crudely / appeared (page 21)
c beloved / sign / the / was / hand-carved / gone (page 21)
d the / booth / corner / in / had / up / set / a / makeshift / been / DJ (page 136)
e gourmet / gone / Cuban / was / cuisine / the (page 136)

2 **Work with a partner. Check your completed sentences in Exercise 1 with the review and answer the questions.**

a Are the sentences in the review different from yours?
b In what way is the word order different from usual?
c In which sentence has a word been dropped? Which word?
d What information has been brought to the front of each sentence? What effect does this have?

3 **Rewrite the sentences to change the emphasis.**

a The peaceful little restaurant we once knew was gone.
b There was a modern monstrosity in its place.
c We didn't know when exactly the change took place.
d The chef lived above the restaurant.
e The path, lit by small twinkling candles, went down to the beach.
f We went home, tired and hungry.

4 **Complete the sentences about a place you remember from your past which has changed a lot since you first went there.**

a Many a time did we ...
b Gone is the ...
c Why ... I don't really know.

Compare your answers with your partner and ask for more information about the place and the changes that have taken place.

5 **Grammar Extra 2, Part 2** page 142. Read the explanations and do Exercise 2.

SPEAKING: ANECDOTE

You are going to tell your partner about the last time you ate out at a restaurant.

- Ask yourself the questions below.
- Think about *what* to say and *how* to say it.
- Tell your partner about your experience.

a When did you last eat out?
b Where did you go?
c Who did you go with?
d Why did you decide to go there?
e What was the place like?
f Did you like the atmosphere? Why? / Why not?
g Do you go there often, or was it the only time?
h What did you order?
i Did you enjoy it? Why? / Why not?
j Was the service good? Did you leave a tip?
k Would you recommend it to someone else? Why? / Why not?

WRITING

1 **Write a review for the restaurant you described in Speaking: anecdote. Before you start, look at the points below and think about what you are going to write and the language you will need.**

a Think about the kind of person who goes to that kind of restaurant and the kind of information they would be interested in.

b Decide what information you are going to include. Look at this list:

- the address and telephone number
- the opening times
- some information about the people who run the place
- anything they said of interest that you could report
- the menu
- some typical dishes
- a description of a particular dish
- a description of the decor
- a description of the atmosphere
- a personal recommendation (a dish? a good time of day to go?)
- some information about the history of the place (how long it's been open? the history of the building?)
- any particular incident that gives an insight into the restaurant
- anything else you'd like to add

c Decide what order to present the information in.

2 **Write a short review of no more than 200 words.**

3 **Work in small groups. Read each other's reviews. Can you guess what kind of person the review is written for? Which restaurant would you like to eat at?**

LISTENING

1 **Work in small groups. Think of one typical dish for as many countries as you can. You have three minutes.**

2 **Compare your answers with the rest of the class and discuss the questions.**

a Have you tried any of the dishes you mentioned in Exercise 1? Do you know what the ingredients are?
b Do you have a favorite foreign dish?
c When you travel, do you make a point of trying the local specialties?

3 1.14-1.17 **Listen to Anne, Kim, Bill, and Steve talking about their eating experiences abroad. Did they like the food in the countries they visited?**

Listen again and list the food vocabulary you hear each person use.

4 **Work with a partner. Compare your lists and discuss the questions.**

a Which countries do you think they are talking about? Check your answers on page 136.
b Which diet appeals to you the most/least? Why?
c How do these foods differ from the food you're used to eating?

PRONUNCIATION

1 **Look at the extracts from the conversation in Listening, Exercise 3. Underline the words and sounds the speakers stress to express their enthusiasm or reservation.**

a Mmm, it's superb, really hot and spicy ...
b Actually, it took some getting used to.
c Well, to tell you the truth, I didn't really like it that much.
d ... and, hmm, I don't really like cabbage that much ...
e ... no, it isn't really my favorite.
f It isn't particularly elaborate, but it's good.

1.18 **Listen and check your answers.**

2 **Listen to the extracts in Exercise 1 again. Pay particular attention to the intonation of the words and sounds that were stressed by the speakers. In which sentences does the speaker use intonation to ...**

a show enthusiasm?
b show that he/she has some reservations?
c soften criticism?
d emphasize good qualities?

3 **Work with your partner. Discuss the questions.**

a How do the sounds of *mmm/hmm* and *really* change according to their meaning?
b Do you use *mmm/hmm* in your own language to do the same thing?
c We often use intonation to communicate what we are thinking or feeling. What other techniques can we use to show enthusiasm or reservation?

4 **Work with your partner. Look at the two short exchanges below. Use the words and intonation in Exercise 1 above and add your own ideas to make the conversations sound a) more enthusiastic and b) less enthusiastic.**

a A: How was your trip?
B: Interesting.
b A: So, how was the food last night?
B: Unusual.

VOCABULARY & SPEAKING

1 **Work in small groups. Answer the questions.**

a How many words can you form from the root word *taste*?
b What verbs or adjectives can you think of that are often used with *taste*?
c The word *taste* has several meanings. How many can you think of?
d Do you know of any sayings or idioms with *taste*?

2 **Complete the sentences with the words and expressions in the box.**

accounting acquired bad taste of her own medicine
poor taste share tastefully tasteless tasty victory

a The new bar is very lively, with very _____ food and a good selection of drinks.
b When they asked him if he had enjoyed the aperitif, he was very diplomatic and said that it was an _____ taste.
c We found a charming little hotel with _____ furnished bedrooms and great facilities.
d "They get along well."
"Yes, they _____ the same taste in music."
e She forgot to put salt in, so the bread was absolutely _____ .
f She's always keeping him waiting, so when he left her waiting in the restaurant for half an hour, she got a taste _____ .
g The new boss left without saying goodbye, which left a _____ in everyone's mouths.
h The joke was in very _____ and quite a few people were offended.
i An orange fake fur coat! There's no _____ for taste.
j They finally tasted _____ when their team won 3-0.

Look at the idiomatic sayings with *taste*. Do you use the same sayings in your own language?

3 **Work with a partner. Write a short definition of *good taste*. Use no more than twenty words. Share your definition with the rest of the class. Which one do you like best?**

4 **Look at the list of actions and decide which of them you consider ...**

a completely unacceptable.
b acceptable in certain circumstances.
c totally acceptable at all times.

- chewing gum
- using your cell phone on public transportation
- kissing in public
- talking in a movie theater
- cursing
- losing your temper in public

5 **Compare your views with your partner. Would your parents have given the same answers? How many of these are you actually guilty of? What other things do you consider "not in good taste"?**

LANGUAGE FOR LIFE

1 1.19–1.21 **Listen to three short conversations. As you listen, answer the questions.**

a Match each conversation (1–3) with one of these topics:

a shopping **b** giving gifts **c** eating out

b Decide who is speaking in each conversation (1–3):

a a married couple **b** co-workers on the telephone **c** a parent and a child

2 **Work with a partner. In each conversation the people are disagreeing about something. What exactly is the nature of the disagreement?**

Listen again and check your answers.

3 **Complete the extracts from the conversations in Exercise 1 with the useful phrases in the boxes. There is one useful phrase too many in each case.**

a That can't be I think you'll find That may be, but

A: Because you could have used the company's dining facilities.
B: Yes, but it was a breakfast meeting with a client.
A: (1) ______ it's company policy.
B: (2) ______ that it's only company policy if we're entertaining in-house guests.

b I suppose you're right No way! That's garbage

A: Well, apart from the fact that it doesn't help the environment, imported fruit doesn't taste as good.
B: (1) ______ . These strawberries are absolutely delicious!
A: What about the environment?
B: OK, OK, (2) ______ , it's not good for the environment, but I couldn't resist them.

c I rest my case I know, it's awful Oh, I don't know

A: I can't believe he got her a vacuum cleaner for her birthday.
B: (1) ______ . It's the thought that counts.
A: No! Come on! He couldn't have given it much thought, if that's all he came up with.
B: You gave me an electric drill on my last birthday!
A: So?
B: (2) ______ .

Listen again and check your answers.

4 **Work with your partner. Look at the useful phrases in Exercise 3 again. Use them to complete the table below.**

Agreement	Disagreement	Closing an argument
strong:	total:	
reluctant:	polite:	

Life Skills: Social Skills

Cultural Awareness of Food

- 1.22 **Listen to an introduction about cultural awareness of food and look at the following elements of eating meals. Work with your partner. What is most common in your culture?**
  - Seating (chairs? special places?)
  - Utensils (cutlery? chopsticks? hands?)
  - Conversation (all topics acceptable?)
  - Timing (arrive early/on time/late? typical starting time?)
  - Dietary restrictions (any unacceptable foods/drinks?)
  - Sharing (individual dishes? group dishes?)
  - Tipping at restaurants (none? specific amount?)
  - Trying food (rude to say no if offered?)

Think about other places or cultures you have visited, know about, or have heard about. Are their food customs the same or different?

MACMILLAN LIFE SKILLS

2 Writing Extra

LETTER TO A NEWSPAPER

1 Work in small groups. Look at the pictures and discuss the questions.

a Do you like wearing jeans? Why? / Why not?
b Do you have any jeans that look like the ones in the pictures?
c Would you wear these jeans, or any other jeans, ...
- to work?
- to class?
- to a job interview?
- to a party?

2 Look at this headline from a local newspaper. What do you think is the story behind the headline?

Schools ban baggy, ripped, and super-skinny jeans

3 Read one woman's reaction to the story. Would you class her reaction as ...

a moderate? b reasoned? c exaggerated? d extreme?

Can you think of any other adjectives to describe her tone?

At last, it's good to see that someone has finally come to their senses! It was about time, too. I'm just surprised that it didn't happen sooner. I'm sick and tired of seeing kids on the streets in their baggy jeans, underwear on show, dragging their feet with their hands in their pockets – looking scruffy and like they're up to no good. Or the opposite – super tight jeans that they can hardly walk in! I do, of course, respect everybody's right to self-expression, however bad their taste in clothes. Having said that, a line should be drawn when it comes to inappropriate jeans in schools. I think that allowing young people to wear clothes to school that are falling apart or don't fit shows disrespect – a very unhealthy disrespect – for their teachers, their fellow students, and their school. I don't think I'm being unreasonable as I have no problem with young people wearing properly-fitting jeans in good condition – that is completely normal in today's society, and I'm not so old-fashioned to expect teenagers to wear suits or ties. If I had my way, all schools would follow suit with the excellent example you wrote about; in fact, I think the wearing of inappropriate jeans in all educational institutions should be banned!

Margaret Morgan

Do you agree with anything the woman says? Why? / Why not? How would you feel if the same ban was suggested in your town?

4 Look again at the woman's reaction to the story in Exercise 3 and find expressions to complete the table.

Expressing agreement or approval	Accepting someone's arguments without necessarily agreeing with them	Expressing disagreement or disapproval
It's good to see that ...		

5 Add these expressions to the table in Exercise 4.

I can sympathize with the view that ...
I take exception to ...
While not in total agreement with ...
I couldn't agree more.
I find it hard to believe that ...
There is doubtless some truth in ...
However, ...

6 Write a reply to the woman's reaction. Use the expressions in Exercises 4 and 5 to help you.

3 City

LISTENING

1 **How much do you know about cities around the world? Take this quiz and find out.**

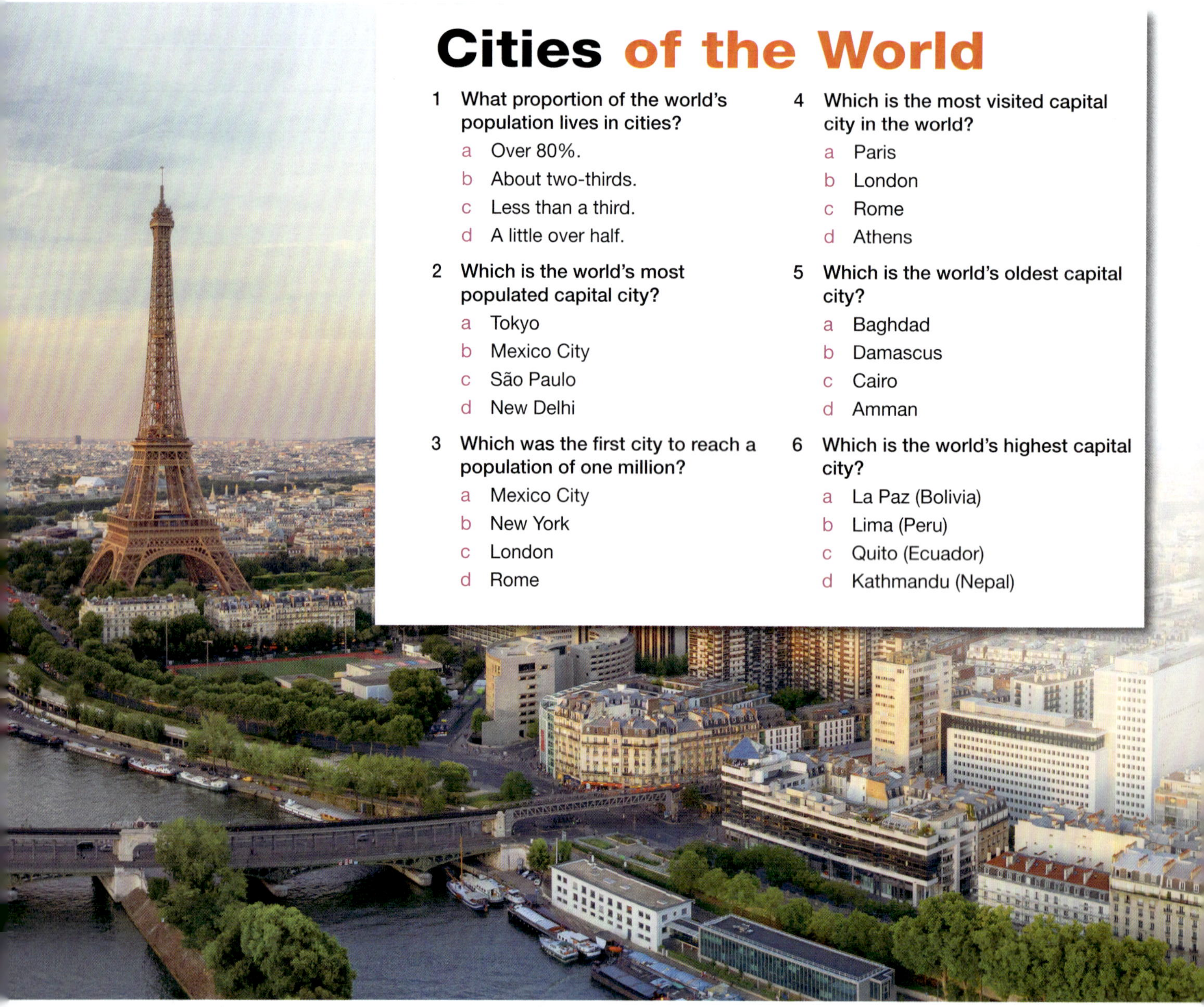

Cities of the World

1 What proportion of the world's population lives in cities?
- a Over 80%.
- b About two-thirds.
- c Less than a third.
- d A little over half.

2 Which is the world's most populated capital city?
- a Tokyo
- b Mexico City
- c São Paulo
- d New Delhi

3 Which was the first city to reach a population of one million?
- a Mexico City
- b New York
- c London
- d Rome

4 Which is the most visited capital city in the world?
- a Paris
- b London
- c Rome
- d Athens

5 Which is the world's oldest capital city?
- a Baghdad
- b Damascus
- c Cairo
- d Amman

6 Which is the world's highest capital city?
- a La Paz (Bolivia)
- b Lima (Peru)
- c Quito (Ecuador)
- d Kathmandu (Nepal)

1.23 **Listen to a professor giving a lecture about cities and check your answers. Were there any surprises?**

2 **Listen to the lecture again. Replace the words in italics with the words used by the speaker.**

- **a** It *seems* that there is a steady movement towards urban areas.
- **b** It is *commonly accepted* that Paris, with its population of over 11 million, is the most visited city in the world.
- **c** Sources *would appear* to suggest that the Syrians are right.
- **d** On the other extreme, there is *absolutely no question* that La Paz, the capital of Bolivia, which stands at four kilometers above sea level, is the highest capital in the world.
- **e** It is *unclear* whether this information is based on popular opinion or on statistical data.

- **Grammar:** Hedging. Inversion after negative and limiting adverbials
- **Vocabulary:** Describing cities. Describing tourist spots
- **Language for Life:** Adding emphasis

GRAMMAR

1 **Work with a partner. Look at the expressions you replaced in the extracts in Listening, Exercise 2 and find expressions that show the writer believes there is ...**

a very strong evidence.
b fairly strong evidence.
c weak evidence.
d unreliable evidence.

2 **Read the sentences (a–e) and look at the information below. Decide if the sentences are true or false. Correct the ones that are false.**

a It seems that most people enjoy life in the countryside.
b It appears that very few people who live in a city would prefer to live in a rural area.
c The results from the first survey seem to suggest that most people are happy to stay in a rural area.
d On the other hand, the second survey would seem to show that most people who live in the countryside would prefer to move to the city.
e Older people are not believed to be as happy with city life as younger people. But there is little evidence in the surveys to back this up.

The results of two new surveys have just been published in which people living in rural and urban areas were asked about how happy they are with where they live. Below are some of the results.

	Survey 1	Survey 2
People who enjoy living in cities	79%	72%
People who live in a city, but would prefer to live in a rural area	35%	43%
People who live in a city, but spend as much time as possible outside the city	47%	29%
People who live in rural areas, but would prefer to live in a city	62%	36%
Percentage of these who are under 30	84%	-
Percentage of these who are over 50	13%	-

Do you think the results would be the same in your country?

Hedging

Use hedging expressions to distance yourself from facts or opinions that you cannot prove are true.

Hedging with verbs

it **seems** that ...
it **appears** that ...
sources **seem to suggest** ...
the results **would appear to show** ...

Hedging with *would*

it **would** seem that ...
it **would** appear that ...

Hedging with the passive voice

it **is** widely **recognized** that ...
there **are** not **believed** to be ...
it **is** not **known** ...

Hedging with noun phrases

there is **no/little/some doubt** ...
there is **no/little/some evidence** ...
there is **some discussion** ...

3 **Look at the sentences (a–e) in Exercise 2 again and underline all the hedging expressions.**

4 **Work with your partner. Rewrite the statements using the words in parentheses.**

a Most young people prefer to live in large cities because of the job opportunities. (seem)
b Older people living by themselves get very lonely in big cities. (little doubt)
c People who live in the countryside are generally more healthy than city dwellers. (some discussion)

Do you agree with the sentences you've written?

5 1.24 **Listen to Sharon and Derek discussing a newspaper story about the survey. Make notes about the reasons why young people prefer to live in a city.**

6 **Work with your partner. Write the story as it would have appeared in the newspaper. Use no more than 120 words. Then compare your story with the version on page 137.**

7 **Grammar Extra 3, Part 1** page 144. Read the explanations and do Exercise 1.

Sharon and Derek

SPEAKING

Work with a partner. Discuss the questions.

a What is the capital of your country famous for? Does it attract a lot of visitors?

b Which capital city would you most like to spend a weekend in?

c Do you live in a city, a town, a village, or out in the countryside? Have you always lived there? Do you like it? Why? Why not?

1 With mountains, valleys, extensive coastlines, and semi-desert fringes all easily reachable via a well-developed transportation network, this city is one of the top tourist destinations in Africa. Nestled between the soaring Table Mountain on one side and the sea on the other, this city enjoys a Mediterranean climate which is perfect for growing the grapes for the region's booming wine industry. It is the most entrepreneurial city of the region.

Despite its beauty and development, there is also a sad past to this city, which it does not deny. In fact, statues of the country's four Nobel Peace Prize laureates, all of whom were involved in the struggle for equality in their country, can be found in Nobel Square along the V&A Waterfront. In this same region, you can get a ferry to visit the island which housed political prisoners and the country's most illustrious son, who later went on to become one of its presidents. Today, the island serves as a museum and a reminder of the country's past. The city has been able, however, to make way for the new, transforming itself into a thriving hub for business and pleasure.

2 This South American city is perhaps the one which most resembles Europe in style, demographics, and architecture. It was settled by waves of migrants, mainly from Italy, Spain, and Germany, but also from other counties like Portugal and Greece. It is home to some amazing architecture in the French and Italian neoclassical styles. One of the most iconic examples is the Teatro Colón, built in 1920.

More than for its architecture, this city is known for its love of football. Here, people root for one of two main teams, and they are very passionate about their teams. This same passion is evident in their most famous style of music and dance, the tango. Tango shows, which often include a lesson and dinner, are very popular among both locals and tourists. Don't be surprised if the show starts late - an early dinner here starts at 10:00 p.m.! In fact, in no other South American city will you find throngs of people so late into the night.

Finally, a visit to the exquisite Museum of Modern Art, which holds one of the finest collections of art in all of Latin America, is a must. Whether you are interested in food, culture, music, art, or sport; whether you are a day person or a night owl, this city will work its magic on you because it has something for everyone.

3 For a small capital, with a population of just over half a million, this city certainly packs a punch! Considered an educational center with four important universities, students make up about twenty percent of the population, but what this city is really known for is its rich historical and cultural heritage. Here, the skyline is dominated by its awe-inspiring castle, which sits atop a hill and can be seen from most vantage points in the city. It is said that the castle, in one form or another, has existed for hundreds of years. It has served as a royal residence, fortress, and military barracks, and has been witness to many historical conflicts. Today, it is the most visited site in the city.

In addition to all its rich history, this city becomes a bustling hive of activity during the summer when it attracts over four million visitors for its famous summer festivals: the Military Tattoo, a parade which takes place in front of the castle every night during the festival; the International Festival, which has theatre and classical music performances; the Festival Fringe, which focuses mainly on comedy acts; and the International Book Festival, where many world-known authors and thinkers get together, making it a wonder for readers. Believe it or not, these are just the more well-known festivals which take place during the summer months! If you are a history or culture buff, you will certainly fall prey to the charms of this city. One thing is for sure, you won't run out of things to do and see in this city.

4 In this capital city, be prepared to become overwhelmed by the sea of humanity and the onslaught of visual stimulation. You should also be prepared for the constant contradictions. While extremely crowded, this city has pockets of calm and quiet areas everywhere, from temples hidden away behind office buildings, to parks with wide lawns, trees, and ponds. You may expect such a crowded city to be a haphazard mass of humanity, but it is actually quite orderly. When walking along the city's sidewalks, everyone stays to the left. On escalators, stay to left if you are standing, but walk on the right if you are in a hurry. In a city this crowded, it is understandable that housing comes at a premium, and people live in minuscule apartments, practically on top of one another.

In stores and restaurants, you are almost assured impeccable service, but tipping is actually frowned upon, so be aware. When entering almost any establishment, you will be greeted with a 'welcome' - smile and give a slight bow of the head in response. When heading back home, be sure to pick up some stationery or origami as a gift. It might seem tacky, but they are in fact beautiful, well made, and so easy to carry that they make the perfect gift.

READING

1 **Work in small groups. Look at the guidebook extracts on page 30. They describe four of the world's most famous cities. Read the descriptions and decide which city is being described.**

Turn to page 137 if you need help.

2 **Read through the guidebook extracts again and underline the information that helped you decide which cities were being described.**

3 **Work with a partner. Discuss the questions about the guidebook extracts.**

a Which description appeals to you most? Why? Choose two or three phrases which you find evocative.
b Have you been to any of these cities? Do the extracts reflect your experiences?
c Do the extracts make you want to visit any of these cities?

VOCABULARY

1 **Match the adjectives (a–f) with the definitions (1–6). Then decide which of the adjectives you would use to describe the noun phrases in the box below.**

a awe-inspiring	1 giving a feeling of respect and amazement
b haphazard	2 full of people who are very busy or lively (especially a place)
c tacky	3 not organized, not arranged according to a plan
d bustling	4 very tall or high in the sky (especially buildings or trees)
e soaring	5 so loud, big, or noticeable that you just can't ignore it
f in-your-face	6 cheap and badly made or vulgar

advertising campaigns coastal resorts collection of people high-rise buildings
market plastic souvenirs scenery tree tops

2 **Find the adjectives (a–f) in Exercise 1 in the guidebook extracts on page 30. What are they describing?**

3 **Work with your partner. Look at the verbs (1–5). Without looking back at the guidebook extracts, match each verb with an appropriate phrase.**

1 to make	a punch
2 to work	prey to
3 to fall	on top of one another
4 to live	its magic
5 to pack	way for the new

Now check your answers.

4 **Complete the sentences with the phrases from Exercise 3. Make any changes to the phrases that are necessary.**

a It's very easy _____ the charm of the market stallholders, and people often end up spending much more than they'd expected to.
b The old town was built on the edge of a cliff overlooking the gorge, using up every bit of spare space. Some houses were even built into the cliff face, and people _____ in a warren of narrow cobbled streets.
c The city seems unassuming at first, but it certainly _____. There is so much to do and see that it is difficult to get everything in on one trip.
d No matter how stressed you feel, once you let the beauty of the beach and the warmth of the sun _____ on you, you will begin to wind down and relax.
e Far too often, historic districts are carved up and charming old buildings torn down _____ .

5 **Work with your partner. Look at the sentences in Exercise 4 again. Have you ever visited a town or city that matches one of the descriptions? Tell your partner about it.**

GRAMMAR

1 **Work with a partner. Look at the adverbials in the box and decide which of them have negative or limiting meanings.**

at once   even in the summer   frequently   never   not a word
not until he'd finished   on no account   only after a long night
only after a long wait   only then   quite often   rarely
seldom   under no circumstances   usually

Inversion after negative and limiting adverbials

Not only was it the most expensive city I'd ever stayed in, it was also the most dangerous.

Seldom have I seen anything more beautiful.

2 **Look at these pairs of sentences and answer the questions.**

1A In no other South American city will you find throngs of people so late into the night.
1B You won't find throngs of people so late into the night in any other South American city.
2A Not until I actually visited the city, did I understand just how culturally rich it is.
2B I didn't understand just how culturally rich the city is until I actually visited it.

a Which sentences, the As or Bs, would be more likely to be spoken?
b What happens to the word order when the adverbial phrase is placed at the beginning of the sentence?
c What effect does this have on the sentence?

3 **Rewrite the sentences, starting with the word or words in parentheses.**

a You will rarely see such a superb example of modern architecture. (Rarely)
Rarely will you see such a superb example of modern architecture.
b I rarely visit a city more than once, but this place is really special. (Rarely)
c I had never seen anything so breathtakingly beautiful before. (Never before)
d You will only be able to experience the heart of this beautiful old town by wandering down its narrow side streets. (Only by)
e You will only begin to understand the special charm of this place after you have spent an evening there. (Only after you)
f You can't really understand exactly how beautiful the view is until you climb to the top. (Not until)
g You shouldn't leave the town without first tasting its famous local delicacies. (On no account)

4 **Work with your partner. Think of a town, city, or area to fit each sentence in Exercise 3.**

5 Grammar Extra 3, Part 2 page 144. Read the explanations and do Exercise 2.

WRITING

1 **You are going to write a short description of a famous town or city in your country.**

- Choose the town or city you are going to write about.
- Decide what kind of tourist or visitor you are writing for. (Young backpackers? Families? Culture vultures?)
- Decide on three or four main points to include in your description.
- Write a short description (about 200 words) in the style of a guidebook. Include **at least one** inversion after a limiting or negative adverbial and **at least three** of the words and expressions from the Vocabulary exercises on page 31. Do NOT include the name of the town or city.

2 **When you have finished writing, work in groups of three or four. Read your description to the group. Listen to the descriptions and try to guess which town or city they are describing. What information helped you get the answer?**

SPEAKING

1 **Work in small groups. Look at the tourist posters, compare them, and discuss the questions.**

   a What aspects of the city are they promoting?
   b What kinds of tourists are they appealing to?
   c Which poster appeals to you more? Why?

2 **Work in your groups. Make a list of the things a city can offer a visitor that the beach, the mountains, or the countryside can't.**

   Which aspects would attract you most? Choose the top three. Compare your answers with the class.

3 **Work in new groups. Discuss the questions.**

   a Which city in your country attracts the most visitors? Why?
   b What is there for them to see and do there?
   c What time of year would you recommend a visitor go there? Why?
   d Do you know of any advertising campaigns for that city? What aspects of the city are they trying to sell?
   e Choose three adjectives to sum up the atmosphere of that city.

4 **Work with a student from another group. Tell each other about the city or cities you discussed in Exercise 3. If you discussed the same city, did you come to the same conclusions? If you discussed different cities, which one do you think is the most successful as a tourist attraction? Why?**

READING & VOCABULARY

1 **Times Square has become a staple in American pop culture, appearing in countless movies, TV shows, and even songs. Match the questions (a-d) with the answers (1-4).**

- **a** Where is it?
- **b** What's with the funny name?
- **c** Why is it so popular?
- **d** Who goes there?

1. Tourists and locals alike stroll along the pedestrian plazas.
2. It was renamed 'Times Square' after the New York Times moved there in 1904.
3. It represents fame, bright lights, and the belief that anything is possible.
4. In New York City.

2 **Read the article and answer the questions.**

- **a** What can you see in Times Square?
- **b** What type of entertainment does Times Square offer?
- **c** What time of year is the most significant at Times Square? Why?

Times Square

Times Square, New York is one of top three (1) ______ tourist attractions in the world. Nicknamed the 'Crossroads of the World' it welcomes millions and millions of tourists every year who tour the bowtie-shaped plaza, (2) ______ the bright, flashing lights of the big city like moths to a flame. So popular is it that it has been featured in literature as well as many movies, television shows, music videos, and video games. (3) ______ throngs of ogle-eyed visitors traverse the streets creating a 24-hour buzz of energy, rubbing shoulders with celebrities, and posing for photos with Elvis impersonators, the human Statue of Liberty, or any of a host of cartoon characters who vie for their tips. Day or night, street performers and artists provide entertainment on demand and not-so-original souvenirs while people-watchers (4) ______ and then some. There is much to see as the square is located in midtown Manhattan in the very heart of New York City and surrounded by skyscrapers, billboards, shops, restaurants, and hotels at every turn. It encompasses several city blocks north from 40th Street, including the now family-friendly 42nd Street at the intersection of Seventh Avenue and the Broadway Theatre District. Flashing theater marquees and multi-story electronic billboards (5) ______ the streets like a giant spotlight, mimicking the stages in its vicinity. A Broadway (or off-Broadway) play is definitely a must-see. Bonus points if it's a musical. (6) ______ nearby also include Madame Tussaud's Wax Museum with over 200 wax figures of A-list stars, world leaders, musicians, sports legends, and more, as well as Ripley's Believe It Or Not if you're fascinated by the odd, the unusual, and (7) ______. However, its most magnificent display is the New Year's Eve Spectacular, featuring star-studded musical performances and the dropping of the ball at midnight, a tradition which began in 1908 by the New York Times, which was then headquartered in the Times Tower. An estimated one million people (8) ______ below-freezing temperatures to converge on Times Square every year for this event while millions more watch worldwide and wish that they were there in the jam-packed crush of humanity. There is indeed nothing like it.

3 **Match the phrases (a-h) with the appropriate places (1-8) in the article.**

- **a** illuminate
- **b** the downright unbelievable
- **c** most visited
- **d** On any given day
- **e** brave
- **f** lured by
- **g** Popular attractions
- **h** get their fill

4 **Work with a partner. You are going to teach your partner some words from the article. Student A: turn to page 137. Student B: turn to page 138.**

5 **Work in small groups. Discuss the questions.**

- **a** Where is the busiest place where you live? What do people do there? Are there street performers or eateries? Which places would you recommend?
- **b** What do you like to do in the city where you live? Where do you go? What do you do? When was the last time you went out? Tell your group where you went and what you did.

LISTENING & SPEAKING

1 **Work with a partner. Do you agree with this statement?**

Life in the city is more dangerous than life in the countryside.

Draw up a list of the main dangers of city life.

2 ▶ 1.25 **Listen to Helen and Robert talking about the city they live in. Do they mention any of the dangers on your list?**

3 **Compare your answers with your partner and discuss the questions.**

a Do Helen and Robert think they live in a particularly dangerous city?
b What precautions do they suggest you should take when walking home at night?
c In what places do they suggest you should take special care with your purse? Why?
d There seems to have been an increase in crime recently. What sort of crime?
e What exactly happened to the group of tourists?
f What do they think the police could do to improve the situation?

Listen again and check your answers.

4 **Work in groups. What advice would you give to ...**

a somebody visiting your home town for the first time?
b somebody going abroad for the first time?

Helen

Robert

PRONUNCIATION

1 **Look at the extracts from the conversation in Listening & Speaking, Exercise 2. Complete them with *just*, *really* or *actually*.**

a As we live in a relatively small city, I don't _____ think it's particularly dangerous.
b _____ like any medium to small city, I think we are much safer than in the big cities.
c _____, come to think of it, I do have a friend who had her purse snatched.
d Well, we _____ shouldn't be complacent because we live in a smaller city.
e Pickpockets _____ tend to target more crowded places.
f But you don't think it's _____ dangerous, do you?
g Well, yes, _____ now you are making me think twice.

▶ 1.26 **Listen and check your answers. Notice the stress on *just*, *really*, and *actually*.**

2 **Add *just*, *really*, and *actually* to the exchanges. Practice reading them with your partner.**

a A: So, what happened?
B: Well, I was coming around the corner when a boy rode past on a scooter. It all happened quickly. Next thing I knew, my purse was gone.

b A: I wouldn't walk home that way if I were you. It's dangerous.
B: I walked home that way last night. It took five minutes. It didn't look dangerous to me.

LANGUAGE FOR LIFE

1 Look at the pictures of an unusual building and discuss the questions with a partner.

- a What do you think it's used for?
- b What does the shape remind you of?
- c Do you like it? Why? / Why not?

2 At the time the building was opened, readers of a blog were invited to comment on the design. Read their comments. Do you agree with any? If so, which ones?

https://buildings.com/interesting-designs.free-blog

Jack	Whether you like it or not, **it does draw attention**. It reminds me of a chocolate Easter egg that's been left out in the sun.
Priya	**What I like about it is** its originality and the beautiful spiral staircase in the main hall.
Flo	Although I can't say I liked it when I first saw it, **it did grow on me** in time, and I found, once I'd had a closer look, that the design wasn't as simple as it looked.
Brigit	**The thing I like most is** the way it looks at night, when it's all lit up.
Pamela	**It's the location** I don't like - right there, next to a historical building! It's a travesty!

3 Look at the comments on the blog in Exercise 2 again. Look at the phrases in bold and match them with the rules (*1* or *2*) on the right.

4 Add emphasis to the sentences using the words in parentheses. You may need to change the structure of the sentence.

- a Although I really didn't like it to start with, I got used to it with time. (did)
- b I like the design best of all. It's really original and eye-catching. (it)
- c I like the simplicity of the design best. (the thing)
- d Initially, people complained about the location. (what)
- e One thing it certainly does is provoke discussion. (do)
- f It needs a more identifiable shape. (one thing)

1.27 **Listen and check your answers.**

Adding emphasis

When we want to add emphasis to a statement we can use:

1 the auxiliary ***do***, ***does***, or ***did*** between the subject and the main verb.

He really **does** like it.
They really **did** come up with a great design.

Notice that the main verb is in the infinitive:

does **like** it (not ~~does likes it~~)

did **come** up with (not ~~did came up with~~)

2 cleft sentences. Cleft sentences emphasize the object of a sentence using expressions with ***what***, ***the thing***, or ***it***.

what I like is ...
the thing I like best is ...
it's the ... I love / object to / don't like

Life Skills: Cultural Awareness

Multicultural Cities

1 How multicultural is your city? Is it easy to meet people from other countries/cultures or people who speak other languages? Are restaurants of various cuisines from different countries/cultures easily accessible?

2 What do you think are the advantages of living in a multicultural city? Do you see any disadvantages?

3 1.28 **Listen to Stella talking about life in the city where she lives. Compare what she says with your answers to questions 1 and 2 above.**

4 Extending the discussion:

- Stella talks mainly about living in a multicultural city. Think about studying and/or working in a multicultural and diverse institution.
- What would be the advantages and disadvantages of working and studying in a multicultural environment? Share your ideas and experiences.

MACMILLAN LIFE SKILLS

LEXICAL SETS AND COLLOCATIONS WITH *CITY* AND *URBAN*

Chongqing, China – the world's fastest growing city

Ny-Ålesund, Norway – one of the northernmost settlements in the world

1 **Look at the pictures and think of two nouns and two adjectives that would best describe each one. Compare with a partner.**

2 **Work with your partner. Look at the words in the box and answer the questions.**

city hamlet megalopolis metropolis outpost satellite settlement town village

a Can you order them from the largest to the smallest?
b Can you think of an example of each in your immediate area? Which do you live in?
c Which words would you be more likely to find in a geography textbook or geography magazine?

Check your answers in Section A on the right.

3 **Complete the sentences with the nouns or compound nouns in Section B on the right to make collocations.**

a The country is undergoing a steady process of ______ , as towns and cities grow at an incredible pace.
b More and more small towns are getting eaten up in the ______ surrounding the capital city.
c A ______ search has begun for the Chicago-based mystery lottery winner.
d The ______ is one of the most impressive buildings in the capital.
e The state has pledged to spend more money on ______ as more and more people move to the cities.
f The country is probably better known for its spectacular ______ than its natural landscapes.

4 **Work with your partner. Look at the sentences in Exercise 3 again. Are these sentences true for your country?**

SECTION A

cit·y /ˈsɪti/ noun [C] ★★★
1 a large important town: *a thriving industrial city on the Tasmanian coast* ♦ **capital city** (=the main city in a country) *Tokyo is Japan's capital city.* ♦ **major city** (=a large and important city) *New and better hotels are springing up in most of Russia's major cities.* **1a.** [usually singular] the political, legal, and ADMINISTRATIVE institutions of a city: *The city has agreed to pay damages to those involved.* ♦ *city employees/officials* ♦ *city hospital/court/legislature* **1b.** the people who live in a city: *a city that is optimistic about the future* **1c.** a European town that has a CATHEDRAL

ham·let /ˈhæmlət/ noun [C] a small village

meg·a·lop·o·lis /ˌmegəˈlɑpəlɪs/ noun [C] a large city, or an area that contains a lot of large cities

me·trop·o·lis /məˈtrɑpəlɪs/ noun [C] *mainly literary* a big city, especially considered as somewhere that is very busy and exciting

out·post /ˈaʊtˌpoʊst/ noun [C] **1** a military camp that is far away from the army **2** a small town far away from other towns, usually where trading takes place

sat·el·lite /ˈsætlˌaɪt/ noun ★★
1 [C] an object that is sent into space to travel around the Earth in order to receive and send information: *a spy/communications/weather satellite* ♦ *France was the third country to launch* (=send into space) *an artificial satellite.* ♦ **via satellite** (=by satellite) *We have pictures of the disaster live via satellite.* ♦ **by satellite** *The new equipment will link vehicles by satellite to their office.* **1a.** a natural object such as a moon that moves around a planet: *Jupiter's satellites*
2 [C] something that is controlled by a larger thing or depends on a larger thing but is separate from it: *She must be working from home or in a satellite office.* **2a.** a town or city that is close to and depends on a larger city **2b.** a country that depends on another, more powerful, country

set·tle·ment /ˈsetlmənt/ noun ★★
2 [C] a place where people have come to live permanently, usually when there were very few people living there before: *They discovered the remains of an early Anglo-Saxon settlement.* **2a.** [U] the process of going to live in a place with few people and starting to make it into a community **2b.** [C] a small town: *a rural settlement in western Minnesota*

town /taʊn/ noun ★★★
1 [C] a place where people live and work that is smaller than a city: *a small town* ♦ *an industrial town in China* ♦ *Mountains overlook the town on three sides.* ♦ *a town on the Mississippi River* ♦ **+of** *the northern Wisconsin town of Rhinelander*

vil·lage /ˈvɪlɪdʒ/ noun [C] ★★★ a very small old town in the countryside, usually in a country outside the U.S. and Canada: *a Scottish fishing village* **a.** the people who live in a village: *The whole village attended the meeting.* **b.** the official legal description of a small town in some U.S. states **c.** [only before noun] in a village or relating to a village: *the village shop/church* ♦ *village gossip*

SECTION B

ˌcity ˈhall noun *Am E* [C] the building where the officials who manage a city work **a.** [U] the officials who manage a city

cit·y·scape /ˈsɪtiˌskeɪp/ noun [C/U] the way that a city looks, or a particular view of a city: *architectural projects that have changed the Paris cityscape*

cit·y·wide /ˈsɪtiˌwaɪd/ adj involving the whole of a city: *Police launched a citywide hunt for the gunman.*

ur·ban·i·za·tion /ˌɜrbənɪˈzeɪʃn/ noun [U] the process by which towns and cities grow bigger and more and more people go to live in them: *The 18th century was a period of rapid urbanization.*

ˌurban reˈnewal noun [U] the process of making areas of a city more attractive and rich by creating new buildings and parks, more business activity, etc.

ˌurban ˈsprawl noun [U] a very large area of buildings, industries, etc. that has spread from a city into the countryside surrounding it, especially in a way that is not attractive: *We drove through several miles of urban sprawl.*

From the *Macmillan English Dictionary (American edition)*

Review A

▶ Grammar Extra pages 142-145

GRAMMAR

1 **Underline the correct alternative.**

I had (1) **waited / been waiting** for ages. I (2) **was getting / had been** really bored. I didn't know how much longer I was going to wait. Why (3) **was he taking / had he taken** so long? (4) **Had something terrible happened / Was something terrible happening** to him? At last I saw him.

"Sorry! There's a demonstration in town. Thousands of people (5) **are protesting / have protested** outside City Hall. They've (6) **closed / been closing** all the streets to traffic."

"Why didn't you call? I've (7) **worried / been worrying** about you!"

"Sorry, but I (8) **hadn't charged / haven't been charging** my cell phone."

When was the last time you had to wait a long time for somebody? Tell a partner what happened.

2 **Work with your partner. Read the pairs of sentences. Explain the difference in meaning between them.**

a 1 I don't particularly want to go.
  2 I particularly don't want to go.
b 1 John only has his telephone number.
  2 Only John has his telephone number.
c 1 I did my work quickly and got ready to go.
  2 I did my work and quickly got ready to go.
d 1 Personally, I don't think he'll apologize.
  2 I don't think he'll apologize personally.
e 1 For a minute I didn't believe him.
  2 I didn't believe him for a minute.
f 1 Just Sam and I went for a drink.
  2 Sam and I just went for a drink.

3 **Write the phrases in the correct order.**

a beautiful / with a delicate / shirt / floral pattern / silk / A
b coat / A / made of 100% / warm / lamb's wool / winter
c A / old pair of / shoes / covered in mud / scruffy / running
d bought / leather / Knee-high / that my mother / for me / boots / in Italy

Do you ever wear anything similar to the clothes described? Write a detailed description of one of your favorite items of clothing. Show it to your partner.

4 **Rewrite the sentences starting with the word given.**

a His name was Harry.
  Harry _____ .
b Gambling was his game.
  His _____ .
c His losses were great.
  Great _____ .
d His car was gone.
  Gone _____ .
e Nobody knew where he had gone.
  Where _____ .

Write a short story about Harry's disappearance. Use fronting where appropriate.

5 **Add words and phrases from the box to soften the statements and reflect your attitude towards them.**

appear believe discussion doubt evidence recognize seem suggest think

a City life is dangerous.
  It is widely recognized that life in some cities can be very dangerous.
b There are no job opportunities in small towns.
c Capital cities are the best places to build a career.
d Quality of life is more important than money.
e Life in a small town is boring.

Work with your partner. Discuss your statements.

6 **Match the sentence halves.**

a Never had she
b Only then did I
c Not only was she
d Not a word did she
e Never again would I

1 understand how strongly I felt.
2 say as I took her hand.
3 looked so beautiful.
4 my best friend, she was also the love of my life.
5 ask such an important question.

What do you think the question was? Discuss with your partner. Write three more sentences to continue the story.

VOCABULARY

1 Complete the descriptions with the words and phrases in the box.

> butting in   drones on and on   flows   gets it across   hog   hunt around   say   the same wavelength

a I think Dylan can be really rude, don't you? He's forever _____ on conversations and it's not even as if he has anything interesting to _____ !

b Ava is very sweet, but she does tend to _____ the conversation – you know, she gets started on a subject and then she just _____ forever.

c He's amazing – the conversation really _____ when we're together. We're always on _____ . I've never met anyone like him before!

d She's really good in meetings. She never has to _____ for words; she always knows exactly what she wants to say and she _____ so clearly. I wish I was like her!

Do you know anyone like the people described above? Tell a partner about them.

2 Complete the sentences with the correct form of the words in parentheses.

a That was probably the greatest _____ of my whole life. (achieve)

b He tackled the problem with _____ and _____ . (competent / efficient)

c I don't think she's particularly _____ of other people's feelings. (consider)

d I get an enormous amount of _____ out of my family. (satisfy)

e She's a very _____ worker and a _____ addition to the workforce. (skills / value)

f Reaching the top of the mountain gave me an incredibly intense feeling of _____ . (fulfill)

3 Match each sentence (a–f) with a response (1–6).

a Have you seen Tim's new hairstyle?

b This coffee is really strong!

c Ann hasn't called me for two days! Do you think she's mad at me?

d He should really apologize.

e It's great to see the boys playing so well together.

f What's up with José? He looks glum.

1 No, she's just giving you a taste of your own medicine.

2 Yes! Just goes to show – there's no accounting for taste!

3 I agree – that comment was in poor taste.

4 Yes, it's definitely an acquired taste.

5 Yes, it's the bitter taste of defeat!

6 Well, it comes as no surprise. They share the same taste in practically everything!

4 Choose the correct words to complete the descriptions.

It was a busy, (1) _____ market town. We arrived at dawn. The bus station was an ugly (2) _____ block set in a (3) _____ back street behind the main square. People were already setting up their stalls. Music (4) _____ from the loudspeakers of one of the trucks. It was a lively scene, and behind it all, the (5) _____ view of the Andes (6) _____ above the town.

	a	b	c
1	a homey	b bustling	c bobbing
2	a concrete	b tacky	c batter
3	a haphazard	b in-your-face	c grubby
4	a sped off	b blared out	c chugged
5	a exquisite	b awe-inspiring	c reverie
6	a thriving	b thrusting	c soaring

PRONUNCIATION

1 Look at some words from Units 1–3. Say the words and add them to the table.

> ~~animated~~   atmosphere   awe-inspiring   efficiency   evocative   exquisite   fulfillment   frustrating   haphazard   hilarious   historical   intricate   meaningful   reverie   satisfying   stimulating

A: □▫▫	B: ▫□▫	C: □▫▫▫	D: ▫□▫▫
		animated	

2 Underline the stressed syllables.

1.29 **Listen, check, and repeat.**

4 Story

SPEAKING

1 **Read the text about six-word life stories. Which is your favorite story and why?**

One Life. Six Words. What's Yours?

Legend has it that the novelist Ernest Hemingway was once challenged to write a story in six words. He came back with, "For sale: baby shoes, never worn." Some say he called it his best work. Others dismiss the anecdote as literary folklore. Either way, the six-word story was born, and it's been around ever since. The following stories were amongst thousands submitted to *Smith* magazine in New York.

I was never the pretty one.
Followed rules, not dreams. Never again.
Found true love, married someone else.
Time heals all wounds? Not quite.
Six words not enough for a
Never lived up to my potential.
Didn't fit in then, still don't.
I write stories. They come true.
I still make coffee for two.

2 **Match the famous people (a–e) with the six-word life stories (1–5).**

a Bill Gates
b Julius Caesar
c Agatha Christie
d Martin Luther King Jr.
e Marilyn Monroe

1 Kept you guessing until the end.
2 My dream came true at last.
3 Died young and beautiful, loved forever.
4 I connected people and got rich.
5 I came, I saw, I conquered.

3 **Work with a partner. Write six-word stories for three famous people. Read them to another pair. Can they guess whose stories they are?**

READING

1 **What do you know about David Bowie's life and career? Read the extract from his obituary on page 41. Which of the facts were mentioned?**

2 **Read the text again. Put the events below in order from first to last (1-8).**

- ☐ He died in his home.
- ☐ He reached the pinnacle of his fame and popularity.
- ☐ He sustained an injury which gave him a distinguishing physical feature.
- ☐ He stopped using his most famous stage persona.
- ☐ He met the woman who was to be his second wife.
- ☐ His first marriage came to an end.
- ☐ The release of a new album coincided with his birthday.
- ☐ He experienced his greatest personal struggles.

3 **Complete the glossary on page 41 with the highlighted words in the obituary extract.**

4 **Which of these six-word stories best describes David Bowie's life for you? Why?**

a Never afraid to be an individual.
b Who was Bowie? We'll never know.
c Ups and downs, always an artist.

- **Grammar:** The future as seen from the past. Discourse markers in writing
- **Vocabulary:** Types of stories. Expressions with *story* and *tale*. Deception and belief
- **Language for Life:** Responding to a story

David Bowie

With a career spanning nearly five decades, it is no wonder that David Bowie's musical persona shifted and evolved with the years. Whether going by the name Davy Jones, Ziggy Stardust, Thin White Duke, Aladdin Sane, or David Bowie, his utter uniqueness and strength of personality have ensured an enduring legacy in popular culture. Like many of his high-profile peers, Bowie was not immune to controversy. By the time of his death his popularity had waned considerably from its apex in the early 1980s. But, with over 140 million album sales, countless accolades, and generations of adoring fans and musicians, it is impossible to deny the value of his global impact as a musical and a cultural icon.

Unlike other pop and rock stars, David Bowie was never known as an amazing technical musician like Jimi Hendrix nor a brilliant dancer like Michael Jackson. Instead, what made him special was his chameleon-like nature and the willingness to go to extremes in the name of his art. With his distinctive eye (the result of a schoolyard fight), penchant for colorful costumes, and total lack of inhibition, Bowie was unlike any other performer of his generation. Take for example his famous Ziggy Stardust persona, a time-travelling androgynous rock star who communicates with extraterrestrial beings. Not only did he come up with this fantastical character for the purpose of an album, but also he would go on to maintain his alter-ego for over another year before abruptly retiring Ziggy in the summer of 1973.

As a result of his constant experimentation, Bowie was to have every conceivable record label attached to his work at one time or another, including those specializing in glam-rock, electronic, rock'n'roll, funk, soul, and more. Similarly, he was called everything from a singer-songwriter, actor, and pioneer, to much less flattering terms by critics of his showmanship and his fluctuating musical style. Bowie's eclectic career resulted in innumerable hits, notably the space-themed 1972 album *The Rise and Fall of Ziggy Stardust* and more mainstream classics like 1983's *Let's Dance*. Regardless of the time, the voice and look were unmistakably his own.

Despite Bowie's dedication to his craft, his outspoken nature and rock-star lifestyle were also the cause of many personal issues he battled during his life. Though it was at a time of great fame, in many respects the mid to late 1970s was an era of deep emotional and physical stress. As a result, Bowie's health deteriorated and he became extremely thin and paranoid from the lack of sleep. His friends said he was on the verge of collapsing. Simultaneously, his behavior turned erratic, with wild swings of emotion. Ultimately, his marriage to Angela Barnett ended in divorce in 1980.

Ironically as it may seem, Bowie would get through this rough patch when his fame was declining. As opposed to his more surreal earlier work, his music turned towards political activism and made a positive impact. In his personal life, meeting the fashion model Iman in 1990 was a blessing, leading to long-lasting and stable relationship. After a brief courtship, they married in 1992, had a child, and would remain together until his death 24 years later.

Bowie's death mirrored his life in many ways – his focus remained on his art. Although he had been diagnosed with liver cancer 18 months prior, this fact was not revealed to the public. Throughout this period, Bowie maintained his dedication to his craft, working on what would become his final album, *Blackstar*. What's more, although it's unknown whether he had been planning on ever performing live again, according to his producer Tony Visconti, Bowie had been thinking of recording one more final album. Also, he was to have published a photobook of objects from his life. But, alas, it was not to be.

On January 10, 2016, two days after *Blackstar*'s release and his 69th birthday, Bowie passed away in his New York City apartment. In line with his wishes, David Bowie was cremated without a funeral, but this did nothing to quell the outpouring of love from his fans, who flocked to memorials around the world. Shortly after his death, his son announced that David Bowie was to have soon become a grandfather.

Glossary

- **a** _____ verb [I]: to become weaker or less important
- **b** _____ adjective: not hidden or secret
- **c** _____ adjective: interesting or unusual because of its variety
- **d** _____ verb [T]: to last for a particular period of time, especially a long period
- **e** _____ noun [C]: the part of your personality that you deliberately show most people
- **f** _____ adjective: changing often, not following a regular pattern
- **g** _____ noun [C]: a feeling of liking something very much or a tendency to do something a lot
- **h** _____ adjective: neither clearly male nor clearly female
- **i** _____ verb [T]: to get rid of thoughts or feelings
- **j** _____ noun [C]: honors given to someone for their work

GRAMMAR

1 **Read the sentences about David Bowie and answer the questions.**

a *... David Bowie was to have soon become a grandfather.*
b *... he would go on to maintain his alter-ego for over another year ...*
c *... Bowie was to have every conceivable record label attached to his work ...*

Which of the sentences express ...

1 a future event, as seen from the past, that took place?
2 a future event, as seen from the past, that did not take place?

Are the sentences formal or informal in register?

2 **Complete the sentences with the verbs in parentheses in an appropriate form, to express the future as seen from the past. Which events took place and which didn't?**

a Bowie _____ (release) *Blackstar* on his 69th birthday.
b He _____ (record) one final album, but he ran out of time.
c His marriage to Iman _____ (provide) stability to his life for many years.
d He was working on a book which *Penguin* _____ (publish) in the near future.

3 **Underline the correct alternatives about events that did not take place.**

a I was going **to get** / **to getting** married, but I realized he was the wrong person for me.
b I had been hoping **of seeing** / **to see** the concert, but I got the flu and had to give away my ticket.
c I was just about **studying** / **to study** in Mexico when my visa fell through and I had to call it off.
d I had been thinking **of going** / **to go** into medicine, but I changed my mind and trained as a lawyer instead.
e I was on the point **of winning** / **to win** the race, but I tripped over and came last.
f I was planning **to buy** / **of buying** a car, but I didn't get my driver's license.
g I was on the verge **to give up** / **of giving up** waiting when the bus finally came.
h I was due **to move** / **for moving**, but the landlord of the new apartment increased the rent, so I decided against it.

Is the register more or less formal than the sentences in Exercise 2? Which sentences refer more to intentions, and which refer more to imminent events?

The future as seen from the past

Events that took place

He **would** / **was to maintain** his alter-ego for over another year.

Events that did not take place

He **was to have (soon) become** a grandfather.

Future plans in the past

It's unknown whether he **was going** / **was planning** to ever perform live again.

It's unknown whether he **had been planning** / **had been thinking** of ever performing live again.

Imminent events in the past

He **was (just) about to** / **due to** collapse. He **was on the point** / **on the verge** of collapsing.

4 **Complete the sentences in a suitable way.**

a I was planning _____ , but it was sold out.
b I was on the verge _____ , but I decided it was too expensive.
c I had been hoping _____ , but my grades weren't good enough.
d I was thinking _____ , but I was too tired.
e I was just about _____ , when the telephone rang.
f I was going _____ , but a friend persuaded me not to.
g I was on the point _____ , but I decided the salary was too low.

Are any of these sentences true for you? Discuss with a partner.

5 **Grammar Extra 4, Part 1** page 144. Read the explanations and do Exercise 1.

VOCABULARY

1 **Work with a partner. Discuss the differences between the types of stories in the box.**

anecdote fable fairy tale legend mystery myth news story short story

In which type of story would you expect to find each of the following sentences?

a Once upon a time, in a faraway kingdom, there lived a beautiful princess.
b Have I told you about the time when I fell into the river?
c Long ago, there lived a brave warrior and his band of soldiers.
d "Let's return to the scene of the crime and see if we can find any more clues," the detective said.
e At 92, Muriel felt she had achieved all she could in life.
f And the moral is: pride goes before a fall.
g Reports are coming in of a forest fire which is spreading rapidly in northern counties.
h Athena, daughter of Zeus, was the goddess of wisdom and warfare.

2 **Tell your partner about one of the types of stories in Exercise 1 you have heard recently.**

3 **Read the definition of *urban myth* on the right. Read the urban myth on page 137. Do you believe it? Do you know any others?**

Urban myth

An urban myth is a funny, scary, sad, or educational story which is supposed to be true. However, you'll never hear one told by the person it actually happened to. Every time an urban myth is retold, it changes slightly.

LISTENING

1 1.30 **Listen to Simon talking about his favorite book when he was a child. What kind of book is it? Why does he like it?**

2 **Work with your partner. Try to complete the sentences about the book in Exercise 1.**

a The story is set ...
b The characters are ...
c It tells the story of ...
d The main character is ...
e Basically, the book is about ...
f The villain is ...
g They have all sorts of ...
h In the end ...
i He enjoyed the book because ...
j Now the book ...

Listen again and check your answers.

3 **If you have read this book, did you enjoy it? Why? / Why not? If you have not read it, does it appeal to you? Why? / Why not?**

SPEAKING: ANECDOTE

You are going to tell your partner about a story you know. It could be a favorite children's story, a traditional tale from your country, or the plot of a novel, short story, or movie or TV show.

- Ask yourself the questions below. Think about *what* to say and *how* to say it.
- Tell your partner about the story.

Note: You can use the simple past tense or the simple present tense to tell a story.

a What kind of story is it?
b Where and when did you read, hear, or see it?
c What is the story about?
d Where and when is the story set?
e Who are the characters?
f What is the plot of the story?
g What happens at the end?
h Why do you like it?

LISTENING

1 **Work with a partner. Read the definition of the word *con*.**
Then look at the pictures (1–4) and discuss what cons they might illustrate.

> **con**[1] /kɑn/ noun [C] ★★
> **1** *informal* a dishonest plan or method for making someone give you money: *The insurance scheme was just a big con.*
> **2** *very informal* a PRISONER
> **con**[2] /kɑn/ verb [T] *informal* to make someone believe something that is not true, especially in order to get money from them: *He conned them into believing he was sick.* ♦ *She was conned out of her life savings.*

2 ▶ 1.31–1.34 **Listen to the four stories of the pictures (1–4). Were you correct?**

3 **Listen again and answer the questions for each person (1–4) in the stories.**

a What deception is described?
b Why did the person fall for it?
c How did they feel about being conned?

What would you have done in the situations described? Tell your partner.

VOCABULARY

1 **Work with your partner. Complete the sentences with words or phrases from the box. Use a dictionary if necessary.**

> a cock-and-bull story a long story an old wives' tale a sob story
> tattle-tale the story of my life to cut a long story short

a They say that eating carrots helps you see in the dark, but personally I think it's just ______ .
b We lost our baggage at the airport, and had to fill in various forms and keep calling the airline. But anyway, ______ , we got it back in the end.
c "Mommy, Ella hit the cat." "Don't be a ______ , Mia."
d I'm afraid you can't believe everything Karen says. She always has ______ about how badly people have treated her.
e When he arrived late he told me ______ about being trapped in an elevator and then being rescued by a news reporter and being interviewed on TV.
f I didn't get the job – they told me I didn't have enough experience. But that's ______ .
g "So how did you persuade your father to lend you the car?" "Well, it's ______ ."

2 **Work with your partner. Discuss which expressions (a–g) in Exercise 1 relate to …**

1 a myth or superstition.
2 a silly story that is hard to believe.
3 a person who tells a story to get someone else into trouble.
4 a sad story designed to elicit sympathy.
5 a story that you don't want to tell in detail.
6 a detailed or complicated story.
7 something unfortunate that often happens to someone.

3 **Work with your partner. Write a short conversation containing one or more of the expressions in Exercise 1. Read it aloud to the class, leaving out the expression(s).**
Can other people guess what they were?

PRONUNCIATION

1 **Read the extracts from the conversations in Listening, Exercise 2. How are the underlined words pronounced?**

1 Q: So, have you ever been conned?
A: I'm ashamed to say I have.

2 Q: Do you have any experiences of being conned?
A: Yes, I do.

1.35 **Listen and check your ideas. Then answer the questions.**

a Which words carry the main stress in each sentence?

b Why are the underlined words pronounced differently in each exchange?

Practice reading the exchanges aloud with a partner.

Weak and strong forms of auxiliary verbs

Have (/həv/) you ...?
Yes, I **have** (/hæv/). /
No, I **haven't** (/ˈhævnt/).

Do (/də/) you ...?
Yes, I **do** (/du/). /
No, I **don't** (/doʊnt/).

Can (/kən/) you ...?
Yes, I **can** (/kæn/). /
No, I **can't** (/kænt/).

Are (/ər/) you ...?
Yes, we **are** (/ɑr/). /
No, we **aren't** (/ɑrnt/).

See *Phonetic symbols* on page 174.

2 **Work with your partner. Decide how the auxiliary verbs are pronounced in these exchanges.**

a A: So, do you ever enter competitions?
B: I have to say I don't.

b A: So, can you cook well?
B: I'm proud to say I can.

c A: So, are you good at managing your time?
B: I'm happy to say I am.

d A: Can you speak Chinese?
B: I'm afraid I can't.

1.36 **Listen and check your answers. Practice reading the exchanges with your partner.**

3 **Ask your partner the questions in Exercise 2. Give true answers. Then ask more questions beginning *Do you ever ...?, Have you ever ...?, Are you ...?, Can you ...?***

VOCABULARY & SPEAKING

1 **Read the situations and complete the sentences with words and phrases from the box.**

con fall for fishy get taken for a ride naive plausible skeptical unfaithful

a I let the used-car salesman _____ me into believing that the sound that the engine makes was nothing to worry about. I shouldn't have been so gullible.

b You can't take Laura in - she's too streetwise to _____ any cock-and-bull story.

c He made out he was a police officer and just needed to check my passport. How was I to know he was a con man? His story seemed completely _____ to me.

d You have to be really on the ball and astute if you don't want to _____ . There are some really unscrupulous people out there.

e Did you really swallow that sob story about his daughter? I can't believe you were so _____ .

f He led me to believe he wanted to marry me. Little did I realize he already had a wife and children back home. It's made me more _____ about men, I'm afraid.

g "I thought that investment deal sounded _____ ." "Yes, I should have realized. The trouble with me is, I'm too trusting - I take everyone at their word."

h Unbeknown to Tim, his girlfriend was cheating on him. He can't seem to find a woman who isn't _____ to him.

Deception and belief synonyms

gullible	=	naive
swallow	=	fall for
unscrupulous	=	dishonest
trick	=	con
make out	=	pretend
astute	=	streetwise
plausible	=	credible
skeptical	=	cynical

2 **Underline the correct alternatives.**

a Are you a(n) **gullible** / **plausible** / **unfaithful** person or are you more skeptical?

b Have you ever been **tricked** / **made out** / **swallowed** into handing over money to a stranger?

c Can you think of a **trusting** / **plausible** / **naive** excuse for forgetting an appointment?

d Have you ever **made out** / **taken in** / **conned** you were sick when you didn't want to go somewhere?

e Would you ever **fall for** / **make out** / **cheat on** a boyfriend or girlfriend behind their back?

Work with your partner. Ask and answer the questions.

READING

1 **Look at the cartoons on page 47. Do you get the jokes? Do you have similar jokes in your country?**

2 **Read the extract from a book on humor. Choose the best title: *a*, *b*, or *c*.**

a English comedy b Lost in translation c The world's funniest jokes

http://jokesaroundtheworld.com

People say that humor is a universal phenomenon, common to all human societies. So, what about the perception of humor between societies? Are the same things funny to people of different nationalities living in different places? And what about jokes – can they even be translated? Let's see if you get these jokes from around the world, translated into English:

1) One fish says to another fish, "Hi!" The other replies, "Where!?" (*from German*)
2) Why do Hawaiians never need to go to the dentist? Good teeth. (*from Japanese*)
3) One road sign says to another road sign, "Are you married?" and the other replies, "No, I'm divorced." (*from Danish*)

And yet, for some brave translators making sure jokes remain funny is a full-time job. Discussing her work with *The Verge*, translator Sabine Sebastian describes the trials and tribulations of translating the classic American sitcom *Seinfeld* for German television. Not only is wordplay a huge part of the series' appeal, but also it has a very specific context (New York), and is full of American cultural references. That is to say, is the character of George Steinbrenner as funny if you don't know anything about American baseball? Unfortunately, in this case, although Sabine loved the show, it didn't really take off in Europe, whereas other story-based comedies, in particular *Friends*, became huge hits.

So what's the best way to translate a joke? According to some experts like Peter Alan Low, it is feasible to translate almost any humor although strictly speaking, only *spoken* humor. To do so, it's important to remember that translating is an art and to not worry about word-for-word accuracy. If two words need to rhyme, for example, you might need to find a different rhyming pair, rather than stay true to translation. As for translating culture-specific humor, it's best not to over-explain and to just leave it as it is. In an increasingly globalized world, people often share a lot of cultural knowledge. Luckily too, sometimes humor really is universal, especially physical humor – it seems a person falling over can cause laughter no matter where in the world you go.

Joke explanations

1) *In German, "hai" means shark.*
2) *In Japanese, the translation for good teeth, "ha wa ii", sounds like Hawai'i.*
3) *In Danish, "skilt" means "sign" and also "divorced".*

3 **Read the text again. Based on the text, decide if the statements are True *(T)*, False *(F)*, or Not Given *(N)*.**

a Translating from English to another language is more difficult than translating from another language to English.
b Because of her own enjoyment of the show, Sabine Sebastian found translating *Seinfeld* easy.
c It is recommended not to alter cultural references for the sake of clarity when translating jokes.
d American comedies are more popular internationally due to audiences' existing familiarity with American culture.

4 **Complete the glossary using words from the extract.**

Glossary

a ______ phrase: the difficulties and problems involved with something
c ______ noun [C]: a television series about a particular group of characters who deal with situations in a humorous way
c ______ noun [U]: clever or funny use of words
d ______ verb [I]: to become successful or popular very fast
e ______ adjective: possible to be done

5 **Work with a partner and discuss: Do you watch comedies that have been translated, either with subtitles or with dubbing? Do you think that the translated jokes are still funny?**

GRAMMAR

1 **Match each discourse marker in the box with one highlighted in the extract on page 46 with a similar meaning.**

in addition particularly say then to be accurate in other words

2 **Where in the sentences could you put the discourse markers in parentheses? Change the punctuation where necessary.**

a Why do different nationalities laugh at different things? (so)
b Some writers, Oscar Wilde, are famous for their wit. (for example)
c Many nationalities enjoy puns, the French. (in particular)
d What is universal about humor? (then)
e Americans love slapstick. Europeans find it hilarious. (too)
f Slapstick leaves me cold. I don't find it in the least amusing. (in other words)

3 **Look at the pairs of sentences. What is the difference in each pair?**

a 1 Some nationalities, **such as** the Mexicans, find this joke absolutely sidesplitting.
2 Some nationalities, **namely** the Mexicans, find this joke absolutely sidesplitting.
b 1 The professor could be regarded as eccentric, **or at least** slightly weird.
2 The professor could be regarded as slightly weird, **not to say** eccentric.
c 1 Canadians find this hilarious; Americans, **by contrast**, simply do not see the joke.
2 Canadians find this hilarious; Americans, **likewise**, are vastly amused by it.

Match each discourse marker in bold with one in the box with a similar meaning.

including on the other hand or at any rate or even similarly viz.

4 **Underline the best discourse marker.**

a I find puns, **particularly / that is to say / such as** jokes involving a play on words, very amusing.
b I love classic comedies, **in other words / on the other hand / in particular** the movies of Woody Allen.
c I don't often tell jokes – **at any rate / on the other hand / namely**, not in a group.
d I like subtle jokes rather than more earthy ones; my family, **say / similarly / by contrast**, tend to have a pretty dry sense of humor.
e I can only tell jokes in two languages, **including / in particular / namely** my own language and English.

Are any of these statements true for you? Compare your answers with a partner.

5 **Grammar Extra 4, Part 2** page 144. Read the explanations and do Exercise 2.

Discourse markers in writing

I love TV comedy shows, ...
particularly the American ones.
for example, *Friends*.
or **at any rate**, cartoon shows.
and funny movies, **too**.

"Waiter, what's this fly doing in my soup?"
"I think it's the breast stroke, sir."

"Waiter, what kind of soup is this?"
"It's bean soup."
"Never mind what it's been. What is it now?"

LISTENING & SPEAKING

1 1.37-1.40 **Listen to the four jokes and write down the punch line. Did you get the joke?**

2 **Listen again and respond to each one using the expressions in the box.**

It's hilarious. It's pretty funny. I find it a little offensive.
It leaves me cold. I find it mildly amusing. I don't get it.

3 **Work with your partner. Student A: look at page 138. Student B: look at page 139. Read the joke and try to remember it. Then close your book and tell it without looking. Does your partner get the joke?**

4 **Do you think the jokes are funny? Do you have any similar jokes in your country? Tell a joke you know to your partner. Do they get it?**

LANGUAGE FOR LIFE

1 1.41 **Listen to the conversation between two friends and answer the questions.**

a What two problems did the speaker have?
b Has anything like this ever happened to you or anyone you know?

2 **Listen again and number the useful phrases in the order that you hear them.**

☐ What a relief! I bet you were happy!
☐ I'm not surprised!
☐ Oh, no!
☐ Oh, good!
☐ Right.
☐ Oh, how scary! You must have been terrified!
☐ Oh, what a nightmare! That must have been awful!
☐ Oh, wow!
1 Really?

3 **Work with a partner. Discuss which part of the story each useful phrase in Exercise 2 was in response to. Check your answers against the audioscript on page 154.**

Which of the useful phrases express ...

a interest? b sympathy? c gladness? d agreement?

4 **Match the useful phrases in the box with the categories in Exercise 3.**

a Uh huh.
b I don't blame you!
c Lucky you!
d Poor you!
e What a shame!
f Totally.
g How awful!
h That's amazing!
i Fantastic!

1.42 **Listen and repeat the intonation of the responses.**

5 1.43–1.47 **Listen to extracts from five stories. What happened in each one? Listen again and respond with appropriate useful phrases.**

6 **Think of an anecdote beginning with one of the following sentences.**

Have I told you about the time when ...

- I went skiing / sailing / fishing for the first time?
- I lost my purse / keys / cell phone / baggage on vacation?
- I went to a café / bar / restaurant without my wallet?

Tell your partner your story. Your partner should respond using appropriate phrases.

Life Skills: Communication

Active Listening

Active Listening: an important life skill which means to concentrate on, understand, remember, and respond to what the other person is saying.

1 **Look at the different elements of active listening below. Decide which category they belong to and write them in the spaces. Write: *NV* for non-verbal signs, *V* for verbal signs, *MP* for mental processes and *A* for things to avoid.**

a Eye contact _____
b Day dreaming _____
c Keeping an open mind _____
d Asking for clarification _____
e Always agree with the speaker _____
f Responses to show interest _____
g Remembering key points and the speaker's name _____
h Smiling and nodding _____
i Face the speaker _____
j Asking questions _____
k Repeating or paraphrasing _____
l Checking your phone _____

2 **With a partner, do Language for Life, Exercise 6 again. While your partner is speaking, practice using active listening, in particular the points you listed as areas for improvement.**

MACMILLAN LIFE SKILLS

4 Writing Extra

DESCRIPTIVE NARRATIVE

1 **What are some of your earliest memories as a child? Tell a partner.**

2 **Read the narrative about a childhood memory. Does it have a happy or a sad ending?**

I remember the day when I got my first pair of in-line skates. I was about eight or nine at the time. I remember I had been asking my parents for about a year to get me a pair, but they had said no, as they were too dangerous. Finally, when my birthday came, I went downstairs to find a huge package on the kitchen table.

(1) _____ , I took off the wrapping paper and (2) _____ found that it contained a pair of brand-new in-line skates. (3) _____ .

I put them on, went outside, (4) _____ , and skated down the sidewalk, only to trip over the curb and fall down. Needless to say, I landed flat on my face and started crying. A neighbor ran out to pick me up as I lay (5) _____ on the ground, but I (6) _____ remember hoping my parents hadn't seen what happened because they were bound to say, "I told you so."

Eventually, however, I had to go back home, carrying the in-line skates which were badly damaged, and (7) _____ admit what had happened. (8) _____ , they didn't tell me off, and didn't say anything about the skates. My elbows and knees were hurt and I had bruises all over and holes in the knees of my new pants. It didn't stop me though, and I eventually became very good at it. I don't know what happened to my skates – I guess my parents gave them away, or maybe they are still somewhere in my parents' attic.

3 **Replace the highlighted words and phrases in the narrative in Exercise 2 with the ones in the box (a–j).**

a clutching	f howling at the top of my lungs
b must have been	g one of my most vivid childhood memories is
c pestering	h proficient
d badly grazed	i refused point-blank
e tore	j went hurtling

4 **Complete the blanks (1–8) in the story with these extra words and phrases (a–h), to add interest.**

a sheepishly
b with my heart beating
c sprawled
d distinctly
e to my delight
f like a rocket
g I could hardly contain my excitement
h to my relief

5 **You are going to write about a childhood memory, for example:**

- your first day at school or in a new house.
- a time you got lost or got into trouble.
- a birthday or a time you got a special gift.
- a visit, outing, vacation, or celebration.
- a memorable meeting.
- the first time you did something – for example, went to the movies, the zoo, the dentist.

Write the story using vivid expressions. Give details of what happened and how you felt.

Exchange stories with your partner. Can they suggest how to make it more detailed or vivid?

5 Bargain

READING & VOCABULARY

1 **Do you enjoy shopping? Why or why not? Discuss with a partner.**

2 **Take the quiz. Then compare and discuss your answers with your partner.**

Money Management - What is Your Spending Profile?

1 Your favorite brand is launching a new leather jacket that would look great on you. What do you do?
- **a** Put aside a little money every month until you can afford to buy it.
- **b** You only buy what you need, and you don't need a leather jacket.
- **c** Run out and buy it on your credit card.

2 Your cell phone is quite old. Although it still works, there are newer phones on the market with new features and modern designs. What do you do?
- **a** Figure out your budget and shop around for the best deal.
- **b** Don't buy the phone and make do with what you have.
- **c** Buy a newer model, even though it is above your budget.

3 How do you do your grocery shopping?
- **a** Plan your shopping list carefully and stick to it.
- **b** Buy low cost brands and in bulk to save money.
- **c** Just go and buy what seems interesting.

4 It's your birthday. How do you plan to celebrate?
- **a** Plan ahead and put some money aside for a nice celebration.
- **b** Get a cake and celebrate with a few friends at home.
- **c** Make a last-minute decision to go on that weekend ski getaway you've been thinking about.

5 Your friends are renting a beach house for the summer and have invited you to rent together with them, but you are broke. What do you do?
- **a** Cut other items in your budget so that you can afford your part of the rent on the beach house.
- **b** Say no because you have other financial priorities right now.
- **c** As long as there is credit limit on your credit card, there's money. Beach house here I come!

3 **Turn to page 138. Check your scores and read the spending profiles. Is your profile an accurate description of your spending habits? Why? / Why not?**

4 **Complete the glossary using words and phrases from the quiz.**

Glossary

- **a** ______ phrasal verb: to save money so that you can buy or pay for something in the future
- **b** ______ phrasal verb: to go to several shops before you decide what particular thing to buy
- **c** ______ phrasal verb: to manage with the things that you have, even though this is not really enough
- **d** ______ phrasal verb: to do something that you decided you would do or that you believe you should do
- **e** ______ phrase: when you buy large amounts of goods each time you buy them
- **f** ______ adjective: having no money
- **g** ______ noun [C]: the maximum amount of money you can spend on your credit card

5 **Look at the words and phrases. Circle the word or phrase in each group which has a different meaning from the other two. Use a dictionary if necessary.**

- **a** budget / overspend / economize
- **b** run up a bill / live within your means / get into debt
- **c** save up / clear a debt / pay off a debt
- **d** frugal / generous / thrifty
- **e** broke / short of cash / tight-fisted
- **f** overdrawn / in the red / extravagant

6 **Write five sentences describing your spending habits or those of someone you know. Read your sentences to your partner. Ask questions to find out more information, and decide what the spending profile might be.**

- **Grammar:** Prepositions in relative clauses. Articles
- **Vocabulary:** Spending and saving. Economizing. Discussing prices
- **Language for Life:** Negotiating, haggling, making a deal

LISTENING

1 1.48 **Listen to six people being interviewed about their shopping habits for a survey. Which question (a–i) are they each answering?**

- a Do you enjoy shopping?
- b What's your earliest shopping memory?
- c What's your favorite store?
- d What was your most extravagant purchase?
- e What was your last big purchase?
- f Who does the grocery shopping in your household?
- g What's the next thing you're planning to buy?
- h Are you an impulsive shopper?
- i What was your best bargain?

2 **Listen again to the six people in Exercise 1 and make notes on their answers. Then choose three of the questions to ask a partner.**

GRAMMAR

1 **Look at the pairs of sentences. Which sentence sounds more informal and which sounds more formal?**

- a 1 When I go grocery shopping, I pick the produce I like the look of.
  - 2 When I go grocery shopping, I pick the produce of which I like the look.
- b 1 Are you the person I should speak to about opening a bank account?
  - 2 Are you the person to whom I should speak about opening a bank account?

In which sentences could you use the relative pronouns *that* or *who*? Is it more or less common to leave them out when speaking?

2 **Rewrite the sentences to make them more informal.**

- a The grocery store at which I do my shopping is very cheap.
- b I have a good friend with whom I like to go shopping.
- c At the moment, there is nothing for which I am saving up.
- d I never buy clothes in which I don't feel comfortable.
- e Being tight-fisted is something of which my friends would never accuse me.
- f I can't remember the last person to whom I gave a gift.
- g The last thing for which I wrote out a check was very expensive.

Are any of these sentences true for you? Discuss with your partner.

3 **Look at this pair of sentences. Underline the relative clause in *b*.**

- a I bought lots of clothes on sale; I'll probably never wear most of them.
- b I bought lots of clothes on sale, most of which I'll probably never wear.

Is it a defining or non-defining relative clause? How do you know? Can *which* be replaced by *that*?

Prepositions in relative clauses

Formal
She's the person **from whom I'm buying the house**.

That's the house **into which I'm moving**.

Informal
She's the person (**that** / **who**) **I'm buying the house from**.

That's the house (**that** / **which**) **I'm moving into**.

Of in non-defining relative clauses
My friends, **many of whom are in debt** / **all of whom are broke**, often want me to lend them money.

I bought several souvenirs, the **most expensive of which** / **the first of which is this necklace**.

4 **Rewrite these sentences to include a non-defining relative clause, as in sentence *b* in Exercise 3.**

- a I earn $200 a week. I spend half of it on rent.
- b I have several close friends. None of my close friends enjoys shopping.
- c There are several restaurants near my house. The nicest restaurant is out of my price range.
- d My cell phone bills are pretty high. I got the latest bill last week.
- e The people in my class can't afford to go out for a fancy meal. The majority of them don't have jobs.

5 **Write true sentences about the stores or restaurants in your neighborhood, using a similar non-defining relative clause. Compare with your partner.**

6 **Grammar Extra 5, Part 1** page 146. Read the explanations and do Exercise 1.

READING & VOCABULARY

1 **Do you look for deals and discounts? What kinds of deals do you look for and how do you search for them? Tell a partner.**

2 **Read the article on page 53 about someone who learnt about all the ways she could save money using the internet. From the article, make a list of the ways she could save money. Can you think of other ways you could save money using the internet?**

3 **Choose the best alternative to complete the statements. Find evidence to support your choices.**

a Sheila **fully embraced** / **did not fully** embrace technology.
b The writer tried to convince Sheila **of the benefits of the internet** / **that the internet is good for checking her emails**.
c Sheila is a **frivolous** / **frugal** spender.
d Free phone calls and text messaging are the **exception** / **rule**.
e Anyone can **learn DIY from the internet** / **do DIY to make money**.
f Air travel has become cheaper because of **discounts from airlines** / **tools made possible on the internet**.
g Sheila **now believes in the benefits of the internet** / **remains an internet sceptic**.

4 **Complete the sentences from the article. Then check your answers.**

a Sheila has shied _____ getting internet at home.
b She gets _____ using the internet at her workplace.
c Sheila collects coupons from newspapers and magazines to cut _____ on her grocery bill.
d Practically anything you want to know how to do can be looked _____ on the internet.
e Many people have opted _____ of paying for these past-times.
f People had to save _____ for family trips and vacations abroad.

Look at the phrasal verbs in the sentences. Write questions using three of the phrasal verbs. Ask and answer with your partner.

5 **Have you used the internet to save money as suggested in the article? Do you agree with these suggestions? What other suggestions do you have for saving money via the internet?**

LISTENING

1 1.49 **Listen to an extract from a radio show in which the speaker gives some money-saving tips. Answer the questions.**

a What are the tips?
b What benefits are mentioned for each tip?

What do you think of the tips? Would they work for you? Discuss with your partner.

2 **Work with your partner. Write a tip to send in to the show. Use one of these money-saving ideas or your own idea.**

- walk/cycle to the station/work
- take a packed lunch to work
- have picnics instead of going to cafés
- make your own clothes, cards, and gifts
- shop online
- avoid the "buy one get one free" trap

Use the prompts to help.

My best tip for saving money is to ...
My suggestion is to ...
It really makes sense to ...
You can make huge savings by ...

Read your tip to the class. Which of the ideas presented in class would work for you? Can you think of other ways to save money?

How the Internet Can Save You Money

While the internet is perhaps the most revolutionary invention of the twentieth century, there are still a few people who have not embraced it or are not aware of its full potential.

Sheila, my friend and co-worker, is a self-proclaimed Luddite. While in theory she appreciates the benefits of the internet, she has shied away from getting internet at home and doesn't even own a smartphone. She gets by using the internet at her workplace 'to check her email and do occasional research'. Since she fancies herself as a bargain hunter and a thrifty shopper, I embarked on a mission to bring her into this decade and convince her that it was worthwhile to invest in an internet connection at home or a smartphone with a data connection for the simple reason that it will save her lots of money and pay for itself many times over. Here are the top five ways that the internet can save her, and you, money.

1 Phone bills. Perhaps the main bill that can be significantly reduced if not completely eliminated by the internet is our phone bill. The internet has made free phone calls and text messaging the rule and not the exception.

2 Grocery bills. As a bargain shopper Sheila knows all about coupons and is diligent about regularly collecting them from newspapers and magazines to cut down on her grocery bill. With access to the internet she would have access to infinitely more coupons and bargains at her fingertips.

3 DIY. The internet has sparked a 'do-it-yourself' revolution. Practically anything you want to know how to do can be looked up, effectively saving you hundreds of dollars a year if you attempt your own basic home repairs: from plumbing and electrical repairs and maintenance to reupholstering furniture and creating your own home furnishings.

4 Entertainment. Let's say on a typical weekend you engage in some form of recreation for example reading, listening to music, or going to the movies. Many people have opted out of paying for these past-times, because through the internet, these hobbies can all be enjoyed for free. There are several websites that provide extensive libraries of free e-books, apps that offer free music-streaming services, and movies are available in high definition on a number of websites at no cost.

5 Travel. In the past people had to save up for family trips and vacations abroad. Nowadays air travel has become much more affordable with the introduction of the internet. There are many sites that compare airfares across airlines and search for the cheapest fares available.

After sharing these tips, I am happy to say that Sheila is now an internet convert.

Glossary

to embrace verb [I/T]: to accept a new idea

Luddite noun [C]: someone who is strongly opposed to using modern technology

fancy yourself phrasal verb: to think of oneself in a specific way, or as having particular attributes

thrifty adjective: careful about how you spend money

embark on verb [T]: to start a new project or activity

diligent adjective: hard-working

do-it-yourself noun [U]: the activity of making or repairing things for your home yourself instead of paying someone to do them for you

plumbing noun [U]: the system of pipes, water tanks and other equipment for supplying and storing water to a building

reupholster verb [T]: to cover a chair with material

READING & LISTENING

1 **Read the tips on bargaining from a tourist guide. Which one is false?**

- Shop around before you make a purchase to get an idea of the average price of whatever it is you want to buy.
- Be prepared to drive a hard bargain - sellers expect it.
- Try to appear casual and indifferent while browsing in stores and markets. Never show enthusiasm for the item you want to buy, as the seller may react by jacking up the price.
- Start the bargaining process by proposing a price considerably lower than the asking price. A good rule of thumb is to halve the price and work upwards from that.
- Try to find and point out as many flaws as possible in the product so you can get a better price for it.
- If the price proposed by the seller is still unacceptable and outside your budget, pretend to walk away. Usually, you will be called back again, and the price you offer may be accepted.
- Avoid paying with small change, as this may annoy the seller. Larger denominations are preferable.

Barney and Maiara

2 1.50 **Listen to Barney and Maiara discussing their experiences of bargaining. Do they discuss a) bargaining abroad? b) bargaining in their own country? c) both situations?**

3 **Read a summary of the conversation. ~~Cross out~~ any factual errors.**

> Maiara saw a rug in Turkey. She really wanted it and it was reasonably priced, but she decided to bargain for it. She did not start by offering a very low price because she was afraid she might lose the rug. In the end, she was able to knock down the seller's price and bought the rug.

> Bill does not like bargaining. He believes that the sellers do not enjoy it either. Generally, he has been unsuccessful in his experiences of bargaining when abroad. However, he feels that his experience of bargaining in the USA has been more successful.

Listen again and check. Then rewrite the summary correctly.

4 **How do you feel about bargaining? Have you had any similar experiences? Tell a partner.**

PRONUNCIATION

1 **Which sound occurs in the words in red in the bargaining tip on the right?**

Are the words in red stressed or unstressed? Practice saying the sentence with your partner, stressing the sounds in bold.

> **Weak forms of common words**
>
> **Try** to **find** and **point out** as **ma**ny **flaws** as **poss**ible in the **prod**uct so you can **get** a **bet**ter **price** for it.

2 **How is *to* pronounced in each of the sentences below?**

a Be prepared to drive a hard bargain.

b Try to appear casual and indifferent while browsing in stores.

1.51 **Listen and check your ideas.**

What is the pronunciation of *to* before a) a consonant sound? b) a vowel sound?

3 **Work with your partner. Practice reading the other bargaining tips from Reading & Listening, Exercise 1, paying attention to the pronunciation of *to* and weak forms.**

VOCABULARY

1 **Put the words and phrases in the box into two groups: *cheap* or *expensive*.**

> affordable   a rip-off   budget   daylight robbery   discounted
> exorbitant   lavish   low-cost   no-frills   overpriced

2 **Work with a partner. Discuss the questions about the words and phrases in Exercise 1.**

a Which are more informal in register?
b Which have negative connotations?
c Which two could not be used before a noun?

3 **Underline the best alternative in the shopping tips.**

a If you want to find **budget** / **discounted** accommodations, go to ...
b If you want a(n) **lavish** / **overpriced** meal, a good place to eat out is ...
c The best place to buy **low-cost** / **budget** souvenirs is ...
d Be prepared to pay **exorbitant** / **lavish** prices for ...
e A good place to find **affordable** / **no-frills** clothes is ...
f A good **no-frills** / **discounted** airline is ...
g Try to avoid shopping **in** / **at** ... It's a complete **rip-off** / **daylight robbery**.

Complete the shopping tips to make them true for a visitor to your town or country. Tell your partner.

SPEAKING: ANECDOTE

You are going to tell your partner about a purchase you have made recently.

- Ask yourself the questions below.
- Think about *what* to say and *how* to say it.
- Tell your partner about the purchase.

a What did you decide to buy and why?
b Was it an impulse buy or had you shopped around?
c Who did you go shopping with?
d Where did you look for the item?
e Where did you find the item?
f What was the item like?
g How expensive was it?
h Did you pay in cash or by credit card?
i How satisfied were you with the purchase?
j How do you use the item now?
k With hindsight, was it a good purchase?

READING

1 **The title of this article was adapted from the saying "to do something one step at a time". What do you understand by the expression "one step at a time"? What do you think the title of the article means? Read the article to confirm your ideas.**

2 **After reading the article, can you suggest an alternative title?**

http://savingtheplanet.com/one-purchase-at-a-time

SAVING THE PLANET ... ONE PURCHASE AT A TIME

As we become more aware of the hazardous effects of human and industrial activity on the environment and of the negative repercussions of our patterns of consumption, our responsibility should be to become mindful consumers and better stewards of our habitat. Environmental sustainability requires that we be aware of the effects our resource consumption produces. Our main aim should be to reduce unnecessary waste.

One practical way we can do this is by lowering our carbon footprint in our purchasing decisions. Opting to buy used instead of new items is a simple but effective way of lowering it. Every consumer item and product that we use has an environmental footprint created from the materials used to manufacture them, the pollution emitted during the process of creating them, and the packaging that inevitably ends up in landfills or improperly disposed of in the wider environment. If you are a conscious consumer you should ask yourself if what you want to buy is something you really need and if it is so, consider buying used instead of new. When opting to purchase second-hand you are effectively saving valuable resources and reducing pollution.

There are several apps that make it easy and convenient to buy second-hand. Two of the more popular ones are *LetGo* and *OfferUp*. Both apps offer a quick, easy, and convenient way to buy and sell used items in your own local community. Buyers can view photos and descriptions of items in various categories, contact sellers through the app, ask questions about the product on sale, and set up a time and place to meet to complete the transaction. We're saving money and the environment one app at a time!

There are some items, such as food, that we cannot buy second-hand. However, there are other ways to ensure that our food purchases are also sustainable and environmentally friendly. "Fair trade" products such as chocolates, coffee, tea, bananas, gold, and even flowers and beauty products mean that everybody involved in the process, from the farmer to the manufacturer, follow a process to ensure sustainability. Let's take chocolate as an example, "fair trade" tells us that the farmers of the cocoa are paid fair wages and are able to take care of their families. It also means that their children can go to school instead of having to work on the plantations.

Buying locally grown produce is another way to help the environment. Products grown far away need to be transported, using cars, trucks, or planes which pollute the environment. Locally grown fruits and vegetables are transported over much shorter distances and are less harmful to the environment. As an added bonus, this also provides jobs within the community and contributes to the local economy.

By following the suggestions above we can live more sustainable lives and help to protect the planet, one purchase at a time!

3 **Read the article again. Answer the questions with a partner.**

- a What is one way the article suggests we can reduce waste and resource consumption?
- b What is an "environmental footprint"?
- c What are the benefits of the apps mentioned in the article?
- d How does buying "fair trade" help farmers?
- e Give two reasons for buying locally grown produce.

4 **Complete the glossary using words and phrases from the article.**

Glossary

- a ______ adjective: dangerous, especially to people's health or safety
- b ______ noun [C/U]: a bad effect something has
- c ______ adjective: careful about or conscious of something
- d ______ noun [C]: someone who looks after something and protects it
- e ______ noun [U]: the ability to continue without harming the environment
- f ______ verb [I]: to make a choice or decision
- g ______ verb [T]: to send something out into the air, especially gas, light, or heat

5 **Work with your partner and discuss: What three items would you like to get rid of right now?**

GRAMMAR

1 Read the Freecycle™ post exchange. What furniture is Harry going to collect?

Hi, I have furniture I need to get rid of (sofa bed and bookshelves) as I'm giving my bedroom makeover. May be of use to someone? It's all in good condition. Mike.

Hi Mike,
If furniture is still available, I'd be very grateful for it, as I'm moving and starting from scratch in my new home. Could you give me information about sofa bed? What size is it, and what color? Also, I'm in dire need of wardrobe if you have one. Harry.

Hi Harry,
Yes, it's all still available. Sofa bed is king-size. Sorry, I don't have wardrobe but I do have dresser, if that's any use. You're welcome to come and collect stuff if you have van. Mike.

Hi – Yes, I'm still interested in everything, including dresser. I'll contact you again as soon as I've got hold of van to pick things up. Thanks a lot! H.

2 Correct the posts by adding the missing articles.

a / an (x7) some (x3) the (x6)

Delete the alternatives below that are incorrect. Then find examples in the text.

- If something is unknown to the speaker, the listener, or both, use **a(n)** / **some** / **the** / **-** .
- If something is known to both the speaker and listener, use **a(n)** / **some** / **the** / **-** .

3 Write a post for Freecycle™ offering an item or items. Exchange posts with a partner and write an email reply.

4 Complete the sentences with *a*, *an*, *the*, or put a dash (-) if no article is necessary.

a What time do you have ______ dinner? When did you last go out for ______ special dinner?
b Do you ever travel by ______ train? When did you last take ______ train?
c When is ______ next long weekend? What are you doing ______ next weekend?
d What is your view of ______ internet shopping? How often do you use ______ internet?
e What is the countryside like ______ north of your town? What is it like in ______ north of your country?
f Do you think ______ English are friendly? Why do you want to learn ______ English?

Work with your partner. Ask and answer the questions.

Articles

Use *a*/*an* before singular nouns

a bed / **an** idea

I need **a** room.

Use *some* / no article before plural and uncountable nouns

things / **some** things
furniture / **some** furniture

I need (**some**) money.

Use *the* before singular, plural, and uncountable nouns

the bed / **the** idea / **the** furniture / **the** things

I'm very pleased with **the** drapes.

How much is **the** rent?

5 ~~Cross out~~ the alternative in each sentence which is *not* possible.

a I'd like a (coffee / cake / juice / beer / bread / chocolate), please.
b I might go to the (bank / movies / gym / theater / store / work) after class.
c This time tomorrow I'll probably be at (school / college / grocery store / home).
d I would be interested in working for the (army / police / business / media / government / press).
e I don't like (rock music / jazz / 17th-century Italian classical music / music of Beethoven).
f Most of the (people I know / people / people in my country / people here) speak English.
g I love (the pasta / fresh pasta / the pasta you make / all kinds of pasta).

Underline alternatives to make the sentences true for you. Discuss with your partner.

6 **Grammar Extra 5, Part 2** page 146. Read the explanations and do Exercise 2.

LANGUAGE FOR LIFE

1 1.52 **Listen to a conversation between a customer and a market trader. Answer the questions.**

a What does the customer want to buy?
b How does she try to get a reduction?
c What is the final outcome?

2 **Work with a partner. Complete the useful phrases.**

a It's a little bit more than _____ pay.
b Could you give me _____ , do you think?
c The _____ is, it's a little chipped.
d I'm afraid it's still _____ .
e I think _____ , thanks.
f Is that your _____ ?
g OK, I _____ .

Listen again and check your answers.

3 **Read the beginning of three conversations in which people negotiate a solution to a problem. Answer the questions (1–3) with your partner.**

1 Karla: Well, it's a beautiful room, and the location is ideal. It's just that I was really looking for something that's furnished, especially since the rent is so high.

2 Brett: Yes, I really like the apartment and I'm very interested. The only problem is, I don't have enough for the deposit right now.

3 Frank: I wanted to talk to you about my essay. I know the deadline is the end of next week, but the thing is, I've been under a lot of stress lately.

1 What is the situation in each case?
2 Underline the expressions the speakers use to introduce the problem.
3 Try to guess how the conversations will continue.

1.53-155 **Listen to the conversations (1–3). Were your predictions correct?**

4 **Match the sentence halves from the conversations.**

a Supposing I were to
b I don't have any objections to
c That sounds like
d There shouldn't be
e I was wondering
f In theory I'm prepared to
g How would it be if
h I should be able

1 any problem.
2 I handed it in on Monday?
3 if I could ask for an extension?
4 grant you an extension.
5 to have it done by then.
6 put in some furniture?
7 a good compromise.
8 deferring the deposit.

Which sentences express a) a request? b) a proposal? c) an agreement?

5 **Work with your partner. Student A: turn to page 138. Student B: turn to page 139. Improvise conversations for the two situations.**

Life Skills: Sustainable Development

Identifying what can be done to the environment

In 2015, the United Nations adopted an agenda of sustainable development to "end poverty, protect the planet and ensure prosperity for all". Amanda, a student at the Fredrick Douglas High School in Baltimore, studied this UN agenda as part of her civics class. She decided to take this lesson beyond the classroom.

- 1.56 **Listen to an interview with Amanda and answer the questions below.**

a How did Amanda put the lesson on sustainable development into action?
b Which UN sustainable development goal were her actions most focused on?
c Can you implement any of Amanda's actions in your school, workplace or home? Which ones? What else can you do to contribute to the UN sustainable development agenda?

MACMILLAN LIFE SKILLS

5 Vocabulary Extra

AMERICAN AND BRITISH ENGLISH

1 **Which variety or varieties of English have you studied? Which do you prefer? Discuss with a partner.**

2 **Read the two advertisements below. What are they advertising? Do you ever shop like this?**

Shopping has gotten a whole lot easier with shoppingexperience.com, the world's largest online shopping list. Why go to your local mall when, from the comfort of your own home, you can access literally hundreds of your favorite stores selling thousands of products, from diapers to cell phones, from baby strollers to drapes? Once you've gotten the shoppingexperience.com habit, you'll never need to go downtown to do your shopping again.

Shopping has just got so much easier with shoppingexperience.com, the world's largest online shopping list. Why travel to your local shopping centre when, from the comfort of your own home, you can access literally hundreds of your favourite shops selling thousands of products, from nappies to mobile phones, from prams to curtains? Once you've got the shoppingexperience.com habit, you'll never need to go into the city centre to do your shopping again.

Which text is written in American English and which in British English? How do you know? Underline differences in vocabulary and spelling.

3 **Look at the words in the box. How would you rewrite these words in British English?**

center color a driver's license gray humor organize pedaling traveled

4 **Work with your partner. Discuss the different meanings of these words in British and American English.**

college gas holiday public school school subway

Read the dictionary extracts on the right and check your ideas.

5 **Work with your partner. Discuss whether the sentences below were said by an American or British English speaker.**

a After I graduate from high school, I want to go to school in France.
b I went to a state school as my parents couldn't afford to send me to a public school.
c At college I majored in math, and graduated summa cum laude last year.
d I use public transportation because the cost of gas is too high.
e We're hoping to go on holiday to Vancouver in the autumn.
f The quickest way to the drugstore is to take the subway. It's only two stops away.

6 **Read the American sentences (a-f). Change them to British English by substituting the words in bold with their British equivalents.**

a I usually take the **elevator** if I have to go higher than the **second floor**.
b I love **French fries** and **potato chips** but I'm not so fond of **candy** or **cookies**.
c My **mom** and dad live in an **apartment building**, so they don't have a **backyard**.
d **On** weekends, I like to **take a walk** in the countryside or go to the **movies**.
e I hate **standing in line** and it makes me **mad** if people **cut in**.
f I always **wash up** before I have a meal.

Which of the sentences are true of you? Discuss with your partner.

7 **Check your own dictionary. How does it show information about American and British English?**

Differences between American and British English: **college**

In the U.S., a **college** refers to a place where people study for their bachelor's degree (=first degree), whether the institution is a **college**, which offers only bachelor's degrees, or a university, which offers both bachelor's degrees and advanced degrees. When British speakers use the word **college**, they usually mean a place where students over 18 are trained in a particular subject or skill, earning a qualification that is not usually an academic degree. Students in the U.K. who are studying for an academic degree go to a university.

Differences between American and British English: **gas**

In the U.S., **gas** often refers to a type of liquid fuel that is used to produce power in cars: *We'd better get gas on our way out of town.* The usual British word for this is **petrol**. **Gas** can also refer to a substance like air that is burned to cook food or to heat your house, and it can be used with this meaning in both the U.S. and the U.K.: *a gas furnace.*

Differences between American and British English: **holiday**

In the U.S., a **holiday** is a single day fixed by law when people do not have to go to school or work: *I forgot that Monday's a holiday.* In both the U.S. and the U.K., this can also be called a **public holiday**, but the usual British word is **bank holiday**. When American speakers say **the holidays** or the **holiday season**, they mean the period of time that includes Christmas, Hanukkah, and New Year's Day: *Have you got any special plans for the holidays?* In the U.K., **holiday**, often called someone's **holidays**, usually means a period of time when you do not go to school or work, and usually you go to a place away from home to relax: *Where are you going for your holiday?* Americans call this a **vacation**.

Differences between American and British English: **public school**

In the U.S. and the U.K., **school** can mean a place where children are taught between the ages of about five and 18. But American speakers also use this word to refer to a college or a university. British institutions that provide education at higher levels are called **colleges** or **universities**. In the U.S., you say that children are **in school**: *The kids will be in school until 3:00 today.* In the U.K., they are **at school**. In the U.S., **in school** can also mean studying at a school or college instead of having a job: *She's still in school, but she's graduating in the spring.*

Differences between American and British English: **subway**

In the U.S., the **subway** is an underground railroad in a city: *Take the subway to 14th Street.* In the U.K., you would call this the **underground** or the **tube**. When British speakers say **subway**, they mean an underground tunnel that people can walk through to get to the other side of a busy road: *It's safest to use the subway to get across at this corner.*

From the *Macmillan English Dictionary (American edition)*

6 Mind

SPEAKING

How much do you know about your brain? Decide if the statements are true or false.

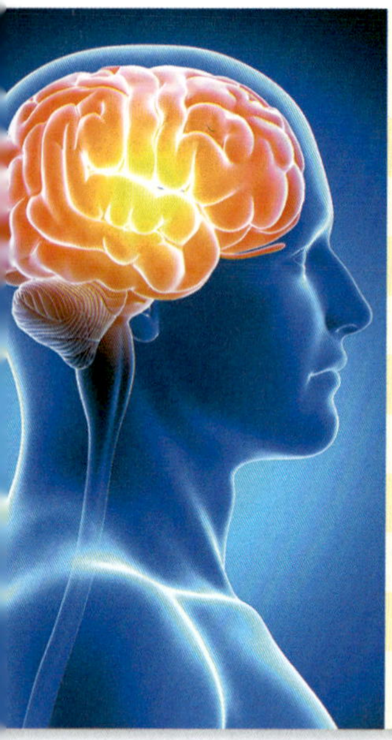

The Human Brain

a On average, the brain weighs 2.8kg in a man and 2.2kg in a woman.
b The brain floats in a liquid in the skull.
c 50% of the average human brain is water.
d Your brain is uniformly pink in color.
e The adult human brain uses up to 25% of the blood's oxygen supply.
f We only use 10% of our brains.
g Your brain cannot feel pain.
h Your brain is more active watching TV than it is sleeping.
i We yawn more when our brains are not being stimulated.
j The human brain continues to send out electrical signals for up to 37 hours following death.

Check your answers on page 138.

LISTENING

1 **Work with a partner. Label the games in the pictures. Order them from the oldest to the most recent. What is the aim of each game? Which do you like playing?**

2 1.57 **Listen to four people answering questions about some of the games in the pictures. Which question (*a*, *b*, *c*, or *d*) was each of them asked?**

a Do you do or play any of these games on a regular basis?
b Which of them do you think requires the most brain power?
c Which of them do you think are a waste of time?
d Which of them did you use to play as a child?

▲ 1 ______

3 **Listen again and make notes on the people's answers in Exercise 2. Then compare your notes with your partner. Do you disagree with anything they said?**

▲ 2 ______

▲ 3 ______

▲ 4 ______

▲ 5 ______

- **Grammar:** Verbs of the senses. Participle clauses
- **Vocabulary:** Verbs of seeing. Collocations with *mind*
- **Language for Life:** Making appropriate requests

READING & SPEAKING

1 **Work with a partner. Look at the words in the box. Which have negative connotations? Write a definition for one of the words with negative connotations and read it to the class. Can they guess the word?**

decay decline fit growth inactivity lack loss stretching training

2 **Use six of the words in the box in Exercise 1 to complete the article about brain training.**

In recent years there has been a barrage of new studies about how to maintain cognitive function as you get older. (1) ______ in cognitive function is a natural process, and everyone experiences deterioration in memory and motor skills as we grow older. However, by taking action now, there are things you can do to ameliorate the process of aging. First and foremost, keeping physically (2) ______ has been shown to improve cognition. Exercise is associated with the (3) ______ of blood vessels in the brain and therefore an increase in the survival rate of new brain cells. (4) ______, on the other hand can have the opposite effect.

Another vital factor is sleep. In fact, the (5) ______ of sleep has been tied to reduced gray matter in the brain and problems with working memory and executive function. Furthermore, sleep is a key part of the process of consolidating learning and memory, so a chronic lack of sleep can actually prevent you from learning.

A third factor associated with improved brain function is (6) ______ the brain through challenging activities, like learning a new language, skill, or musical instrument. When doing these activities we go beyond what we can already do and we force our brain to be active.

There are a host of other ideas for preventing the reduction of brain function, from meditation to diet, some proven and others still to be ratified by research, but as people live longer, increasing the quality of life through better brain function promises to become a growth field.

3 **Work with your partner. Discuss the questions.**

a Choose two adjectives from the box to describe the article in Exercise 2.

censorious chatty critical factual funny
argumentative informational sarcastic serious casual

b Where do you think the article might come from?

c Has it inspired you to do some brain training?

4 **Check your brain power by answering as many of the questions below as you can in three minutes.**

Calculate your Brain Power

1 What was the day and date you started this class?

2 What was your teacher wearing last class? (The more detail you give, the more points you get.)

3 How many *R*s are there in this sentence?

Red rhinoceroses are a rarity in Rochester although they have been observed in Rome.

4 How many circles do you have to move to turn this triangle upside down?

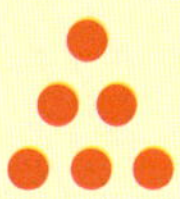

5 Complete this table so that all the rows and columns add up to nine.

5		2	
	3	2	
1		0	
			1

6 Study these words for one minute, then close your book and write them down.

sold rare very today tree about
radio paint book tried mix next
brief could dish

Check your answers on page 139.

READING

1 **Work with a partner. Look at the picture on the right. Discuss the questions.**

a Have you ever heard about Phineas Gage or his story?
b What do you think happened to him?

2 **Read the article about his life on page 63. Label the extracts (1–4) with the headings in the box.**

The criticism The recovery The effects The accident

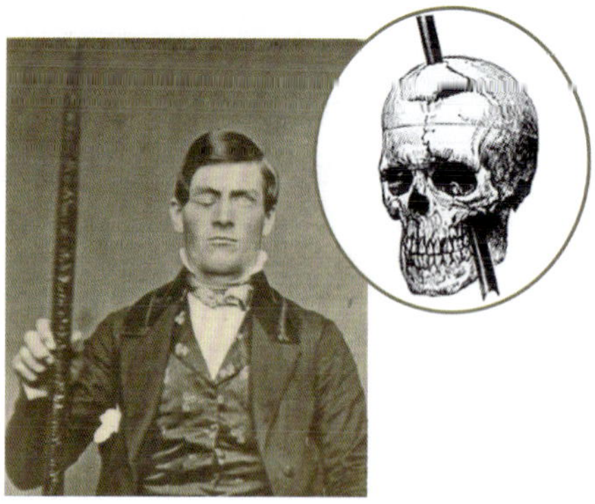

3 **Read the article again. Work with your partner. Discuss the questions.**

a What happened immediately after the accident? How did Phineas react?
b What treatment did the doctor provide Phineas? How would his injury be treated nowadays?
c What were the physical effects, both short-term and long-term, of his injury?
d What did science learn about the human brain as a result of this case?
e How did Phineas' later life cast doubt on some of the stories about his 'new' personality?
f Do you believe that his personality permanently changed? Why? / Why not?

VOCABULARY

1 **Look at the highlighted verbs in the article. Try to guess the meaning from context and complete the glossary.**

Glossary

a ______ verb [I]: to look steadily at something for a long time
b ______ verb [T]: to notice
c ______ verb [I/T]: to move suddenly and quickly
d ______ verb [T]: to spend time looking at something
e ______ verb [T]: to know what something is when you see it again
f ______ verb [I/T]: to look at or over something quickly to get a general impression
g ______ verb [T]: to look closely or analytically at something
h ______ verb [T]: to become aware of someone or something using your eyes

2 ***Observe*, *recognize*, and *see* have more than one meaning. Look at the sentences (a-f) and match the verbs in italics with the meanings (1-6).**

a I *recognize* I'm not perfect.
b I *see* what you mean.
c You should *observe* the customs of the country you are visiting.
d Are you still *seeing* Peter?
e "That wasn't very clever," he *observed*.
f As I *see* it, she's making a big mistake.

1 understand
2 date someone
3 admit
4 follow/obey a law/rule
5 have an opinion
6 comment

3 **How would you translate *observe*, *recognize*, and *see* into your own language? Do the translations have multiple meanings?**

4 **Write a paragraph using *observe*, *recognize*, and *see*. Use each word once. Show it to your partner and ask them to figure out the meanings of the verbs you have used.**

So You Think You're Having a Bad Day?

1 ________

If you do then you might find some comfort in the story of Phineas Gage. One day, in 1848, Phineas, like many other young men, was working in Vermont for the railroad company. As part of his job, he would get the ground ready to build the railroad by blasting the rock. To do so, he had to put blasting powder into a hole, cover it with sand, and then pack it all down with a big iron rod. As legend has it, Phineas was momentarily distracted when he recognized the other workers' voices nearby, and his eyes darted away from his work to see what they were doing. In that split second, an accidental spark lit the blasting powder, and Phineas' life would never be the same.

Propelled by the explosion, the iron rod hurtled up and through his jaw, through his left eye, and finally out the top of his skull. And yet miraculously, after only a few minutes, he was able to talk and even walk without assistance. The other workers must have surely gazed in amazement as this scene unfolded, shocked that he hadn't been immediately killed. He was then quickly hurried in a cart back to the town where he calmly sat outside his hotel and waited for the doctor to arrive, his brain partially visible for all the world to see.

2 ________

Now you must remember that this was in 1848, when medical practices were not as sophisticated as those today. So it should come as no surprise that there was no opportunity for brain surgery to repair the damage. Instead, the doctor did what any of us would do with a minor wound – first, he examined it, then he cleaned it and bandaged it! To be fair, in this scenario, he also put back some pieces of skull, and finished off the procedure with a nightcap to hold everything in. Apparently, at the time, Phineas told the doctor that would be back at work in only a few days although he didn't want to see his friends!

As it turns out, Phineas was a little overly overoptimistic in his prognosis, but nevertheless he did manage a remarkable recovery. Only ten weeks after his traumatic injury, he was healthy enough to return home. One can only imagine what he must have thought about as he traveled by carriage, taking in the countryside, reflecting on his life and his lucky escape. He had lost sight completely in his left eye and had partial paralysis of his face, but all things considered, he was lucky to be alive and by all accounts was still a handsome man.

3 ________

Remarkable though the accident was, perhaps if his story had ended here, he would not have maintained the fame that he does today. Equally amazing as his survival is actually what transpired next, and what would fascinate doctors, psychologists, and the public imagination for many decades to come. In addition to the obvious physical damage, the destruction of his left frontal lobe appeared to have impacted Phineas' personality in very noticeable ways. Described as a healthy, hard-working man before his accident, afterwards his friends famously said that he was "no longer Gage". As the legend goes, Phineas was observed to become very rude, with a lack of self-control and no sense of embarrassment. What's more, he started to make immediate, impulsive plans, only to just as quickly abandon them. Overall, the implications of such changes were momentous, providing evidence that specific parts of the brain affect aspects of personality.

4 ________

So how much are we to believe of Phineas' story? In some ways it is hard to tell, and in the 150 years since it happened, rumors and exaggerations have spread regardless of the facts. To give an example, it has been said that he mistreated his wife and child. One problem though – he never married or had children! To complicate matters further, very little was known about Phineas prior to his accident, so comparisons are tricky. Also, although his personality may have been temporarily altered, over time he seemed to have regained most of his lost social and personal skills, becoming a skilled and responsible stagecoach driver in Chile until health issues forced him to stop. Some experts theorize that his structured profession and routine during this period of his life may have been exactly what he needed to provide him with the stability he required.

Ultimately, however, he could not overcome the long-term effects of his trauma, and in 1860, twelve years after that fateful day, Phineas passed away in his mother's home in San Francisco after numerous seizures. His legacy lives on though, as anyone who has scanned a psychology coursebook can attest to. His infamous skull also continues to draw great interest, with visitors coming to see it on display at the Harvard Medical School in Cambridge, Massachusetts.

LISTENING

1 **Work with a partner. Discuss the questions.**

a How many senses do we have?
b Which sense do you think is the most important to you in your everyday life?
c Which sense would you be able to cope best without?
d Which sense triggers the most memories?
e Have you ever lost the use of one of your senses temporarily?
f Do you think any of your senses is especially well developed?
g Which sense do we most take for granted?

2 ▶ 1.58-1.62 **Listen to Mike, Maria, Helen, Nick, and Petra answering some of the questions in Exercise 1. Which question is each person answering? Which senses do they mention? Compare your notes with your partner. Were the speakers' answers similar to yours?**

GRAMMAR

1 **Work with your partner. Look at the verbs in the box. Which can a) only be used with a stative meaning (referring to an ability or a sensation)? b) only be dynamic (referring to an action)? c) be used with either a stative or a dynamic meaning?**

feel hear listen look see sense smell taste touch watch

Verbs of the senses

see, feel, taste, smell, hear, sense

I **can't see** without my glasses.

I**'m seeing** Luis tomorrow.

I think I **can hear** the telephone.

I **must be hearing** things. My telephone's turned off.

2 **Complete the extracts from the speakers' answers in Listening, Exercise 2 with the correct form of some of the verbs in the box in Exercise 1. Some of the verbs are used more than once. You may need to add a modal verb or a negative.**

a If you're blind, if you ______ , then although you can lead a full life and all that, I think it does make you more vulnerable.
b I would really hate it if I ______ what things or people looked like.
c I read an article about a man who went deaf and then his hearing was restored to him, and he talked about how isolating it can be if you ______ .
d He really missed ______ to music, that was the worst part, he said. That, and not being able to ______ his wife's voice.
e I ______ the palm trees, ______ the food, ______ the sun on my skin.
f They ______ the vibrations of the drums, even though they ______ them.
g I can ______ things that nobody else even notices. For example, when someone cooks for me, I can tell which spices were used.

▶ 1.63 **Listen and check your answers.**

3 **What modal auxiliaries were used in the sentences in Exercise 2? Were they used with a stative or a dynamic meaning? What other verb phrase was used with the same meaning?**

4 **Work with your partner. Look at the pairs of sentences below and discuss the difference in meaning of the verbs in italics.**

1A I *can see* John. He's right over there, standing next to the bar.
1B I*'m seeing* John tomorrow. I'll let him know what we've decided.

2A I *could hear* strange sounds coming from downstairs, so I decided to go and investigate.
2B I*'ve been hearing* great things about you recently. You must be doing really well.

3A I*'m not feeling* very well. I think I'm going to go and lie down for a while.
3B That heater's really good! I *can feel* the heat from here.

4A I*'m just tasting* the soup to see if I need to add any more salt.
4B I really *can't taste* the difference between butter and margarine.

5 **Pay careful attention to what's going on around you, both inside and outside the classroom. Write down what you can hear, smell, and touch. Compare your answers with the class.**

6 **Grammar Extra 6, Part 1** page 146. Read the explanations and do Exercise 1.

READING & VOCABULARY

1 Work in small groups. Discuss the questions.

- **a** Have you ever had a pet? What was it? How long did you have it for?
- **b** Why do you think people keep pets? Do you think pets serve a useful function? If so, what function?
- **c** Do you think some people get too attached to their pets?
- **d** What is it that differentiates humans from the animals around us?

2 Match the terms (a-e) with the definitions (1-5).

a sentience	**1** an instinctive or intuitive feeling
b cognition	**2** the capacity to feel perceive or experience
c consciousness	**3** the state of being awake and aware of one's surroundings
d emotion	**4** the mental action or process of acquiring knowledge and understanding
e empathy	**5** the ability to feel and share the feelings of others

Which of these faculties do you think are more common in animals and which in humans?

3 Read this article and identify the faculties that animals demonstrate. Do you think animals really have these capacities, or is it a case of projecting human qualities onto non-human objects or beings (anthropomorphism)?

Do Animals Think and Feel?

Tilting his head to one side, Scooby stares at me with that quizzical, questioning look of his. I can almost hear him asking me to repeat myself. "Yes, I asked you if you want to go for a walk." Springing to life from his doggie bed, he runs to get his leash and quickly returns and barks.

What is going on in his head? What was the thought process from hearing the word "walk" to fetching the leash? Is Scooby happy? Is it wrong for me to attribute human feelings and thoughts to my pet?

We all know that animals differ from humans, not in kind, but in degree. They have the same faculties; but these faculties are more or less developed compared to human beings, and proof can be hard to come by. We cannot unequivocally know what any person is thinking, much less what an animal might be thinking, though animal behavior gives us a window into animal thought and feeling. I'll cite just two cases:

- Having been fed by humans for years, wild dolphins at a resort in Australia began throwing fish to humans. They were not rejecting food but offering it to the humans. We can read this behavior in several ways: we can see empathy, generosity, reciprocity, and perhaps even humor or pity if we believe that the gift was motivated by our incompetence as fishermen!
- After losing his mate to a poacher, a bull elephant stops eating and, crying copiously, slumps to the ground, never to rise again. Other elephants attempt to comfort the prostrate elephant, but to no avail. Has the elephant literally died of a broken heart? Witnessing this scene, it is difficult not to conclude that elephants feel compassion and heartbreak.

No matter how you justify their behavior, we have to conclude that there is some degree of feelings in them that can be related to a certain extent to human beings. Perhaps, we should pause and think about the way mankind has treated animals over the millennia. It is time to see all animals, not just Scooby, as living beings capable of feeling and thinking, and most importantly as creatures that deserve all our love and respect.

4 Work with a partner and discuss the meanings of these expressions in the case history.

- **a** tilting his head (line 1)
- **b** springing to life (line 3)
- **c** not in kind, but in degree (line 8)
- **d** hard to come by (line 10)
- **e** slumps to the ground (line 18)
- **f** to no avail (line 19)

5 What are the author's views on what animals think and feel? Do you agree or disagree with the author?

GRAMMAR

1 **Make three sentences using one clause from each box: A, B, and C.**

A	a	Having left his trusty companion to keep an eye on the shiny new van,
	b	Waking up with a jump,
	c	Numbed by the efficiency of his new air-conditioning system,
B	d	he's often spotted scouring the streets between deliveries,
	e	Willy sat up to greet his owner
	f	Mr. X returned from dinner to find
C	g	and barked with excitement.
	h	that his new mode of transportation had been completely remodeled.
	i	under the protection of a warm blanket.

Now check your answers.

2 **Work with a partner. Look at the participle clauses in Box A in Exercise 1 and answer the questions.**

- a Which contains: a present participle? a past participle? a perfect participle?
- b What is the subject of each participle clause?
- c Look at the sentences below and answer the questions.
  1 *Having been fed by humans for years, wild dolphins at a resort in Australia began throwing fish to humans.*
  2 *Because wild dolphins at a resort in Australia were fed by humans for years, they began throwing fish to humans.*
  - Which sentence, 1 or 2, is more likely to be spoken?
  - Which was used in the pet case history on page 65?
  - What has been added to sentence 2 to replace the participle clause?

Participle clauses

Present participle clause
Seeing the dog, she braked sharply.

Past participle clause
Encouraged to write from an early age, she published her first book when she was twelve.

Perfect participle clause
Having seen the house, she knew it wasn't worth the price they were asking.

3 **Rewrite the sentences using participle clauses.**

- a When I graduated from college, I went on a long vacation.
- b Because I live alone, I don't really do a lot of cooking.
- c I don't eat candy because I'm on a diet.
- d I like to spend the weekends relaxing when I'm tired after a long week at work.

Are these sentences true for you, for anyone you know, or anyone in your class?

4 **Look at this sentence. Where should the word "not" go?**

Rejecting food, but offering it to people, dolphins showed empathy and generosity towards humans.

5 **Work with your partner. Look at the sentences and add *not* if necessary.**

- a Discouraged by the long climb ahead of them, they set off at dawn.
- b Wanting to offend people, they decided to extend the guest list to include both family and friends.
- c Having completed the form, please send it, with a photograph, to the address below.
- d Knowing that arriving on time would make a very bad impression, he left with plenty of time to spare.

6 **Rephrase your answers to Exercise 5 without using participle clauses. You may need to add linking words.**

- a *They were not discouraged by the long climb ahead of them, and they set off at dawn.*

7 **Grammar Extra 6, Part 2** page 146. Read the explanations and do Exercise 2.

VOCABULARY

1 **Work with a partner. How many collocations with the word *mind* do you know?**

2 **Look at the collocations in the sentences (a–i). How many of your collocations from Exercise 1 are in the list? Look at the collocations again. Is *mind* a verb or a noun in each one?**

- a She can't **make up her mind** whether to buy those shoes or not.
- b They pay really well. They can afford to, **mind**.
- c I wish Bill would **mind his own business**. He's always asking personal questions.
- d Jen's invited me to go on vacation with her, but I'm **of two minds about** going.
- e A good night out will help you **take your mind off** your exams.
- f I'll go **out of my mind** with boredom if I have to stay in this job.
- g **Great minds think alike**!
- h Do you believe that healing is a question of **mind over matter**?
- i A vacation is **the last thing on my mind** right now.

3 **Match the collocations (a–i) in Exercise 2 with the definitions (1–9).**

1. the least important problem to deal with right now
2. make you stop worrying or thinking about something
3. make a decision
4. to add a comment that makes something you've already said less strong, or general
5. (humorous) used for saying that you are both very clever when you and another person have the same idea
6. to be uncertain about something or to have difficulty in making a decision
7. not interfere in other people's affairs
8. crazy, insane
9. the belief that our minds are stronger than our bodies and that we can control pain or other unpleasant situations through mind power

Which of the collocations would you like to learn? Write a sentence for each of them to help you remember.

PRONUNCIATION

1 1.64 **Listen to a conversation between three people and answer the questions.**

- a What do you think the relationship is between them?
- b What do you think they're talking about?

2 **Look at the sentences from the conversation in Exercise 1. Complete them with collocations with *mind*.**

- a ______ scooting over a little?
- b ______ not sitting there?
- c ______ your own business!
- d I haven't ______ yet.

Listen again and check your answers.

3 **How do the speakers pronounce the underlined sections?**

- a Would you mind ...
- b Do you mind ...

4 **Work with your partner and discuss the questions. Think carefully about the pronunciation of the underlined sections.**

- a Do you mind if people keep you waiting?
- b Would you mind if someone borrowed something of yours without asking?
- c When was the last time you spoke your mind? Did you offend anyone?
- d Do you find it difficult to make up your mind?

LANGUAGE FOR LIFE

1 **Work with a partner. Look at the requests (1-8). Order them from the most polite to the most informal.**

1 Do you mind if I lie down here for a while?
2 Is it OK if we pick you up at six?
3 Would you mind lending me ten dollars?
4 Can I copy your homework?
5 May I have my book back, please?
6 Give me a pen!
7 Please sign here.
8 Would you mind if I asked you to write that report again?

2 **Match the requests (1-8) in Exercise 1 with the most appropriate responses (a-h). Note that some of the responses can be matched with more than one request.**

a I'm cool with that.
b I hope you're kidding!
c What book?
d I don't think you can do that here.
e What do you mean, sign?
f Anything else?
g It depends.
h Well, to tell the truth, I'm not really comfortable with that.

1.65 **Listen and check your answers. Did any of the responses seem inappropriate?**

3 1.66 **Listen to the complete conversations. Do the speakers know each other well? Are they just acquaintances or are they complete strangers? What is the request in each?**

4 **Work with your partner. Look at the pictures (a-c). Act out one of the situations.**

Change partners. Choose another situation and change the relationship between the speakers. Act out the conversation in front of the class. Can they guess the relationship between you?

5 **Work in small groups. Discuss the questions.**

a What other useful phrases do you know for replying to requests?
b Do you find it difficult to say no? What tactics do you use to avoid saying no outright? What tactics were used in the conversations?
c What excuses have you made to get out of doing something?
d What sorts of requests get on your nerves?

6 **Write down a request. Think of at least six ways of making this request. Ask everyone in the class your request, but vary the way you make it.**

7 **Work with your class. Discuss the questions.**

a How successful were you in making your request?
b Which manner of making your request was the most successful?
c What was the politest negative response you heard?
d What was the most common response?

Life Skills: Learning Skills

The Pomodoro Technique

"Never do today what you can put off until tomorrow". **Use the Pomodoro Technique to make optimal use of time and reduce the desire to put things off. It is a cinch to learn!**

First, divide your study time into chunks of thirty minutes. Turn off all distracting devices and focus entirely on the task at hand for 25 minutes, followed by a 5-minute rest period. You just did one Pomodoro! When you have done four Pomodoros, that is, two hours, take a longer rest of up to 30 minutes. Then you can keep going. Once you get the hang of it, you can customize the length of your Pomodoros to fit your pace. The difference, especially for hardcore procrastinators, can be stunning!

- **Think of the advantages to the technique. Work with a partner to explain the benefits below.**
  - Instant success
  - Time flies
  - Customizable
  - Keeping fresh
  - Efficiency
  - Accomplishment

MACMILLAN LIFE SKILLS

6 Writing Extra

EMAILS MAKING AND DECLINING REQUESTS

1 Work with a partner. Read the emails below and decide ...

a who the sender might be.

b what requests were made of them.

1

Subject: RE: Can you do me a favor?

You've gotta be kidding! I've just had new carpet put down and you know what my apartment's like – I don't even have a backyard. Why don't you try asking Izzy?

2

Subject: Ref 3256

Dear Mr. Holman:

Thank you for your email on 9/23/18. While we make every effort to ensure that your trip is trouble-free, some delays are beyond our control. On the day in question, floods in Missouri resulted in the cancellation of all rail services. Regrettably, we are unable to reimburse the expenses you incurred as a result of these cancellations. However, it may be possible for us to reimburse the cost of your ticket. Please call into your local station and fill in a request form.
We hope that this will not discourage you from using our services again.

Our best regards,
Ms. K. White
Head of Customer Services

3

Subject: RE: Cinderella's party

I'm really sorry, but I can't. I have a big test on Monday and I need to study all weekend. Any other time and I'd love to help out. Have you tried Ellen? I know she takes care of Bob's kids sometimes.

Good luck!
Tx

2 Look at the emails again. Underline the phrases used ...

a to refuse the requests.

b to soften the refusal.

3 Read the emails. Which one would you find the most difficult to refuse? Why?

Subject: Interview in LA

Hi there!
How's it going? Are you still as busy as ever?
I've just been told that our company has to downsize, and to cut a long story short, I'm now out of a job. Fortunately, I have a couple of job interviews lined up, which is the reason I'm writing – one of them is in Los Angeles a week from tomorrow at 9:00 in the morning. I was wondering if I could stay with you the night before? I can sleep anywhere and even bring my own sleeping bag! It would be one less thing to worry about if I knew I didn't have to get up at 4:00 in the morning.

Thanks,
Paul

Subject: Weekend shifts

We have received an unexpectedly large order from one of our biggest buyers. It is really important that we are seen to be efficient in today's harsh economic climate. We therefore need all production-line managers to work an extra shift over the weekend. Please specify a minimum of two shifts you'll be able to cover. We appreciate this is very short notice but feel sure that every one of you will do your best to make sure we deliver.

Please get back to me asap with your availability.

Guy Hardy
Sales and Production Manager

4 Work with your partner. Write a reply to one of the two emails refusing the request and explaining why. Use the expressions you underlined in Exercise 2 to help you.

5 Exchange your email with other students in the class and answer the questions.

a Which email are they replying to?

b Which reply was the most inventive?

c Which excuses were the most unbelievable and which were the most likely?

Review B

▶ Grammar Extra pages 144-147

GRAMMAR

1 Put the words in the correct order to form sentences.

a supposed to / to the beach / be going / the car / we didn't go / We were / so / broke down / but
b I didn't feel / so / but / going to / last night / do my homework / to bed early / I was / very well / I went
c due to / heavy fog / We were / by six hours / the plane was / at 8:30 / delayed / leave / but / and / there was

Have you ever found yourself in a similar situation? Tell a partner about it.

2 Underline the correct alternative.

Children will laugh at almost anything, (1) **for example** / **not to say**, a funny face or a strange sound. (2) **By contrast** / **Similarly**, they love slapstick and farce, things (3) **including** / **such as** people walking into doors or falling into holes. They will even laugh at things they don't really understand, (4) **strictly speaking** / **that is to say**, jokes aimed at adults full of sophisticated word play. They're not laughing because of the joke, (5) **or at any rate** / **particularly**, not because of the content of the joke, but because everybody else is laughing, and they simply want to join in.

Do you agree with the text? Why? / Why not?

3 Work with your partner. Choose the correct alternative. Sometimes both alternatives are possible.

a I once bought a pair of expensive designer jeans **that** / **which** I really couldn't afford.
b My best friend is the kind of person **who** / **which** shops until they drop.
c On Sunday I went shopping with my family, **that** / **which** was good fun, but not a good use of my time.
d I found a real bargain **that** / **who** I couldn't let slip through my fingers.

Are any of these sentences true for you? Tell your partner.

4 *A*, *some*, and *the* have been removed from the article. Put them back in.

Are you shopaholic? Think of your last trip to stores or mall. What did you buy? Did you take list and buy only things you came for? Or did you come home laden down with lots of new - but totally unessential - items? There's very little difference between treating yourself to something new and compulsive shopping. Difference lies in your attitude towards shopping. Compulsive shopper can't stop thinking about shopping. **(1)** They think about it all time and only really find relief when they are actually in store, choosing their next purchase. **(2)** As addiction grows, so does deceit. **(3)** It could be anything: CDs, new pair of shoes, expensive make-up. Men are just as vulnerable as women. Men tend to buy electronic goods or sports equipment, but need to shop and guilt are just same. **(4)**

5 Sentences (a-d) are from the article in Exercise 4. Match them with the appropriate places (1-4) in the article.

a Having brought their purchases home, they'll hide them in the back of the closet.
b Feeling guilty about the money they've spent, they'll lie about the price.
c Finding pleasure in spending money, shopping soon becomes an addiction.
d Once addicted to shopping, they can spend hours at the mall, comparing prices and specifications.

Underline the participle clauses. Rewrite them as full clauses.

6 Work with your partner. Look at the pictures (1-3). Which sense is being used in each picture? What is it being used for?

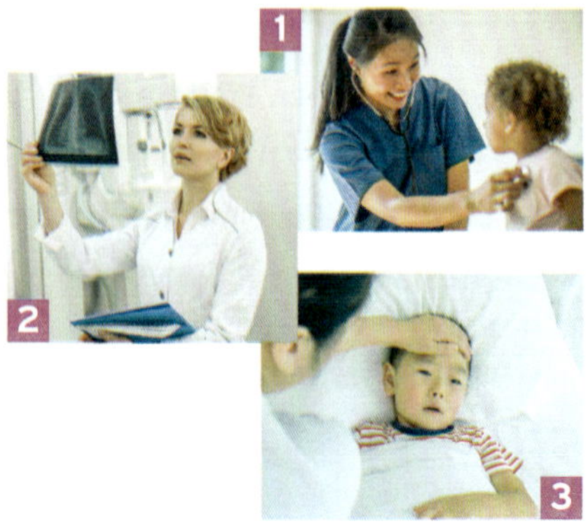

VOCABULARY

1 **Complete the expressions with *story* or *tale(s)*.**

a He told me some cock-and-bull _____ about the dog eating his homework.
b I hate kids who are tattle-_____.
c A: So, what happened?
B: Don't ask! It's a long _____ !

Do you have similar expressions in your language?

2 **Complete the adjectives then answer the questions below.**

a g_ll_ bl_
b pl_ _ s _ bl _
c n _ _ v _
d sk _ pt _ c _ l
e tr _ st _ ng
f f _ shy
g _ nf_ _ thf _ l

Choose three adjectives and write definitions for them. Use the expressions in the box to help you.

cheat on   con   fall for   make out
swallow a story   lead someone to believe
take someone in   take someone at their word
take someone for a ride   trick

Read your definitions to the class. Can they guess what adjective it is?

3 **Complete the sentences with the phrases in the box.**

down payment   impulse buys   in bulk
overpay   shop around

a I don't think it makes sense to buy _____ - especially not with food - you end up throwing most of it away.
b We made a _____ on a house last week! It's our first home; I'm so excited!
c I always _____ before buying anything, from a TV to a loaf of bread.
d I try not to make _____ - but it's so difficult to resist the temptation, especially when it comes to shoes.
e I never _____ for anything - I just don't have enough money!

Are any of these sentences true for you? Tell your partner.

4 **Complete the questions with a preposition.**

a How much money do you need a month to get _____ ?
b How much do you usually run _____ in bills for your telephone and other services?
c Do you think it's better to pay _____ a credit card bill all at once, or in installments? Why?
d Are you saving _____ for anything special right now?
e If you are, does that mean you have to cut _____ on your spending?

5 **Look at the verbs in the box. Which would you (or your eyes) do when you ...**

dart   examine   gaze
observe   recognize   scan

a look through a newspaper to find a particular piece of information?
b look hurriedly around a room to find your keys or cell phone as you're leaving to go out?
c look for a long time into the eyes of someone you love?
d look carefully at a contract or official document?
e see someone you know in a crowd?
f watch something interesting take place, without being directly involved?

Have you done any of these things recently? Tell your partner about what you were doing and why.

PRONUNCIATION

1 **Look at some words from Units 4-6. Say the words and add them to the table.**

~~addiction~~   aggression   competition
disappointment   eccentric   economize
emotion   exorbitant   extravagant   necessities
observation   recognize   sheepishly
sidesplitting   superstition   sympathy

A: Ooo	B: oOo	C: oOoo	D: ooOo
	addiction		

2 **Underline the stressed syllables.**

1.67 **Listen, check, and repeat.**

7 Digital

SPEAKING

Work with a partner. Look at the pictures and discuss the questions.

a Which of the phones represented the biggest breakthrough at the time it came out?
b How many cell phones have you owned? How often do you update?
c Are you happy with the one you have now? Why or why not?

READING

1 **Work in small groups. Discuss ...**

a the functions a cell phone could perform ten years ago.
b the extra functions it can perform today.
c other functions you think it might be able to perform in ten years' time.

2 **Read the article about cell phones in the future on page 73. As you read, check (✓) the functions you came up with in Exercise 1 and write an asterisk (*) next to the ones you didn't mention.**

When you're finished, compare your notes with your partner. Which functions would you find most useful? And least useful? Do any of the developments described in the article worry you?

3 **The sentences and phrases (a-e) are from the article. Match them with the appropriate places (1-5) in the article.**

a First of all, don't throw away your cell phone just yet.
b The next wave will be marked by the rise of augmented reality.
c It was not so long ago that human communication was very different.
d What is perhaps frightening is the vision of the longer-term future that some futurists have.
e Given that, it hardly seems possible that a device so ubiquitous could go the way of the dinosaur.

4 **Do you agree with the article? Or do you think other devices will come to the market?**

- **Grammar:** Complex sentences. Speculating about the future
- **Vocabulary:** Compound nouns. Informal expressions
- **Language for Life:** Discussing implications

Bring on the Demise of the Smartphone!

1 ______ On March 7, 1876, Alexander Graham Bell was granted a patent for the telephone. Since then, successive innovations have culminated in the invention of the smartphone and the number of mobile devices has surpassed the population of the world. Mobile gadgets are growing at a pace five times faster than the human population.

2 ______ Yet, it is inevitable. After all, a glance back at the recent past will reveal a veritable graveyard of technology, from typewriters to the floppy disk to pagers and fax machines. There was a time when the Walkman was cutting-edge. Who in the 1980s suspected its demise? What are the factors that will lead to the downfall of the smartphone and what new device will take its place?

3 ______ You'll still be using your cell phone for now, but what will change is how you interact with it. Two important advances that are already beginning to have an impact are voice recognition and artificial intelligence. Handling your phone, i.e. typing out messages with our thumbs, swiping and tapping our devices, or cleaning greasy finger-printed screens – all this will seem as old-fashioned as the DVD. Because you will command your phone by voice, you will receive immediate feedback from an AI powered virtual assistant, and you will never be disconnected, making any interaction instant and constant. If you think people multitask now, think again! The incidence of people walking down the street talking to themselves will skyrocket. The keyboard will die out and the screen will be used only for playing media, not for inputting commands.

4 ______ The screens of our phones will be replaced by a direct visual interface in which what we see in our real world is blended with the digital world in real time. In this scenario the cell phone screen will become obsolete. Phones will take the form of wearable technology, like watches, bracelets or glasses. Increasingly, we will have direct visual interaction with objects. In this internet of things, there will be a steady stream of information unobtrusively pulsing between human and object. The role of the smartphone will be reduced to providing processing power for our wearable technology; the device itself may look somewhat different. From here, the end of the line for the smartphone is clearly visible.

5 ______ The next stage in the evolution of technology involves the implantation thereof directly onto the brain. How can you misplace your device or have it stolen if it is actually inside of you? Though for some this is going altogether too far and may sound like the prelude to a dystopian world of half-human half-machine cyborgs, the logic of it is undeniable. We will have become completely autonomous, computer-augmented beings, with instant access to a virtual universe. No searching for wi-fi, no forgetting devices at home, no tangle of power cords, only perfect integration. What brave new worlds will await then?

5 Complete the words in the glossary with words or phrases from the article.

Glossary

- **a** ______ verb [I]: vibrating or sounding rhythmically
- **b** ______ adjective: describing a place that is bad or degraded
- **c** ______ verb [T]: passing a finger or card over a surface
- **d** ______ adjective: the most up-to-date and technologically advanced
- **e** ______ adjective: describing something that cannot be questioned
- **f** ______ noun [C]: a continuous flow
- **g** ______ verb [I]: to increase at a rapid rate
- **h** ______ noun [C] a confused mass of something twisted together
- **i** ______ noun [U]: the speed at which something happens
- **j** ______ noun [U]: a loss of power, prosperity or status

VOCABULARY & LISTENING

1 **Work with a partner. Look at the compound nouns in the box. Match them with these patterns.**

1 adjective + noun   2 noun + noun

card reader   cell phone   cellular coverage   central heating   communication device
data network   evening meal   grocery shopping   home-entertainment system
payment system   remote alert   remote control   security center   speech recognition
travel schedule   voice call   voicemail

2 **Match these definitions with five of the compound nouns in Exercise 1.**

a a system which is used to protect your home and alert you to any intruders
b a device you use to listen to music or radio shows, or to watch movies or TV shows
c a system for storing and retrieving messages left, for example on your phone
d supper or dinner
e the act of going out to buy food

3 **Work with your partner. Take turns explaining five of the remaining compound nouns in the box in Exercise 1. Do not use either component of the compound noun.**

A: You can program it to keep your house warm.
B: Central heating.

4 **Work with your partner. Look at the picture of a new gadget. What features do you think it will have?**

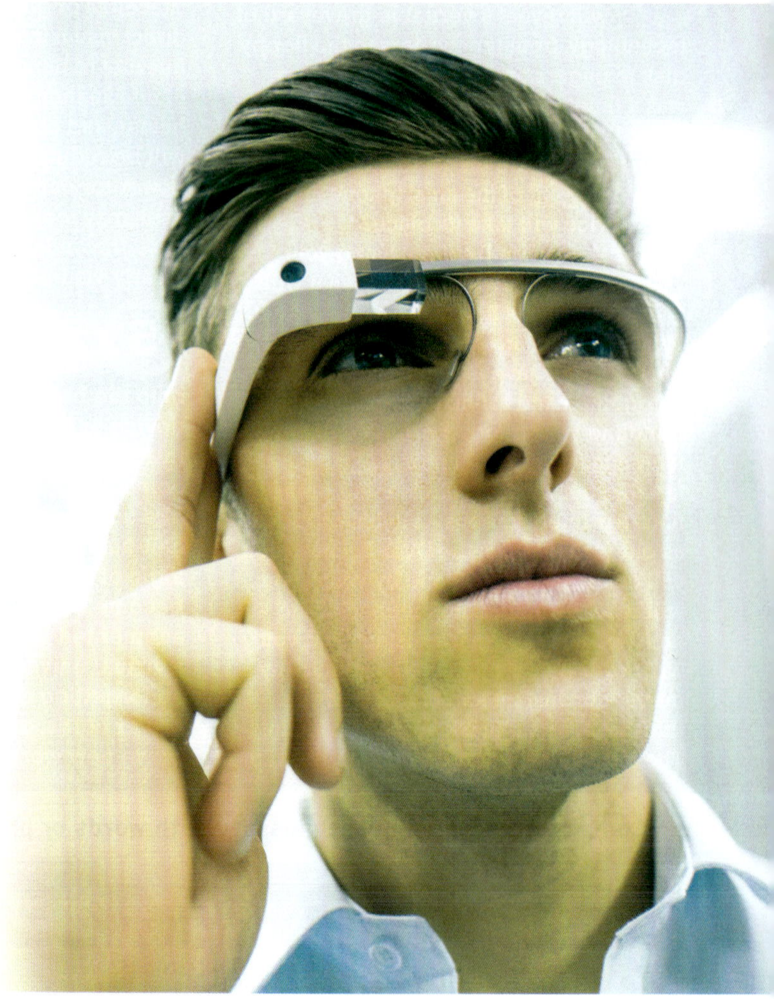

5 2.02 **Listen and check the features that the gadget offers.**

- ☐ Separate keyboard
- ☐ Touch screen
- ☐ Earpiece
- ☐ Low cost
- ☐ Voice control
- ☐ Connects with other devices
- ☐ Wi-fi connection

6 **Complete the description of the device with the words in the box.**

accessible   earpiece   swiping
touch screen   bugs
link up   hands-free

The newest version of the glasses has a lot going for it, starting with the fact that it enables users to be completely (1) _____ . There is no physical interaction with the device, no (2) _____ to be splotched with fingerprints. All commands are done either by voice or by (3) _____ with the eyes. The glasses include the nearly invisible (4) _____ that allows you to hear your virtual assistant. The glasses are fully compatible with other devices and easily (5) _____ with phones and smart watches. Though we love the functionality and it is a huge upgrade over the previous version, it still has some (6) _____ to be worked out, and the price is as yet not (7) _____ to most tech consumers. Wait for the next version if you can!

7 **Compare your answers with your partner. Which innovation or innovations do you think would be most popular? Why?**

GRAMMAR

1 **Work with a partner. Look at this sentence from the article on page 73. How many clauses does it contain? Are the clauses ...**

a main clauses?
b subordinate clauses?

Because you will command your phone by voice, / you will receive immediate feedback from an AI-powered virtual assistant, / and you will never be disconnected, / making any interaction instant and constant.

Break the sentence down into simple one-clause sentences.

a You will be able to command ______ .
b You will be able to receive ______ .
c You will never ______ .
d You can make instant and ______ .

2 **Compare the original sentence in Exercise 1 with the shorter sentences. Circle any differences in the longer sentence and find examples of ...**

a use of linkers.
b dropping subject pronouns and auxiliaries.
c use of participle clauses.

What is the advantage of the longer sentence?

Complex sentences

Simple, one-clause sentence

Your phone can re-program the central heating.

Complex, multi-clause sentence

It can control your home, re-programming the central heating and alerting you if the home security system is triggered.

3 **Put the words in the correct order to form complex sentences.**

a when I can't find them / and generating voice directions, / where I've left them. / I'd love to have a device that locates my car keys / to let me know / by sending a signal to my GPS
b constantly making recommendations / or searching for information, / and generally interfering in my life. / I would not want technology / to be implanted in my brain / without my asking
c A virtual assistant will be a great way / as I am often on the road / to have constant access to my contacts / without having to actually grab my phone / and don't always have time to stop my car.

Underline the main clauses. Which feature appeals to you most? Why?

4 **Write a multi-clause sentence explaining what you'd like from your cell phone. Compare your sentences with the class.**

5 **Grammar Extra 7, Part 1** page 148. Read the explanations and do Exercise 1.

PRONUNCIATION

1 **Look at the words in the box. Say the words and add them to the table according to their pronunciation.**

~~familiar~~ interactive prototype recognition technology traditional transparent

A: □☐□	B: ☐□□	C: □☐□□	D: □□☐□
/ə/ /ə/ familiar			

Look at the words again and write /ə/ above the unstressed syllables where appropriate.

2 ▶ 2.03 **Listen and check your answers to Exercise 1. Listen again and repeat the sentences.**

READING

1 **Work with a partner. What does 'Artificial Intelligence' mean?**

2 **Read the highlighted sentence on page 77 and see if your definition from Exercise 1 is the same. Then, answer the questions.**

a In what ways does A.I. play a role in our lives at present?
b How will A.I. change society in the future?

3 **Read the article on page 77 about Artificial Intelligence and see if your answers are the same as the author's.**

4 **Read the article again and decide if the statements (a-f) are True (T), False (F), or Not Given (N).**

a Despite its long history, A.I. did not see widespread adoption until much more recently.
b A.I. in the employment sector is unlikely to lead to significant changes.
c Targeted marketing and entertainment will soon become a reality.
d Bioengineering is only one of many uses for A.I. in the medical field.
e There is a trend towards people building closer personal relationships with robots.
f One concern about A.I. is that humans might lose control.

5 **Complete the words in the glossary with words or phrases from the article.**

Glossary

a *coin* verb [T]: to use a word or phrase that no one has used before
b ______ adjective: independent and able to make their own decisions
c ______ verb [T]: to produce the features of something in a way that seems real but is not
d ______ adjective: impossible to avoid or ignore
e ______ adjective: describes an action or change that has a very big effect
f ______ noun [C]: a new business or activity
g ______ adjective: very common
h ______ noun [C]: a set of rules for solving problems or doing calculations

6 **Work in small groups. Look at the four areas in the article again. Which do you think would ...**

a have the most dramatic impact on our way of life? Why?
b potentially lead to problems for humanity? Why?

READY OR NOT, HERE A.I. COMES!

Although the term was first coined in the 1950s, Artificial Intelligence, or A.I., is now more prevalent than ever. Whether you realize it or not, A.I. is all around us, inescapable and continuing to grow. Already, the programs and websites we take for granted, like those for searching online or watching videos, use A.I. to anticipate our desires. And with top tech companies all investing heavily in A.I., it doesn't look like this trend will be slowing down anytime soon.

But first, what exactly is A.I.? Basically, it is the concept of a machine which can simulate any feature of intelligence which was traditionally unique to humans. For example, in recent years, one type of A.I., machine learning, has developed at a staggering rate, creating networks that can imitate the way neurons work in our own brains. Looking ahead to the future then, it's impossible to predict exactly how A.I. will shape our world. With that said, it's a safe bet that we can expect heavy A.I. influence in the following areas:

1 At work: For generations people have worried about machines taking human jobs, but with A.I., whole industries may soon become automated. Self-driving cars would replace drivers, automatic translators would replace language teachers and translators, and A.I. writers could replace news journalists. On the bright side, dangerous jobs like defusing bombs would also likely be handed over.

2 Daily lives: Already our phones speak to us and the internet tries to predict ads we might like. We can expect this trend to continue, with activities related to shopping, listening to music, and cooking being influenced by A.I. It has even been suggested that we will soon be able to pay for products just by using our face! When you enter a store, A.I. would recognize you and charge any purchases directly to your account.

3 Our bodies: The image of a half human, half robot is a scary one, but A.I. wouldn't necessarily lead to anything so drastic. Rather, A.I. in medicine could help people with missing limbs to regain mobility, assist the elderly with reminders about their medicine, or provide more accurate diagnoses based on advanced algorithms and big data.

4 Our relationships: In many sci-fi movies, A.I. interacts with humans and even builds relationships. And while we may not have C3PO from Star Wars any time soon, we do interact with 'chatbots' all the time. Just consider the last time you called a bank or airline – did you speak to a human immediately? We can only hope that robot relationships won't replace real ones!

Of course, although the possible benefits of A.I. are immense, so too are the dangers. What would happen, for instance, if A.I. became completely autonomous? Would an independent A.I. know how to achieve its goals without bringing harm to humans? Or if we became completely reliant on A.I., what would happen to our ability to complete even basic tasks? These are but some of the questions facing us as we venture into this brave new world, questions which we must all grapple with in the coming years.

GRAMMAR

1 **Work with a partner. Look at the verbs and phrases in bold in the predictions (a–c). Match them with the three categories (1–3).**

a Travel by teleportation and force fields **could** become scientific realities within decades.
b Time travel **will definitely** be possible in the future.
c Telepathy, force fields, and invisibility **are likely to** become reality at some point in the future.

1 certain (you are sure this will happen)
2 fairly confident (you are almost sure this will happen)
3 uncertain (you think it's possible but you aren't sure)

Make the sentences (a–c) negative. What do you notice about the position of *definitely* in sentence *b*?

Which predictions do you agree with? The ones in the original sentences or the ones in the negative sentences you just wrote?

Speculating about the future

Modals

Teleportation **will** / **may** / **might** / **could** / **should** be possible within the next fifty years.

Adverbs with *will* and *won't*

Invisibility devices **will (almost) certainly** / **definitely** / **easily** / **probably** be perfected within our lifetime.

Invisibility devices **(almost) certainly** / **definitely** / **probably won't** be perfected within our lifetime.

Adverbs with *may*, *might*, or *could*

Time travel **may possibly** / **(very) well** / **easily** be a reality for our grandchildren.

Phrases

It is **sure to** / **bound to** / **(highly) likely to** / **(highly) unlikely to** happen in the next ten years.

2 **Look at the phrases in the box. Which could be used to replace ...**

a *could?* b *will definitely?* c *are likely to?*

could easily is bound to is sure to may may very well might should will almost certainly will probably

3 **Rewrite the sentences using the words in parentheses.**

a Self-driving cars will replace human drivers by the middle of the century. (definitely)
b A cure for cancer could easily be within our reach in the next decade. (highly likely)
c The Earth will eventually be destroyed by overpopulation. (sure)
d It may well become possible to colonize Mars before the end of the century. (we should)
e Anyone could soon be incubating babies using artificial wombs. (will)
f Coastal cities like Miami and Rio de Janeiro may soon be adversely affected as sea levels rise. (likely)
g Organ donors are likely to become things of the past, thanks to advances in stem cell technology. (easily)
h Many jobs will be done by computers, creating more free time for human beings. (bound)

Change the sentences you don't agree with. Compare your new sentences with your partner.

4 Grammar Extra 7, Part 2 page 148. Read the explanations and do Exercise 2.

5 **Work in small groups. What will the world be like in twenty years' time? Make predictions about the following topics. Use a variety of forms from Exercises 1 and 2.**

- the kinds of jobs available to young people
- the size and shape of your home town
- new gadgets and appliances in your home
- the kind of food we'll be eating and the kinds of clothes we'll be wearing
- changes to the way people meet, date, and fall in love

Share your ideas with the class. Whose predictions are the ...

- most conservative?
- most outlandish?

LISTENING & VOCABULARY

1 2.04 **Listen to two people on a radio show discussing the gadget in the picture. Answer the questions.**

- a What exactly is the gadget? What can it do?
- b How do the two people feel about it?

2 **Listen again and make notes on ...**

- a the arguments put forward in favor of the device.
- b the arguments put forward against the device.

3 **Look at the extracts (a–f) from the radio show in Exercise 1. Who is speaking each time: the man or the woman? What do the words and expressions in bold mean?**

- a What cool new gadget are you going to **wow** us with today?
- b Books have **gone digital**.
- c You've been reading too much **hype**!
- d I really don't think any device, no matter how **slick** and quick and easy to use, can possibly replace a much-loved book.
- e Not to speak of the mountains and mountains of newspapers **trashed** every single day.
- f You're definitely **sold on the idea**.

4 **Work in small groups. Discuss the questions.**

- a Who does the device appeal to? Would you like to try it? Why? / Why not?
- b Do you think they'll become as popular as smartphones?
- c Do you think paper books will disappear from our bookshelves? Why? / Why not? If they did, how would that affect your everyday life and the world around you?

SPEAKING

1 **Work in small groups. Discuss the questions. Prepare to justify your choices to the rest of the class.**

- a What do you think were the top five scientific breakthroughs of the last century? Write them in order of importance.
- b What do you think will be the top five scientific breakthroughs of our present century? Again, write them in order of importance.

2 **Present your lists to the class. Then discuss the questions.**

- a Which of the past breakthroughs has had the biggest effect on your life and lifestyle?
- b Which could you happily live without?
- c Which future breakthrough will have the greatest impact on life as we know it?

LANGUAGE FOR LIFE

1 **Work with a partner. Look at this list of decisions. Discuss what the future implications of each decision might be.**

- getting a tattoo
- choosing which college to go to
- quitting your job
- having cosmetic surgery
- coloring your hair bright blue
- running for election

Are you an impulsive decision-maker or do you usually consider all the implications beforehand? Give examples of decisions you've had to make recently to your partner.

2 2.05-2.08 **Listen to the conversations (1–4). What decisions are the people talking about? Match the conversations with the pictures (a–d).**

3 **Look at the extracts (a–i). Which conversation (*1*, *2*, *3*, or *4*) do they come from?**

a It's **not such a big deal**, is it?
b Once I've had a chance **to think things over** ...
c Once you get one, **there's no going back**.
d I should stop **dithering** all the time.
e I obviously hadn't **thought through all the possible consequences**.
f I keep **going around and around in circles**.
g Why don't you **sleep on it**?
h **It isn't the end of the world**.
i You know, **what's done is done** and all that.

Listen again and check.

4 **Look at the useful phrases in bold in Exercise 3. Which useful phrases mean ...**

1 to consider something carefully?
2 not very important?
3 a decision cannot be reversed?
4 to waste time being unable to make a decision?
5 to postpone making a decision?

5 **Work with your partner. Student A: look at page 139 and read about the situation. Student B: look at page 140 and read about the situation. You are going to take turns helping your partner discuss a difficult decision. Use the useful phrases in Exercise 3.**

Life Skills: Interpersonal Skills

Tech Fast

1 **Class discussion:**

a Look at the pictures. What do they illustrate?
b Do you think these behaviors should be considered natural or should we avoid them?
c What kinds of restrictions do you think should be put on children's technology use, if any?

2 **In groups, come up with three no-tech activities you could do during a tech fast and share them with the class. Compare.**

MACMILLAN LIFE SKILLS

7 Vocabulary Extra

ACRONYMS AND COLLOCATIONS

1 **Work with a partner. Look at the acronyms and abbreviations in the box and answer the questions.**

a Do you know what the letters stand for?
b Do you know how to say them in English?
c Do you use the same acronyms in your language?

4G GPS MP3 PC PIN wi-fi

Match them with their definitions on the right.

2 **Match the gadgets and systems in the box in Exercise 1 with the tasks (1-10). Some can be matched with more than one task.**

1 connecting to the internet
2 checking your email
3 instant messaging
4 downloading a podcast
5 paying for goods and services
6 watching a movie
7 texting
8 playing games
9 finding your way around
10 keeping up with the news

How many of the gadgets or systems do you use at least once a day? What for?

3 **Read the article and find out the difference between a *digital native* and a *digital immigrant*. Which are you? Compare your answer with your partner.**

Digital technology has been part of everyday life for many years now, so logically there's a whole generation of individuals for whom concepts such as the internet and wireless technology are just humdrum, because they've never lived in a world where they didn't exist. These are the so-called **digital natives**, generally anyone born from 1980 onwards. **Digital immigrants** are their antithesis, being the folks born earlier who, either reluctantly or enthusiastically, have adapted to the digital world and incorporated its tools into their lives. Observation of contrasts such as these has led to what is referred to as **digital nativism**, the idea that those who have grown up in the digital world have an advantage, not only in terms of using technology, but also because of enhanced cognitive skills developing from a multitasking, "always-on" way of life.

4 **Work with your partner. Look at the words in the box and answer the questions.**

a Which (if any) do not collocate with *digital*?
b What does each collocation in a) mean?
c What did we have before the digital version?

banking broadcasting camera display entertainment friend images learning library life shopping sleep technology thermometer TV universe world

Look at the words in the box again. How many can you combine with *cyber*, *e-*, or *online*?

5 **Tell your partner how you would update the technology you use in your everyday life if money were no object. What could you live without?**

Acronyms

1 ______ stands for personal computer.

2 ______ stands for global positioning system – most frequently used in satnavs (satellite navigation systems) in cars, buses, and taxis.

3 ______ stands for MPeg audio player 3, a method of compressing the size of a computer file that contains sound, especially music, so that it can be sent quickly by email or over the internet.

4 The ______ stands for wireless, the ______ does not actually stand for anything but simply creates a catchy name with the rhyme. It echoes the use of hi-fi used for high fidelity music systems.

5 ______ is a personal identification number, used most frequently with bank cards to get cash from an ATM.

6 ______ stands for fourth generation, a technology that gives you a high-speed connection to the internet, video, and multimedia on your cell phone.

cyber- /saɪbər/ prefix relating to computers and the Internet: used with some adjectives and nouns

dig·i·tal /ˈdɪdʒɪtl/ adj ★★
1 storing information such as sound or pictures as numbers or electronic signals: *a digital recording* ♦ *digital technology* —compare ANALOG 2
2 *technical* relating to your fingers or toes
3 a digital clock or instrument shows information as a row of numbers

e- /i/ prefix on or using the Internet: used with some nouns for making new words: *e-business* ♦ *e-finance* ♦ *e-learning*

on·line /ˈɑnˌlaɪn/ adj *computing* ★★
1 connected to or available through a computer or a computer NETWORK (=a group of connected computers), especially the Internet: *an online bookshop* ♦ *companies with an online ordering service*

From the *Macmillan English Dictionary (American edition)*

8 The law

SPEAKING

1 **Read the statements with some blunders made in real-life courtrooms. What did they really want to say?**

The following exchanges all occurred in US courts of law. The questions are accompanied in some instances by the responses of the quick-witted – and usually exasperated – witnesses.

- *"And the youngest son, the 20-year-old, how old is he?"*
- *"Was it you or your younger brother who was killed in the war?"*
- *"You say the stairs went down to the basement?" "Yes." "Did they also go up?"*
- *"Are you qualified to give a urine sample?" "I have been since early childhood."*
- *"All your responses must be oral, OK? What school did you go to?" "Oral."*
- *"Now, Doctor, isn't it true that when a person dies in his sleep, he doesn't know about it until the next morning?"*
- *"Were you present when your picture was taken?"*

VOCABULARY

1 **The words and phrases in the box are all connected to the theme of the law. Work with a partner and categorize them under the headings in the table.**

arson attorney award damages burglary community service cross-examine embezzlement fine jail sentence lawsuit libel manslaughter probation return a verdict solitary confinement speeding sue the accused to sentence weigh up the evidence

Crimes	Punishments	People	Legal processes

2 **Complete the sentences with words and phrases from Exercise 1.**

a Slander is when you say something about someone which isn't true. _____ is when you publish it, and that's when people generally take action.
b If a person is on trial, the media must refer to them as _____ .
c You _____ someone to claim money from them if they have harmed you in some way.
d The jury has to listen to the case, _____ , and then _____ .
e An _____ is the person who represents you in court.
f _____ can be anything from teaching kids to play soccer to cutting the grass. Obviously, it's not paid.
g Once the prosecution has questioned a witness, the defense has the possibility to _____ him or her.

3 **Choose another three words or phrases from Exercise 1 and write three sentences like the ones in Exercise 2. Give them to your partner to complete.**

- **Grammar:** Paraphrasing. Using modals to talk about the past. Inversion after *neither/nor, so/such*
- **Vocabulary:** Legal vocabulary. Collocations with *law*. Formal vocabulary
- **Language for Life:** Expressing surprise or disbelief

LISTENING & GRAMMAR

1 2.09-2.11 **Listen to three conversations about crimes. Which of the crimes in Vocabulary, Exercise 1 are the speakers talking about?**

2 **Look at the sentences. Which of the conversations (1–3) do they come from?**

a The verdict we returned was unanimous: guilty.
b That's a lesson I won't forget in a hurry.
c The best person to ask is Mike Zurack.
d It was fascinating, seeing how a court works.
e It's been almost three weeks since they published the article.

3 **There is always more than one way of saying something. Paraphrase the sentences (a–e) in Exercise 2 starting with the words below.**

1 We ...
2 I ...
3 Mike Zurack ...
4 Seeing ...
5 They ...

Compare your answers with a partner. Are there any differences between your sentences?

Paraphrasing

Paraphrasing is expressing the same thing using different words.

A strange case was brought before the court.

The case which was brought before the court was **a strange one**.

It was **a strange case** that was brought before the court.

4 **Look at the picture and read about a court case in the Caribbean island of Barbados during British colonial times. Rewrite each sentence twice, starting with the words given.**

a A court case was held in Barbados.
  1 It was ... 2 Barbados ...
b In the witness stand stood a Barbadian who was accused of shoplifting.
  1 A Barbadian ... 2 Accused ...
c He was defended by a Barbadian attorney.
  1 Defending ... 2 The attorney ...
d Towards the end of the trial, the attorney asked the judge if he could speak to the jury in Bajan, the Barbadian dialect.
  1 "May I ... 2 The attorney ...
e The judge agreed because he didn't wish to appear biased towards English.
  1 Not wishing ... 2 In order not to ...
f The jury returned a verdict of not guilty.
  1 A verdict ... 2 Not guilty ...
g The judge was puzzled, because the defendant was obviously guilty.
  1 What puzzled the judge ... 2 The defendant ...
h The judge didn't speak Bajan, so he hadn't understood what the attorney had said.
  1 Not being able ... 2 As the judge ...

The attorney had said to the jury: "The prosecutor is British, the prosecution counsel is British, the judge is British. But the prisoner is a Barbadian, I am Barbadian, and you are Barbadians. Do your duty."

5 **Use the sentences you have written in Exercise 4 to write an account of the court case for a newspaper as if it had happened recently. Make any changes or additions that you think are necessary.**

Compare your story with the one on page 139. What differences are there?

Grammar Extra 8, Part 1 page 148. Read the explanations and do Exercise 1.

SPEAKING & LISTENING

1 **Put the crimes in the box in order of seriousness. Compare your answers with a partner and decide what punishment should be given for each crime.**

graffiti identity theft inciting violence internet piracy jaywalking littering pollution crimes shoplifting spreading computer viruses tax evasion

2 2.12-2.17 **Six people were asked what punishment they would give people guilty of some of the crimes in Exercise 1. Listen and answer the questions.**

a Which crime is each person (1–6) talking about?

b What punishments do the speakers suggest?

"I'm in for forgery."

3 **Listen again and answer the questions.**

a Which speaker, in your opinion, has the most lenient approach?

b Which punishment do you think would be the most effective?

c Which speaker holds views most similar to your own?

4 **Work in small groups. Discuss the questions.**

a Do you think punishment is an effective deterrent to crime? If yes, what kinds of punishments do you think are most effective? If not, how would you prevent crime?

b Can you think of any cases that have been in the media recently? What was the crime? What was the punishment?

5 **Work with your partner. Read each case and discuss the questions that follow.**

Case 1

A driver swerves to avoid a child crossing the road. The driver goes off the road and injures a pedestrian.

a What is the driver guilty of, if anything?

b Who should pay for the pedestrian's medical expenses?

c Who should pay for the damage done to the car?

Case 2

A soccer player trips up an opponent deliberately. The opponent breaks a leg and is unable to play soccer for a long time. He sues the other player for loss of earnings.

a Should the player pay? Why? / Why not?

6 **Turn to page 140 and read the rulings for the two cases. Do you agree with the judge? Do you think the rulings are fair? Do you think these rulings would be possible in your country?**

LISTENING

1 **Work with a partner. Discuss the questions.**

a Have you ever had anything stolen? If you have, what was it? Did you get it back? Were you insured? Was the thief caught?

b If you haven't, what would cause you the most inconvenience if it was ever stolen? Why?

2 ▶ 2.18 **Listen to Anna telling Tim about a time she had something stolen. Answer the questions.**

a What was stolen?

b Who stole it?

c Was she insured against theft?

d What happened in the end?

Anna and Tim

3 **Listen again. Are the statements true or false?**

a Anna's car was stolen by a band of car thieves.

b Her insurance documents had disappeared from the car.

c Her insurance didn't cover accidents after theft.

d She had read the contract carefully before signing it.

e She thought something fishy was going on with the insurers.

f Her friend finds it difficult to believe the story.

g Her insurance company paid up in the end.

h She eventually split up with her boyfriend.

4 **Work with your partner and answer the questions.**

a What would you say were the three most important points in Anna's story?

b What details do you think made the story more interesting or dramatic?

c Do you think there's any truth in Anna's conspiracy theory?

PRONUNCIATION

1 **Work with your partner. Look at the extracts from the conversation in Listening, Exercise 2. Are the underlined consonants pronounced, or are they silent?**

a a brand-new car

b they just didn't want to pay up

c maybe buy a used one

d what did you do?

e they said it didn't matter

f I was insured against theft

g I should have

h you could have asked a friend

2 ▶ 2.19 **Listen and check your answers. Then match the two halves of the pronunciation rules.**

a When a word ending in consonant + /t/ or /d/ is followed by a word starting with a consonant other than /t/ or /d/ ...

b When a word ending in /t/ or /d/ is followed by a word starting with a vowel ...

c When a word ending in /t/ or /d/ is followed by a word starting with /t/ or /d/ ...

1 we only pronounce the /t/ or /d/ in the second word, or sometimes neither.

2 we often drop the /t/ or /d/.

3 the /t/ or /d/ is always pronounced.

Find examples for each rule in the extracts in Exercise 1.

3 **Look at the questions. Work with your partner and decide how the final /t/ and /d/ sounds are pronounced.**

a Why is it important to read everything you sign?

b When was the last time you signed an official document? Are you sure you read it all before signing?

c Have you ever had to go to a police station? What for?

Discuss your answers to the questions.

GRAMMAR

1 **Work with a partner. Underline the modal verbs in the sentences (a–j). Match them with the functions (1–3) below.**

- a The insurance company wouldn't pay up.
- b I couldn't believe it when I saw it!
- c You really should have read it before signing it.
- d I suppose with the benefit of hindsight I should have.
- e Couldn't you have asked your boyfriend to check it over for you?
- f They're standard forms, so I thought it would be fine.
- g They might have just checked the box themselves so they didn't have to pay the equivalent of $8,000.
- h They wouldn't have done that, would they?
- i You must have been upset at the time.
- j They can't have just stolen the documents like that!

1. reporting speech or thought
2. speculating / making deductions
3. commenting/criticizing

Using modals to talk about the past

modal + infinitive
He **couldn't/wouldn't drive**.

modal + *have* + past participle
I **should** / **ought to have checked**.

They **might/could/may have taken** them.

They **wouldn't have done** that.

That **can't/must have happened**.

2 **Look at the sentences. In two of them the modal verb is being used incorrectly. Correct the sentences which are wrong.**

- a Anna mustn't have been very happy when she found her car had been stolen.
- b Her boyfriend must have worked hard to win the case.
- c The boys couldn't have known how to drive very well.
- d Anna can have made a mistake about the insurance company.

3 **Rewrite the sentences using an appropriate modal verb phrase.**

- a I believe they stole the documents.
- b It's possible that they changed the original contract.
- c You were not very smart signing a contract without reading it first.
- d I think it's possible that you were wrong.
- e The garage owner had the opportunity to take the documents.
- f The boys' parents refused to take any responsibility for the boys' actions.

4 **Work with your partner. Look at the pictures (1–3). What do you think happened? Write sentences with *might have*, *could have*, *must have*, or *can't have*.**

1

2

3

Compare your answers with the rest of the class. Who came up with the most original explanation? And the most realistic?

5 **Work with your partner. Think of something ...**

- a you should have done last weekend, but you didn't.
- b you could have done last night, but you didn't.

Tell your partner why you didn't do these things. Do you wish you had? How would things have been different if you had done these things?

6 **Grammar Extra 8, Part 2** page 148. Read the explanations and do Exercise 2.

VOCABULARY

1 **Match the collocations using the word *law* (a–i) with their meanings (1–9).**

a against the law
b a law unto herself
c the letter of the law
d in trouble with the law
e law-abiding
f the long arm of the law
g nobody is above the law
h take the law into your own hands
i laying down the law

1 suspected of having committed a crime
2 she doesn't follow rules
3 we are all equal in the eyes of the law
4 take revenge without using the legal system
5 bossing people around
6 the ability of the police to catch criminals
7 illegal
8 obeying and respecting the law
9 exact words used in a law

2 **Complete the sentences with the collocations in Exercise 1.**

a Police officer: You were doing 160 kilometers per hour.
Woman: Yes, but do you know who I am?
Police officer: Yes, but ______ .
b After years as a ______ citizen, John decided to rob a bank and flee the country.
c There was a police officer here earlier. I think Mark's ______ again!
d I was tempted to ______ and wring his neck.
e "Do this! Do that! Be back by ten!" My father was always ______ .
f You can never tell what Bob's going to do. He's ______ .
g He thought he'd gotten away with it, but ______ finally caught up with him ten years later.
h Since Jenny had never been arrested before, they gave her a warning instead of following ______ .
i In some countries it's ______ to chew gum.

3 **How many of the collocations in Exercise 1 are similar in your language? In English we talk about making and breaking laws as if they were material objects. Do you use the same metaphors in your language?**

SPEAKING

1 **Work in small groups. Look at these proposals for laws and discuss with your group which would affect you personally. Which of these laws do you think would make the world a better place?**

a All major cities should provide free wi-fi access in all public places.
b Politicians should be allowed to stay in office for a maximum of eight years and only after they've had a job in the "real world" for at least five years.
c Nobody should work more than thirty-two hours a week.
d Families should not be allowed to have more than one car.

2 **Are there any laws in your country that you would like to change or introduce?**

READING

1 Read a legal anecdote based on a real-life case. In one sentence each, summarize ...

a the plaintiff's case: ______

b the defendant's case: ______

c the judge's solution: ______

In a small claims court in the United States, a peculiar lawsuit was brought before a judge, involving a pet and its owners. In this case, the plaintiff (let's call her Mallory) was suing the defendant (let's call him Aidan). However, unlike most plaintiffs, Mallory was not seeking money, nor was she asking for property. Instead, she wanted her dog back, a small Chihuahua named Poppy.

Standing before the judge, she tearfully described how she came to lose her dog.

"Well, your honor, I was in my backyard with Poppy when I heard my oven timer go off, so I went in for a second to take my pie out of the oven. I heard Poppy barking, which isn't unusual, and when I got back out, Poppy was gone. I have a fence so I know she couldn't have escaped – she must have been stolen!"

"So, how do you know this man has your dog now?" asked the judge.

"I saw him, your honor, a year later, just walking down the street with my Poppy! He insisted I was wrong, but I would know Poppy anywhere. We almost got into a fight, but I took his license plate number and contacted the police."

Turning to the defendant, the judge asked for his side of the story.

"Your honor, this woman's crazy – she's trying to take my dog Lolita from me. I bought her fair and square and have all the vet records since she's been with me. She's clearly not a five-year-old Chihuahua, more like a three-year-old mutt. I bought her from a woman on Craigslist for $30 who was moving and couldn't look after her. It was a good deed on my part, and now look what's happened!"

The judge pondered the situation for a moment before addressing both parties.

"I find myself in a predicament here, as both your testimonies are credible, and there is no physical evidence to prove or disprove either side's version of events. I am no dog expert and am unable to determine the exact age or breed of the animal, and neither can either of you."

Then the judge made an unexpected request.

"Aidan, can you please bring the dog into the courtroom?"

Slightly shocked, Aidan nevertheless did as the judge had asked, and carried in the small dog in his arms.

"Now put him on the ground," ordered the judge.

Immediately upon doing so, a chaotic scene unfolded in the courtroom. The dog made a bee-line for Mallory, running at full speed, and jumped straight into her arms, yipping with glee and covering Mallory with licks. So overcome with emotion was Mallory that tears began to flow down her cheeks. The defendant started to loudly protest, clearly overwrought himself.

"That means nothing – she does that to everyone!" he exclaimed. "We've had her for over a year and she's part of our family."

But his entreaty was to no avail. "I'm sorry sir, but that is all the evidence I require. That is her dog. Case closed," and with a bang of his gavel, the verdict was final.

2 Read the anecdote again and find formal words or phrases to complete the glossary.

Glossary

a ______ adjective: strange
b ______ verb [I]: to happen
c ______ noun [C]: judgment
d ______ verb [T]: to speak directly to (sb)
e ______ verb [I/T]: to think carefully
f ______ phrase: without getting the desired effect
g ______ adjective: extremely emotional or upset
h ______ noun [C]: difficult situation
i ______ verb [T]: to try to get something
j ______ adjective: believable
k ______ verb [T]: to calculate something
l ______ phrase: description of what happened

3 Write questions starting with the prompts.

a Why did ...
b Why was ...
c What did ...
d What happened when ...
e What was the result of ...
f Why do you think ...

Work with a partner and ask him/her your questions. Check their answers.

GRAMMAR

1 Look at the sentences. Which come from the anecdote on page 88?

- **a** He could not believe what was happening and **neither** could he stop it.
- **b** Mallory wasn't seeking money, **nor** was she asking for property.
- **c** **So overcome** with emotion was Mallory that tears began to flow down her cheeks.
- **d** **Such** was the predicament that the judge could not find an obvious solution.

2 Look at the sentences in Exercise 1 again. What do you notice about the position of the verb and the subject after *nor*, *neither*, *so* (+ adjective), and *such*?

3 Rewrite the sentences in Exercise 1 using the words given.

- **a** He couldn't believe what was happening or ...
- **b** Mallory wasn't seeking money or ...
- **c** Mallory was ...
- **d** The predicament meant ...

Which form of the sentence is more formal, the one in Exercise 1 or the one you have just written?

> **Inversion after *neither/nor*, *so/such***
>
> They weren't hungry, **nor were they** thirsty.
>
> He wasn't seeking recognition, and **neither did he** appreciate it when it came.
>
> **So** disgusted **was he** by the service, he decided to complain.
>
> **Such was the weather** that even the most daring windsurfers stayed at home.

4 Match the sentence beginnings (a–d) with the endings (1–4).

- **a** They didn't release the prisoner
- **b** He isn't young and he isn't good-looking either,
- **c** They were so happy with the results
- **d** There was such an outcry over the new proposals

1. but he is very popular.
2. that they have recommended the company to all their co-workers.
3. and they didn't let his family see him.
4. that the government is reconsidering its plans.

5 Rewrite the sentences in Exercise 4 using inversion. Make any other changes that are necessary.

They didn't release the prisoner, nor did they let his family see him.

6 Work with a partner. Look again at the sentences you wrote in Exercise 5. Invent a context for each of the sentences.

VOCABULARY

1 The anecdote on page 88 contains a lot of formal vocabulary. Use some of the formal words and phrases from the glossary on page 88 to complete the newspaper headlines. Make any necessary changes to the word forms.

- a Mayor _____ resignation after bribery scandal
- b Actress _____ United Nations in heartfelt speech
- c Mystery surrounding plane crash continues to _____
- d Judge delivers shocking _____ in Jones case
- e Tragedy strikes as rescue divers risk lives _____
- f Victims sue the hospital _____ maximum damages

2 Work with your partner. Look at the headlines in Exercise 1 again. Which stories are about a law being broken? What do you think happened? Do you know of any other stories in the news right now that involve laws being passed or broken?

LANGUAGE FOR LIFE

1 2.20 **Listen to two co-workers discussing some news. Answer the questions.**

a What's the news?

b What's their reaction to the news?

2 Listen again and complete the conversation with the useful phrases in the box.

Did I hear you right · I never · Who'd have thought it · You don't expect me to believe that · you never can tell · you've got to be kidding

A: Have you heard about Matt?

B: No, what?

A: He's been arrested!

B: What? (1) ______ ? Arrested? But he **wouldn't hurt a fly**. What are they charging him with?

A: Embezzlement.

B: Come on, (2) ______ . Embezzlement? Old Matthew? (3) ______ , do you?

A: Well, that's what they're saying. Seems it's been going on for a while. Hundreds of thousands, they're talking about.

B: Well, (4) ______ ! (5) ______ ? But what did he do with all the cash? I mean, he hardly **lives in the lap of luxury**!

A: Well, it seems **you can't judge a book by its cover**. Apparently he bought himself a house in Florida ... and a convertible to go with it.

B: Wow! Well, it just goes to show, (6) ______ ...

A: Yeah, but it's always the quiet ones, isn't it? **Still waters run deep** and all that ...

What do the missing useful phrases have in common? Do you have the same expressions in your language?

Look at the four idiomatic expressions in bold. What do they mean?

3 2.21 **Listen to extracts from four conversations. What's the news in each one?**

4 Listen again and make a note of the useful phrases used to express surprise or disbelief. Can you think of any other useful phrases used to show surprise or disbelief?

5 Work with a partner. Take turns breaking one of the pieces of news from the list below. Respond using useful phrases from Exercises 2 and 3.

a You're quitting your job/studies and going to work for a charity in Africa.

b Your grandfather has just won a million dollars in the lottery.

c Your boss/teacher has published a best-selling novel under a pseudonym.

d The government is going to prohibit the use of cell phones on buses.

e Your boss is going to give everybody a huge raise and three weeks' vacation.

Life Skills: Communication and Critical Thinking

Giving Evidence

1 Look at the phrases for giving evidence in the box on the right. Decide if they are more formal (*F*), informal (*I*), or neutral (*N*).

Discuss your answers with your partner.

Research suggests that ...
When you consider that ...
Perhaps the most convincing reason for this ...
There is evidence that ...
... results/arises from ...
You only have to think of ...
To illustrate my point ...

2 Student A: choose one of the topics below and make a statement expressed as a fact. For example, *There should be stricter penalties for people who litter in public places.*

Student B: Agree or disagree with your partner's statement and give evidence for your opinion. Use language from 1, for example, *Yes, there is evidence that stricter penalties do make an impact in terms of ...*

Then, switch roles.

Law · Food · Travel · Entertainment · Technology

MACMILLAN LIFE SKILLS

8 Writing Extra

NEWS STORIES

1 **Work with a partner. Student A: read news report *a*. Student B: read news report *b*. Tell each other about your article. Decide which one was published first.**

a

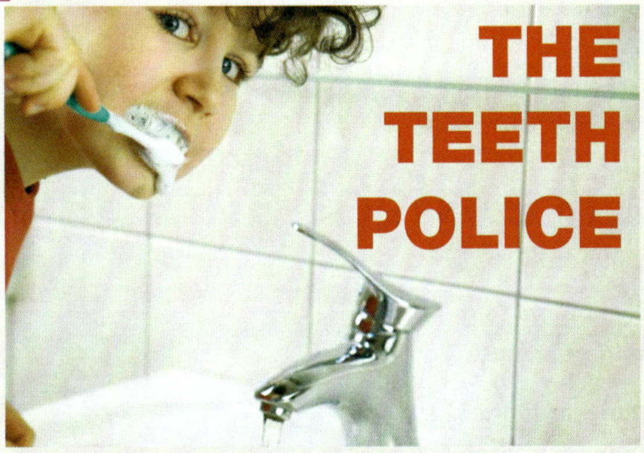

THE TEETH POLICE

PARENTS **are outraged after a new regulation in Massachusetts went into effect last week, *FORCING children* to brush their teeth at school.**

Created by the Massachusetts Department of Early Education & Care, the new regulations promote dental care at an early age, but not everyone sees it that way. One mother we spoke to said to us, "**I don't want some other person, even a teacher, sticking their hands in my kid's mouth!**"

Teachers too are up in arms – with limited time already, they say it is a huge hassle to fit in the new teeth-brushing time.

While government intervention is a hot-button issue, at least in this case, parents can choose to opt-out. Only time will tell us whether mandatory brushing will catch on elsewhere or will eventually be dropped altogether.

b

Teeth brushing law goes into effect

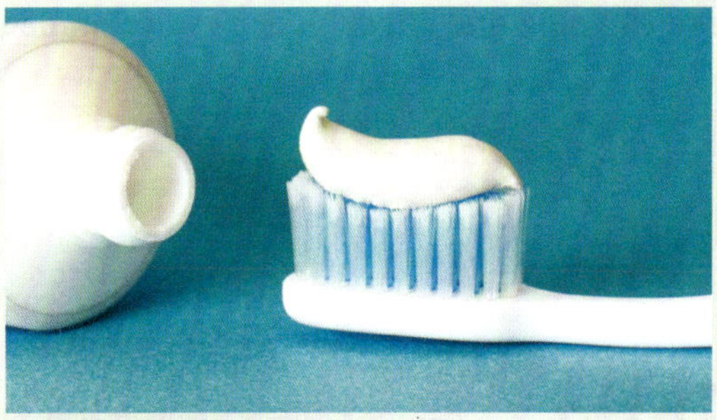

New controversial regulation has been enacted in Massachusetts requiring all children in daycare to brush their teeth

Starting next week, all daycare centers in Massachusetts will be mandated by state law to include teeth brushing as part of their daily routine. When contacted, a government spokesperson said the regulation was created based on the latest evidence in child development and dental hygiene.

Government and schoolboard officials admit that there may be an adjustment period, but that the health benefits will outweigh any potential inconvenience. Opponents of the regulation are critical of what they deem to be unnecessary governmental interference and additional work for teachers.

2 **Work with your partner. Which article do you think was published in the popular press? And which in a serious newspaper? Look at the notes explaining the difference between the two and check your ideas.**

Serious newspapers

Newspapers in which the news is reported in a formal style. The items reported are generally of a factual nature and cover issues of national and global interest. Examples of US quality newspapers include *The New York Times*, *The Washington Post*, and *The Chicago Tribune.*

POPULAR PRESS

Tabloids and magazines which contain bold headlines and large photographs. The writing style is informal and often subjective; sentences are short; and dramatic vocabulary, exclamation points, and capital letters are used to grab the reader's attention, especially in the headlines. Popular titles include *People* and *The National Enquirer.*

3 **Match the phrases (a-d) from the articles in Exercise 1 with the phrases (1-4) that have similar meanings.**

a reached out to
b a hassle
c forced to
d hot-button

1 an inconvenience
2 controversial
3 mandated to
4 contacted

Can you find more examples of differences in style between the two articles?

4 **Work with your partner. Look again at article *b* in Exercise 1. Rewrite it in the style of a tabloid. Use no more than 100 words.**

9 Night

READING & SPEAKING

1 **Take the quiz and check your results on page 140.**

Quiz

Sleep Patterns - Like Night and Day

1 It's a typical work day and you have to get up at 6:00 a.m. because of a long commute. You ...

a) usually wake up before the alarm goes off.
b) set multiple alarms at 5-minute intervals to ensure you eventually get up by the third one.
c) keep the alarm clock across the room to force yourself out of bed so you don't sleep in.

2 You have an important meeting that requires you to be alert and focused. What is your preferred meeting time?

a) The earlier the better.
b) You like to hold your meetings at lunchtime.
c) You are gearing up as the sun sets.

3 It's the weekend and you have no commitments today. What time would you naturally wake up?

a) At sunrise or shortly after.
b) You rise when the sun is already blazing and almost everyone has had breakfast.
c) Lunch IS breakfast on the weekend.

4 Your friends invite you out for a night on the town to celebrate a birthday. You ...

a) have to have a power nap or coffee before leaving the house.
b) make it to midnight before your energy declines, you begin to doze off, and you call it a night.
c) decide the night is young at 2:00 a.m. and keep going strong.

5 Your friend is looking for an early-morning running buddy and asks you to join them at 5:00 a.m. for a 5K jog. You ...

a) jump at the chance; you love to see the sun rise.
b) suggest a 30-minute lunch hour treadmill stint instead, at the gym downtown.
c) decline because you prefer to exercise at night when your energy is at its peak.

6 What time do you usually wind down for the evening?

a) Any time between dinner and 9:00 p.m. I need my beauty sleep.
b) I am usually tucked in bed between 10:00 p.m. and midnight.
c) Long after midnight.

2 **Work with a partner. Discuss the meaning of the highlighted words and phrases. Check in a dictionary if necessary.**

3 **Compare your answers to the quiz in Exercise 1 in small groups. How does your energy pattern compare and fit in with those of your friends or family members?**

- **Grammar:** Concessive clauses and adverbials. Regrets and past conditionals
- **Vocabulary:** Times of day and night. Expressions with *night*
- **Language for Life:** Making and responding to invitations

VOCABULARY & SPEAKING

1 **Work with a partner. Put the times of day in chronological order.**

dawn   dusk   mid-afternoon   mid-morning   midnight   noon   sunrise   sunset

2 **When are these times? Discuss with your partner. Which phrases are literary in style?**

at the crack of dawn   daybreak   first thing in the morning   in the middle of the night   in the small hours   last thing at night   midday   nightfall   twilight

3 **Work with your partner. Tell each other about the following:**

- your favorite time of day
- when you usually feel most and least alert
- what you generally do first thing in the morning and last thing at night
- the last time you got up at the crack of dawn
- being woken up in the middle of the night

LISTENING

1 **Work in small groups. Discuss what the words and phrases in the box mean.**

body clock   circadian rhythms   jet lag   nocturnal and diurnal creatures

2.22 **Listen to a radio show in which these words are discussed, and check if you are right.**

2 **Read the sentences and decide if they are true or false, according to the radio show in Exercise 1.**

a The normal circadian rhythm is twenty-four hours in length.
b Nocturnal animals do not live according to circadian rhythms.
c A body clock is responsive to changes in the environment.
d A body clock changes our feelings of tiredness and wakefulness.
e People are born with individual differences in their circadian rhythms.
f Young children need more sleep than adolescents.
g Older adults tend to get up later than younger adults.
h Jet lag is caused by lack of sleep.

Listen again and check your answers. Is there anything that surprises you about what the scientist said?

READING

1 Read the article on sleep. What are your sleep patterns like?

How Well Do You Sleep?

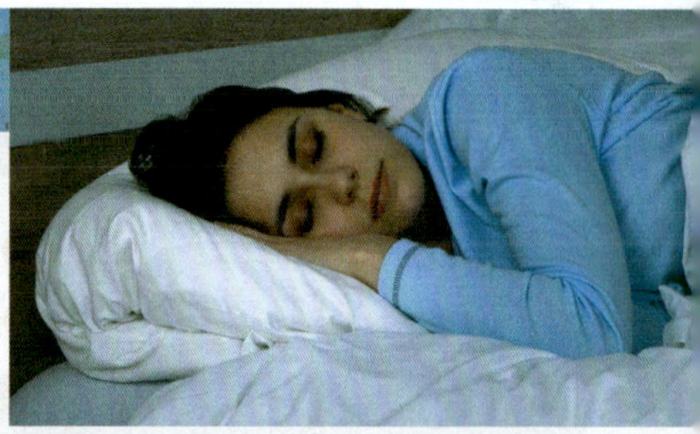

How many of us wake up feeling tired and cranky, despite sleeping for ten hours? How many of us are confident that we are getting enough sleep? While an average of seven to eight hours of sleep is the recommended rule of thumb, even people who tend to go out like a light and sleep like a log may respond negatively to these questions. Why? A study published in the *Journal of Psychosomatic Research* concluded that, although the quantity of sleep is important, the quality of sleep is actually more important when it comes to feeling rested and rejuvenated.

Sleep is essential to overall health and wellbeing. Recharging your batteries is necessary for muscle repair, cardiovascular health, hormone and blood pressure regulation, immune function, brain function (specifically learning, concentration and memory), weight and metabolism management, and mood modulation. As a result, poor sleep patterns can have serious, damaging effects on your body and mind.

How many times have you woken up in the morning but felt like you didn't get a wink of sleep? The National Sleep Foundation has determined that people are not only sleeping less overall but also their sleep quality has decreased. What causes poor sleep quality? When we spend too much time in light sleep and not enough time in deep sleep we experience poor sleep quality. Throughout the night our bodies go through a sleep cycle from light sleep to deep sleep and back to light sleep several times.

To get to deep sleep, your body must progress from light sleep to deep sleep. So, although you may have been in deep sleep, waking up interrupts the cycle and, to get to deep sleep you must start all over again. The more often you wake up, the less time your body spends in deep sleep. As a result, while you may simply describe yourself as a light sleeper, it may mean that your sleep is of poor quality.

Poor sleep quality can manifest itself in many, often subtle and overlooked, ways. Even though you may get eight hours of sleep, symptoms such as irritability upon waking up and a lack of energy during the day indicate poor quality of sleep. Other symptoms include leg cramps, trouble concentrating, sleepiness during the day, and waking up in the middle of the night and having trouble falling back to sleep. If these things happen with regularity it may be time for an intervention. While more serious sleep disorders like apnea, insomnia, snoring and narcolepsy require a medical intervention, there are simple ways that can improve your sleep:

1 Create a regular sleep schedule, allocating 7-8 hours for uninterrupted sleep and going to bed and getting up at the same time every day. Being consistent reinforces your circadian rhythm, makes you more alert during the day, and makes you less likely to be groggy.

2 Beware of your diet in general and especially of what you ingest before bed. Avoid going to bed hungry or stuffed or having large meals within a couple hours of your bedtime. You should also abstain from nicotine, caffeine, and alcohol, all of which can have negative effects on your sleep quality.

3 Creating a soothing environment, conducive to sleep, is an imperative. Preferably, your bedroom should be cool, dark, and quiet. Prolonged use of LCD screens before bed should be avoided. Creating a calming bedtime routine with a bath or meditation to help you wind down is suggested.

4 Curtail daytime napping to a minimum. If you must, have power naps during the day which shouldn't be longer than 30 minutes.

5 Exercising regularly can promote better sleep by improving your mood and reducing stress. Get moving! It can be a great aid in helping you drop off within 20 minutes of going to bed.

Everyone's body has its own individual sleep requirement. Some need less than the recommended eight hours while others need more in order to function properly. It is important to monitor one's own sleep patterns and determine how much sleep your body needs as well as to identify and improve your sleep quality so that the hours count and are effective.

2 Read the article again. Identify which statements are True (T) and which are False (F).

- **a** Sleep is fundamental for building and maintaining our intellectual capacities.
- **b** It is as important to get high quality sleep as it is to get enough sleep.
- **c** There is more than one type of sleep, each with its own function.
- **d** The only way to improve our sleep is with medical help.
- **e** Every day is a different day, and we should sleep when we feel like it.
- **f** There are many factors which affect our sleep, diet being one of them.

3 Complete the glossary with the highlighted words and phrases from the profiles.

Glossary

- **a** ______ verb [I]: to fall asleep immediately
- **b** ______ verb [I]: to sleep soundly
- **c** ______ verb [I]: to take a rest
- **d** ______ verb phrase [I]: to have a sleepless night
- **e** ______ noun [C]: a person who wakes up regularly
- **f** ______ adjective: wide awake
- **g** ______ adjective: drowsy
- **h** ______ verb [I]: to relax
- **i** ______ noun [C]: a siesta
- **j** ______ verb [I]: to fall asleep

4 Work with a partner. Describe your own sleep habits and how they can be improved, following the advice in the article above.

GRAMMAR

1 **Read the sentences (a–d). Are they the same or different in meaning?**

a I slept for ten hours, **yet** I still felt tired the next day.
b **Although** I slept for ten hours, I still felt tired the next day.
c I slept for ten hours. **However**, I still felt tired the next day.
d **Despite** sleeping for ten hours, I still felt tired the next day.

2 **Underline four concessive clauses or adverbials in the article on page 94 that express a similar contrast.**

3 **Rewrite the sentences using the words in parentheses.**

a Despite going to bed early, I was still groggy the next day. (Even though)
b I don't usually oversleep. All the same, I prefer to set the alarm clock. (though)
c The bed was very uncomfortable. Nevertheless, I slept like a log. (In spite of)
d I'd like to get by on six hours a night, but I can't manage on less than seven. (Although)
e Even though I'm normally an early riser, I like to sleep in on Sundays. (Saying that)

Concessive clauses and adverbials

Even though / Although I tried hard, I couldn't get to sleep.

Despite trying / In spite of my efforts / Although I tried, I couldn't get to sleep.

I tried hard. **Even so / Yet / However / Saying that**, I couldn't get to sleep.

I tried hard. I couldn't get to sleep, **though**. / **All the same**, I couldn't get to sleep.

Try as I might, I couldn't get to sleep.

Strange as it may seem, I couldn't get to sleep.

4 **Reorder the underlined words to make concessive clauses.**

a was / as / exhausted / I, I couldn't get to sleep.
b may / strange / seem / it / as, I can't get by on less than ten hours' sleep a night.
c it / be / as / may / hard, we need to get up at the crack of dawn tomorrow.
d might / try / I / as, I couldn't wake him up.

5 **Read the post to a website. What is the person's problem?**

http://community.blog/how-to-deal-with-noisy-neighbors

Does anyone have any suggestions for what to do about persistently noisy neighbors? The people in the apartment above mine have their music on at full blast until the small hours most nights, and it's driving me crazy. (1) ______ my polite requests to turn the music down, so far they haven't taken any notice. I've tried using earplugs, I've tried banging on the ceiling – all to no avail, (2) ______ . My boyfriend thinks I'm being unreasonable. (3) ______ , I do think everyone is entitled to a good night's sleep! Patient (4) ______ I am normally, I'm at the end of my rope.
Can anybody help?

Complete the post with appropriate words or phrases.

Have you ever been in a similar situation? If so, what did you do? What advice would you give to the writer?

6 **Work with a partner. Write a similar post for one of the problems. Use at least three different concessive clauses.**

- I keep oversleeping in the morning.
- I'm always drowsy in the afternoon.
- I always wake up at five in the morning and can't get back to sleep.

Show your post to another pair. What advice do they have?

7 **Grammar Extra 9, Part 1** page 150. Read the explanations and do Exercise 1.

LISTENING & PRONUNCIATION

James

1 ▶ 2.23-2.25 **Listen to James, Rosie, and Phillip describing experiences of staying up all night. For each person, make notes on the following questions.**

- **a** Where did the experience take place?
- **b** What did the person do during the night?
- **c** Did they enjoy the experience? Why? / Why not?

Which of the nights would you *most* and *least* like to have shared? Why? Discuss with a partner.

Rosie

2 ▶ 2.26 **Listen to some extracts from the experiences in Exercise 1 and complete the sentences with adverbs. Sometimes there is more than one adverb in a sentence.**

- **a** The hours just passed, you know, just talking about the sky, _____ .
- **b** It's just _____ wild. The whole experience is crazy.
- **c** So there's _____ no point in going to bed because everybody's up anyway.
- **d** It was _____ worth it.
- **e** _____ , there were about, I think, twenty people there in front of us.
- **f** We were going to see this show – _____ our hero.
- **g** We slept out the whole night and spent the whole night there and didn't even get to see the show, _____ .
- **h** We were _____ upset.

Phillip

3 **Which adverbs in the sentences (a–h) in Exercise 2 ...**

1. add emphasis?
2. express regret?
3. suggest that something is obvious?
4. express surprise?
5. emphasize the main point, not specific details?
6. stress exact details?

4 **How many syllables are there in each of the adverbs in the box? Practice saying each of the words.**

actually basically especially eventually generally ironically
literally particularly practically usually

▶ 2.27 **Listen and check.**

5 **Write true sentences about your experience of parties, concerts, or festivals using some of the adverbs in Exercise 4. Practice reading them aloud to your partner.**

SPEAKING: ANECDOTE

You are going to tell your partner about a time you stayed up late or all night, for example working a night shift, traveling overnight, attending a party or festival, writing an essay, or studying for an exam.

- Ask yourself the questions below.
- Think about *what* to say and *how* to say it.
- Tell your partner about the night.

- **a** Where and when did the experience take place?
- **b** Why did you stay up all night?
- **c** Who were you with?
- **d** What happened during the night?
- **e** What did you see, hear, or do?
- **f** What feelings did you experience?
- **g** How did you feel at the end of the night?
- **h** Was it a worthwhile experience?

SPEAKING

1 Match the two halves of the proverbs about night.

a Wait for the night
b If you befriend a mosquito,
c No matter how long the night,
d Red sky at night, shepherds' delight;
e If in doubt about what is right,
f He who does not lose his way by night,
g At night, all cats
h The road to Heaven is well signposted,
i The night hides a world,

1 will not lose his way by day. (Nigerian)
2 but reveals a universe. (Iranian)
3 are gray. (Dutch)
4 but it is badly lit at night. (Irish)
5 before saying that the day has been beautiful. (Bengali)
6 it will still attack you at night. (African)
7 red sky in the morning, shepherds' warning. (English)
8 consult your pillow overnight. (Mexican)
9 the dawn will break. (African)

2 Work with a partner. Discuss the questions about the proverbs in Exercise 1.

a Are there any proverbs you don't understand?
b Which do you like best, and why?
c Do you have similar sayings in your own country?

3 Work with your partner. Complete the sentences to create proverbs of your own.

a No matter how long the journey, ...
b However good the teacher, ...
c Wherever you live, ...
d Even if ...

Compare with another pair. Which proverbs do you like best?

VOCABULARY

1 Work with your partner. Complete the sentences with words from the box.

long nightcap nightclub nightlife overnight town

a I'm absolutely exhausted. I worked *all night* _____ yesterday.
b "Would you like *a* _____ before you go home?" "I'd better not, I'm driving."
c We had *a night on the* _____ last night. We went to a _____ and didn't get back until the small hours.
d I'm going to get the _____ *sleeper*, so I'll arrive first thing in the morning.
e I think you'll like New Orleans. The _____ is amazing!

Discuss the meaning of the words and expressions in italics with your partner.

2 Work with your partner. Choose one of the questions to discuss.

a Imagine you've just passed your final exams. Where would you go to have a night on the town? Who would you invite? What would you do?
b Imagine your best friend, who you haven't seen for six months, is coming to visit you from out of town and staying at your house overnight. What would you do?

The Midnight Sun

The Midnight Sun has been hailed as a surreal, twilight experience where the sun never quite sets and darkness is replaced by a golden glow bathing everything in its mystical light. In the winter there are the Polar Nights and stretches of darkness when the sun hardly shows its face.

1. _____ For someone born near the equator, with twelve hours of daylight and twelve hours of night time throughout the year, nothing could be stranger than my first spring and summer in Norway. As the chill of the winter thaws and we progress towards spring, the days become longer, reaching its apex on the longest day of the year. The summer solstice, on the 21st June every year, is celebrated in real Scandinavian style. There are music festivals and open-air markets, but most people head to the beaches and rivers to enjoy barbecues or roast marshmallows on an open fire.

2. _____ The town of Ålesund, which we visited for the summer solstice celebration, is famous for its huge bonfire. For several days leading up to the big day, a huge tower made of wooden crates is erected. This tower becomes a raging bonfire on the night of the celebrations, and it is the centerpiece of the town's celebrations. The fire is said to "wake up" the earth, providing warmth and encouraging fertility. The fire represents the sun, which on this day is at its highest in the sky and thereafter will start to wane, with progressively shorter days and longer nights.

3. _____ However, this doesn't mean that the sky is pitch black. Instead, what is experienced is several hours of weak daylight which gives the impression of an extended hours-long sunset or sunrise. It is followed by twilight or the 'blue hour' - an ethereal, arctic light that fills the sky and everything below it in a cozy glow created by the reflection of light by the ocean and snow. This magnificent spectacle is as much a tourist attraction as the aurora borealis.

4. _____ The days (or rather the daytime heavenly spectacles) get progressively longer until the Midnight Sun period takes over from May to July when, conversely, the sun never sets. However, despite general belief and studies on seasonal affective disorder (SAD)[1], research suggests surprisingly low rates thereof among locals. Many attribute this inconsistency to a variety of factors, from cod liver oil to 'wake-up lights' simulating sunrise. Participation in the wealth of cultural festivities also has its effect as well as a broad range of leisure activities available year round. All these combined encourage people to spend more daily hours outdoors than would ordinarily be the case under similar conditions. Perhaps the secret lies in the beautiful colors of the sky and the soft blue light that pervades the atmosphere, creating a form of natural visual therapy.

1 SAD, also known as the winter blues, i.e. depression in those who reside in extreme latitudes caused by the dearth of natural sunlight

Glossary

a _____ adjective: seeming like a dream
b _____ adjective: supernatural
c _____ noun [U]: highest point
d _____ verb [I]: to decrease in duration and strength
e _____ noun [C]: an extraordinary occurrence
f _____ adjective: heavenly or celestial
g _____ adjective: according to general agreement
h _____ noun [U]: scarcity, lack
i _____ verb [T]: to assume the appearance of

READING

1 **Read the traveler's account of a trip to Norway to experience the Midnight Sun on page 98. Do you think a trip to Norway or somewhere similar would be worthwhile? Why or why not?**

2 **Match the first lines (a-d) with the paragraphs (1-4) in the account.**

a In fact, fire is central to the celebrations of the summer solstice in Norway.
b On the other extreme, the Polar Night is the period in winter during which the sun fails to rise, essentially remaining below the horizon and thereby creating the phenomenon of over 24 hours of night.
c In some parts of Scandinavia, in the regions closest to the North Pole, the sun doesn't set for several weeks of the year in the days leading up to the summer solstice.
d In Tromsø, located 200 meters north of the Arctic Circle, Polar Night lasts all winter - from November to January - and the sun never rises.

3 **Find evidence from the account to support the statements about the Midnight Sun and Polar Night.**

a There are many options available of things to do during the summer when the days are longer.
b The absence of the sun in the sky does not necessarily mean that the sky is completely dark.
c Locations above the Arctic Circle experience a longer Polar Night.
d Norwegians have several methods of combating winter depression.

4 **Complete the glossary with words and phrases from the account.**

5 **Would you like to go on a trip like this? Why or why not? What are the top three experiences on your bucket list?**

LISTENING & GRAMMAR

1 2.28 **Listen to Ken talking about a trip to Machu Picchu. What was disappointing and rewarding about the experience?**

2 2.29 **Listen again to extracts from the recording. Complete Ken's sentences.**

a I ______ there in the low season.
b I think if ______ those altitude pills I ______ OK.
c It's too bad ______ for longer.

3 **Read the sentences about Ken's regrets and underline the correct alternatives.**

a I wish I'**d gone** / **went** / **could have gone** in the low season.
b I regret **taking** / **having taken** / **not taking** / **not having taken** altitude pills.
c If you **came** / **'d come** / **would have come** with me, it **'d been** / **'d have been** / **might have been** more fun.
d **If I'd been** / **Had I been** / **If I was** feeling well, I **'d** / **could** / **should** have got up to see the sunrise.
e **But for** / **Except for** / **If it hadn't been for** the rain, I **'d have had** / **'d** / **'d have** some pictures now.

4 **Rewrite the sentences using the words in parentheses.**

a I'm sorry I didn't go in the low season. (I wish)
b What a shame I wasn't able to go with you. (I regret)
c I didn't see the sunrise, which was a shame. (I would have liked)
d It was packed with tourists, so I didn't get a feel for the atmosphere. (If)
e If only I had taken some good picures! (It's too bad)
f My altitude sickness meant I couldn't get up to see the sunrise. (But for)
g It was a great experience, though - that's why I want to go again. (If)

5 **Tell your partner about a trip you have been on. Use the language in Exercises 3 and 4 to express things you regret or things you were glad about.**

Regrets and past conditionals

I wish I'd / If only I could have gone for longer.

I'd have liked to go for longer.

I regret (not) going in the low season.

If I had stayed for longer, I'**d/could/might** have seen the sunrise.

If it hadn't been for the rain, **I'd have seen** the sunrise.

Ken

6 **Grammar Extra 9, Part 2** page 150. Read the explanations and do Exercise 2.

LANGUAGE FOR LIFE

1 **Read the exchanges (1-4). What is the problem with B's responses?**

1 A: What are you up to tomorrow night?
B: Nothing.

2 A: Are you doing anything tonight?
B: No.

3 A: Do you feel like coming to a jazz concert tonight?
B: I don't like jazz.

4 A: I was wondering if you'd like to come over for a bite to eat this evening?
B: Yes.

2 **How could you improve the exchanges in Exercise 1 using the useful phrases (a-f)?**

a To tell the truth, I'm not a very big fan of ...
b No, what did you have in mind?
c That sounds great!
d I'd love to!
e Nothing special - why do you ask?
f That's really nice of you, but ...

3 2.30 **Listen to the exchanges and compare your answers with the recording. Then practice the exchanges with a partner.**

4 **Look at the responses to the invitation. Which one is more formal than the others?**

I'm having some friends over on Sunday afternoon. You're very welcome to join us.

a Thanks very much for asking, but I'm afraid I can't make it.
b I'd really like to, but I have something planned. I'm going to my parents'.
c I really appreciate the invitation, but unfortunately I have a prior engagement.
d I'm tied up on Sunday, sorry. Thanks anyway.

5 **Work with your partner. Invite each other to do something tomorrow, on Friday evening, and on the weekend. Accept the invitation or give an excuse if you turn it down. If you accept, make clear arrangements to meet.**

Life Skills: Organization

Time Management

1 **Below is a definition of time management. Can you add anything else to this definition?**

Time management is a set of actions and techniques employed to organize and plan how one's time is divided among all the activities and tasks to be completed.

2 **There are many techniques we can use to help us manage our time more effectively. Below we look in detail at some of them. Complete the table by adding two more steps to each technique. Compare with your partner.**

TIME MANAGEMENT TECHNIQUE	STEPS YOU CAN TAKE
Manage interruptions	Turn your phone off to stop receiving messages when you are working on something important or need to meet a deadline. ...
Make "to do" lists	Make a "master list" for the week and then divide up the tasks, with a few tasks to be done each day. ...
Manage emails	Set aside a specific time and number of minutes or hours for checking and responding to emails. Restrict yourself to these time slots. ...
Use your smartphone as your ally	Download a time management app to help manage your activities. ...

MACMILLAN LIFE SKILLS

9 Vocabulary Extra

PHRASAL VERBS

1 **Underline the verb and circle the particle in the phrasal verbs in the sentences (a–e). What is the general meaning of *up* and *off* in the phrasal verbs?**

a You're still up and wide awake way after midnight.
b What time do you plan to get up?
c Can you remember a time when you stayed up all night?
d I am up and down all night until I eventually feel tired enough to drop off.
e I generally start nodding off at about nine o'clock.

2 **Work with a partner. Match the meaning of the phrasal verbs with *up* (a–e) in bold with the dictionary extracts (1–5).**

a Do you always remember to **do up** your seatbelt before you travel by car?
b Do you **tear up** letters when you're done reading them?
c Do you usually **clean up** before you leave the house?
d When did you last **go up** to someone on the street to ask a question?
e Do people ever ask you to **speak up** because they can't hear you?

Ask your partner the questions.

up[1] /ʌp/ function word ★★★
1 moving near to sb/sth moving near to someone or something and then stopping: *One of the salespeople came up and asked if she could help.* ♦ **+to** *Two women ran up to us, shouting in Spanish.* ♦ *Just go up to him and say hello.*
2 when an amount increases 2a. at or toward an increased number, level, or amount: *Total new car sales were up $3 million over last year.* ♦ **go up** *Early last month, fuel prices went up by 3 percent.* **2b.** becoming louder, stronger, or more active: *Billy, will you turn the volume on the TV up – I can't hear anything.* ♦ *Competition between the production groups is heating up rapidly.*
3 in or into smaller parts divided or broken into small pieces or equal parts: *The prize money will be divided up among the team members.* ♦ *Divorce settlements often involve property that can't be split up easily.*
4 completely completely done or used so that there is nothing left: *Eat up all your dinner.* ♦ *I think it was selfish of me, using up all her free time like that.* ♦ *The stream dries up in summer.*
5 fastened fastened or closed completely: *She kept Albert's letters in a bundle tied up with ribbon.* ♦ *Did you lock the house up before you left?*

From the *Macmillan English Dictionary (American edition)*

3 **Find three more phrasal verbs in the dictionary extracts on the right and write sentences that are true for you. Compare your ideas with your partner.**

4 **Choose the correct particle from the box for each pair of sentences.**

down	in	off	on	out

a 1 If I run _____ of money, I usually ask a friend to lend me some.
2 A lot of species of plants and animals are dying _____ in my country because of pollution.
b 1 I tend to keep _____ working even if I feel tired.
2 I'd like to stay _____ here next year to study more English.
c 1 It will feel so good to take _____ these shoes.
2 Ian is always showing _____ his new car.
d 1 I generally note _____ English words when I come across them.
2 If I don't write things _____ on a list, I tend to forget to do them.
e 1 I like to sleep _____ on Sunday mornings.
2 I have to fill _____ all these forms.

Are any of these sentences true for you? Discuss with your partner.

5 **Work with your partner. Complete the sentences with the prepositions in the box.**

up (x2)	down	on	out

a Can you cut _____ the cake so that there's a piece for everyone?
b I'm afraid all the tickets for tonight's concert have sold _____ .
c Can you put my name _____ for the trip to the museum on Sunday?
d At the end of the boat trip, we tied _____ the boat and got out.
e If you want to know what happens in the rest of the story, you'll have to read _____ to the end of the book.

6 **Check in your own dictionary. Look up meanings of one of the particles *in*, *on*, *off*, *out*, or *down*. Choose three uses with different verbs to learn.**

Review C

▶ Grammar Extra pages 148-151

GRAMMAR

1 **Rewrite these complex sentences as simple single-clause sentences. The number of single-clause sentences is in parentheses.**

- a Having had a particularly stressful day at work, I got home, switched on the TV, and promptly fell asleep! (4)
- b I really enjoy taking time out, maybe buying a newspaper and finding a quiet café where I can order a coffee and spend an hour or so quietly catching up on the news. (5)
- c After a long day of intensive study, I always try to do some exercise in order to clear my mind and renew my energy levels. (3)
- d Going to the movies really helps me unwind, taking my mind off my problems and letting me escape into another world for at least a couple of hours. (3)
- e Some people say that shopping is relaxing, but I just think it's another source of stress, often leading to overspending, which in turn can cause financial problems. (4)

Write a complex sentence explaining what you like to do to relax. Show it to a partner.

2 **Work with your partner. Look at the ideas below. Which do you think are a) highly likely to happen in the next ten years? b) may happen sometime but you don't know when? c) will probably never happen?**

- a Your country's leader will be a woman.
- b Your home town will double in size.
- c Cars will become a luxury that only a few people can afford.
- d Chinese will take over as the world's number one most-studied foreign language.
- e Water will become the most precious commodity on Earth.

Write three or four sentences summarizing your discussion. Use the words and expressions in the box.

might	could easily	bound to
probably won't	almost certainly will	
should	to our minds	unlikely that

3 **Write a second sentence that means the same as the first, using the words given.**

- a A man contacted me.
  I ______ .
- b Strangely, he refused to tell me his name.
  The strange thing ______ .
- c He said he was an old friend of the family and that he had a message for me.
  What he did tell me ______ .
- d The message was from my father, who had disappeared five years ago.
  It was ______ .
- e He asked me to meet him outside the church at six o'clock so he could give it to me personally.
  In order to ______ .
- f I arrived at the church as the clock struck six.
  As ______ .
- g There was a dark figure standing in the doorway.
  A dark figure ______ .

Work with your partner. Discuss what happened next. Write the next three sentences of the story.

4 **Work with your partner. Read the story in Exercise 3 again. What do you think had happened to the father? Complete the sentences with some of your theories.**

- a He must have ...
- b He may have ...
- c He can't have ...
- d He should have ...
- e He might not have ...
- f He wouldn't have ...

5 **Complete the sentences with words or expressions from the box.**

Despite having	Even so	even though
However	in spite of	Try as I might

- a I could still hear the noise of the traffic outside, ______ I was wearing earplugs.
- b ______ had less than five hours sleep, I felt fresh and ready to start the day.
- c ______ , I just couldn't get to sleep.
- d I usually like to get to bed fairly early. ______ , last night was an exception.
- e I got a good night's sleep ______ all the noise.
- f I had a really good night's sleep. ______ , I still couldn't get up when the alarm went off!

Which sentence best describes how you slept last night?

VOCABULARY

1 **Match a word from column *A* with a word in column *B* to form compound nouns.**

A	B
cellular	coverage
ear	pad
key	piece
music	player
touch	recognition
voice	screen

Work with a partner. Think of five more compound nouns associated with objects or gadgets.

2 **Complete the article with the words and phrases in the box. Make any changes that are necessary.**

wow go digital hype slick trash sold

The manufacturers obviously thought we'd all be (1) _____ by this particular digital gadget. And with everything in the world (2) _____ , it doesn't surprise me that someone has produced a digital coffee machine as well. The (3) _____ claims that this (4) _____ machine is the latest must-have gadget for all modern kitchens. But I'm not (5) _____ on the idea. I love my old Italian coffee maker and its simple, functional shape. And I must admit that I was really happy to find a review that completely (6) _____ the idea of the new digital version. But who knows, maybe the writer was just another old fogey like me?

Would you like to have a digital coffee maker? Why? / Why not?

3 **Complete the sentences with one word. The first letter has been provided for you.**

a He thinks that just because he's in a position of power, he's somehow a_____ the law and can do anything he wants.
b We were really surprised when we heard the news. We'd always thought he was a very quiet, law-a_____ kind of person.
c She may be a rebel, but she's never been in t_____ with the law.
d There was nobody there to help them, so in the end they were forced to t_____ the law into their own hands.
e Their father was far too lenient and it was always their mother who had to lay d_____ the law.

Can you think of anybody in the news, or in your life, who matches the descriptions above? Tell your partner.

4 **Choose expressions from the box to answer the questions below.**

dawn daybreak dusk mid-afternoon
mid-morning midnight nightfall
noon sunrise sunset twilight
the middle of the night the crack of dawn
the small hours first thing in the morning
last thing at night

a What time is it now?
b When did you last go to bed really late? What time was it?
c When did you last get up very early? What time of day was it?
d What time do you find you study best? Why?
e When are you at your least productive? Why?
f What time of day do you think is the most romantic? Why?

PRONUNCIATION

1 **Look at some words from Units 7-9. Say the words and add them to the table.**

adolescent attorney coverage decision
deprivation digital embezzlement
entertainment manslaughter nocturnal
pedestrian probation prominent
sensational situation telepathy

A: □□□	B: □□□	C: □□□□	D: □□□□
			adolescent

2 **Underline the stressed syllables.**

2.31 **Listen, check, and repeat.**

10 Footprints

READING & SPEAKING

1 **Read the two sides of an argument about reducing human's impact on the environment. Are they really that different? What do they have in common and how do they differ? Then complete the texts with the words and phrases in the box.**

consumption | greenhouse gas emissions | lack | citizens | atmosphere | resources | developing world | household appliances | Research and Development | fossil fuels

Humans need to decide what kind of footprint we want to leave on the planet.

Ordinary **(1)** ______ have a pivotal role to play concerning what kind of footprint they leave on this planet. Unraveling the many strands of climate change will be a grassroots, bottom-up movement. People have been hypnotized by the media and convinced of their helplessness on this issue. They need to feel that they have the power to change things. It is critical that the measures taken are felt to be feasible and effective, and that reverting climatic trends means neither personal deprivation nor the end of our natural **(2)** ______.

What can we do? We can make sure that our **(3)** ______ meet the highest efficiency standards. We can install solar panels and buy electric cars, so soon we will no longer need **(4)** ______ to generate energy. We can reduce our **(5)** ______ of water by using rainwater recapture systems and lowering volume flush in toilets and in showerhead flow.

More importantly, we can band together with like-minded neighbors to build communities which cherish our planet. We must embrace agency, for "We are the music makers, and we are the dreamers of dreams," as written in the poem *Ode* by Arthur O'Shaughnessy.

The footprints of technology lead away from the abyss

Thomas Malthus famously theorized that the boom in the Earth's population would outstrip our capacity to produce sufficient food thereby leading to a (6) ______ of food and starvation. Has his prediction, presented in 1798, come close to reality? The answer is a clear 'no'. So, what has happened? Great improvements in agriculture productivity have been accomplished, and food is more than abundantly supplied for the billions of new Earth dwellers. Any shortfalls are on the distribution side rather than the production side.

What many fail to grasp about climate change is that, while many predict Malthusian doomsday scenarios due to global warming, new solutions are provided and new technologies are implemented to guarantee the continuance of mankind on this planet. Therefore, it is imperative that massive investments in (7) ______ be made.

Solar, nuclear, wind, tide, geothermal, and other yet undreamed technologies will allow us to cut (8) ______ to zero. Furthermore, as these new technologies are transferred to the (9)______, bypassing 20th century technologies entirely, they will reduce even further the carbon dioxide currently being pumped into the (10)______. Clearly, the footprint of a brighter future bears the impression of innovation.

2 **Work with a partner. Discuss the questions.**

a Have you ever calculated your carbon footprint or your ecological footprint?

b Do you know what your country's carbon or ecological footprints are? Can you guess?

c Is it helpful to use measurements like this? Why? / Why not?

- **Grammar:** Passive structures. Comparative structures
- **Vocabulary:** Ecological expressions. Expressions with *foot* or *feet*. Shoes
- **Language for Life:** Persuasion and responding to persuasion

VOCABULARY & SPEAKING

1 **Take the lifestyle quiz. Score 2 for "Usually," 1 for "Sometimes," and 0 for "Never."**

How eco-friendly is your lifestyle?

Check how often you do these things.

	Usually	Sometimes	Never
I walk, cycle, or use public transportation to go to work or college.	☐	☐	☐
I avoid flying whenever possible.	☐	☐	☐
I turn off lights when I leave a room.	☐	☐	☐
I use a laptop rather than a desktop computer.	☐	☐	☐
I keep my internet use to a minimum.	☐	☐	☐
I do not leave household appliances on standby.	☐	☐	☐
I do not leave my cell phone charger plugged in.	☐	☐	☐
I do not leave the water running while I brush my teeth.	☐	☐	☐

	Usually	Sometimes	Never
I do not spend more than two minutes in the shower.	☐	☐	☐
I recycle glass, cans, and paper.	☐	☐	☐
I buy recycled paper and stationery.	☐	☐	☐
I reuse plastic bags.	☐	☐	☐
I only buy what I really need.	☐	☐	☐
I buy locally produced food whenever possible.	☐	☐	☐
I buy organic products.	☐	☐	☐
I buy products made from sustainable sources.	☐	☐	☐
I avoid eating meat or fish.	☐	☐	☐

2 **Work with a partner. Add up your score and discuss the questions.**

a How did you score on the quiz? High scores are more eco-friendly.

b In your opinion, which of the activities mentioned in the quiz is the most important in reducing a person's footprint?

3 **Cross out the word or phrase in column *B* which does not collocate with the word or phrase in column *A*.**

	A	B
a	locally grown	produce / fruit and vegetables / apples / meat
b	energy-efficient	washing machine / paper / dishwasher / refrigerator
c	solar-powered	emissions / central heating / car / house
d	recycled	paper / glass / central heating / plastic
e	organic	glass / cotton / meat / produce
f	sustainable	farming / development / forests / light bulbs
g	renewable	energy / resources / food / power

In what way are the items eco-friendly? Which of these items form a part of your lifestyle?

LISTENING

1 2.32 **Listen to Chloe and her mother, Barbara, discussing eco-friendly lifestyle choices. Answer the questions.**

a How are their attitudes different? b Which of the quiz topics do they mention?

Listen again. Note down the facts Chloe mentions to support her ideas.

Chloe and Barbara

2 **Work with your partner. Discuss the questions.**

a Who do you agree with most in the conversation in Exercise 1, Chloe or her mother?

b Would you consider making any changes in your lifestyle to reduce your footprint? Why? / Why not?

READING

1 Read the headline and look at the pictures. Work with a partner. Discuss the questions.

a Can you identify the sites below and the ancient civilizations associated with them?
b What are the traditional tools of archeology?
c What footprints might be left by non-invasive tools?
d With the tools we have today, is it still justifiable to do physical excavations? Why?

2 Read the article and check your answers to the questions.

Archeologists Are Uncovering Our Past without Leaving a Footprint

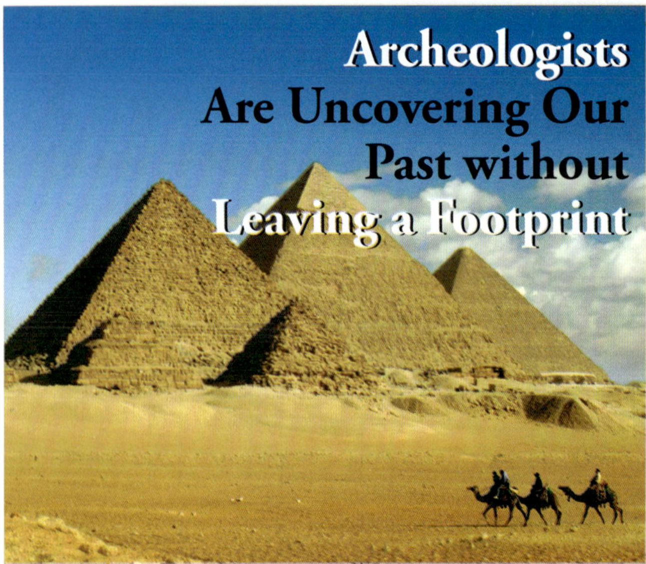

Archeology has come a long way. In 1817, when the pyramid of Cheops was excavated, dynamite was used to do the job! Now a relic of the past, dynamite produced irreparable damage to archeological settings. Even simple digging can generate damage to a site. Luckily, there is a plethora of new tools, which have been deployed throughout the globe, that make archeology much less invasive, like for example satellite imagery, drones, ground penetrating radar, and muon tomography.

In 2017, it was reported that muon tomography had been used in the discovery of a 30 meter deep hollow chamber in Cheops Pyramid, the same pyramid which had been dynamited 200 years earlier. Muon tomography is a non-invasive technique that measures how muons deflect off different materials; by checking those deflections scientists are able to detect anomalies. There are great debates about the next step to be taken. Some scientists have suggested drilling a 3 centimeter hole and inserting camera probes into the chamber; but whatever is decided to be done, the Egyptian authorities need to approve it first.

In Portugal, the Roman ruins of Ammaia, located in a protected nature reserve, were off-limits to physical excavation. Due to restrictions, multiple non-invasive technologies were employed instead to yield a virtual model of the city. Ground penetrating radar revealed what lay below the surface and helikites - a cross between a helium balloon and a kite - were used to scan the countryside from above. The result of the multi-year project was a 3D model of the ruins that allows the site to be explored virtually but leaves the physical site untrampled.

In northern Guatemala, LIDAR (Light Detection and Ranging) is being utilized to penetrate the thick canopy and unveil a colossal Mayan megalopolis. With over 60,000 structures found to date, scientists reason that 10 to 15 million Mayans may have been housed there at its height. This would be much larger than originally thought and casts the Mayan empire in an entirely new light. LIDAR images are produced by shooting pulses of radar from planes surveying the area, giving scientists precise topographical information and enabling them to detect structures like a seven-story pyramid buried beneath dense vegetation. It is hoped that by avoiding physical excavation of the site, it will be safeguarded from degradation by the jungle itself.

Not only do the new technologies grant scientists access to fragile or remote sites, but they also promise to be cheaper and faster. Sites that have been degraded before the development of new technology are forever damaged; however in the future, scientists will be able to explore and preserve sites simultaneously, thereby guaranteeing the integrity of our cultural heritage.

3 Underline the correct alternative in each sentence.

a Cheops was once dynamited in order to **destroy** / **explore** / **repair** the site.
b Scientists want to explore Cheops further, but need to get **permission from the government** / **up-to-date technology** / **more funding**.
c Ammaia was mapped by scientists by using **drones flying over the site** / **radar to look under the site** / **3D models to walk through the site**.
d It is hoped that the end result of these new technologies will **be less damaging** / **prevent destruction by the elements** / **slow the rate of exploration**.
e LIDAR technology is **flown over the site** / **drilled into the ground** / **buried beneath the jungle**.

4 Discuss the meaning of the highlighted words and phrases with your partner. Use a dictionary to check your answers.

5 Work with your partner. Discuss the questions.

a What is the importance of exploring archeological sites? Is it worth the expense?
b Have you ever visited an important historical site? What were your impressions?

GRAMMAR

1 **Read the extract about global warming. What will happen if temperatures rise by 3 °C? Which cities will be affected?**

> Meteorologists have estimated that if temperatures rise by 3 °C, global warming will destroy several cities. In fact, global warming is already drowning cities worldwide little by little. Waves have lapped cities such as Alexandria in Egypt. Scientists say that the Asian countries are the most affected. Natural disasters will probably affect Osaka in Japan. This phenomenon will also reach Miami and New York. Sea levels will reshape populated areas. As a consequence, geographers will have to redraw the world map.

Passive structures

LIDAR images **are produced**

LIDAR **is being** utilized

dynamite **was used** to do the job!

Cheops **had been dynamited**

which **have been deployed**

muon tomography **had been used**

to allow the site **to be explored**

it **will be safeguarded**

any work **would have to be approved**

Reduced passive clauses

With over 60,000 structures **found** to date

structures like a seven-story pyramid **buried** beneath dense vegetation

2 **Are the verb structures in the text active or passive? Is it more natural to use the active or passive in a text like this? Why?**

3 **Rewrite the text in Exercise 1 by changing the verbs into the passive form. Omit the agent if this is not known, irrelevant, or obvious.**

4 **Look at the two sentences. Underline the relative clause and reduced passive clause. What is the difference between them?**

a Cities which are located in the coastline will be the most affected.
b Cities located in the coastline will be the most affected.

5 **Combine the sentences below to include reduced passive clauses as in the examples in Exercise 4. Where appropriate, make other verbs passive or omit the agent.**

a Remains of a stone wall revealed evidence of the settlement. A storm uncovered the remains.
b Tools and artefacts have shed light on life in prehistoric times. Archeologists have excavated the tools and artefacts.
c Archeologists are restoring some of the artefacts. The ocean eroded the artefacts.
d They have found buildings. They think the buildings date back nearly 2,500 years.
e The artefacts provide an insight into a unique way of life. The Jarlshof museum displays the artefacts.

6 **Work with a partner. Student A: look at the text on page 140. Student B: look at the text on page 141. Write a brief report and tell your partner about the site. Use passive structures.**

7 **Grammar Extra 10, Part 1** page 150. Read the explanations and do Exercise 1.

LISTENING & SPEAKING

1 2.33 **Listen to a hiker describing her experiences of hiking. Overall, was it a positive or negative experience?**

2 **Listen again and make notes under the headings (a–f).**

a Why the speaker was a walker.
b The benefits of walking.
c Why the speaker started hiking.
d The equipment needed for hiking.
e The challenges she faced with hiking.
f The benefits of hiking.

3 **Work with a partner. Discuss the questions.**

a Would you like to try hiking? Why or why not?
b Imagine you are hiking in the following situations:

- For the first time
- Up a steep mountain
- Through a snowy forest
- Without a guide

Describe what it would feel like, the dangers you might experience, and the benefits and disadvantages of each situation. How many of these have you or your partner actually experienced? Where and when? What was it like?

PRONUNCIATION

1 **Work with your partner. Discuss the questions.**

a When do you read aloud, either in your own language or in English? What sort of things do you read?
b Which of these tips do you generally follow when preparing to read aloud in English?

- Check the meaning and pronunciation of unknown words before you read.
- Divide the sentences into chunks and decide where to pause.
- Decide which words carry the main stress in each chunk.
- Practice reading several times before you read to an audience.

2 **Read the transcript of part of the recording. What do you think the slashes represent?**

I was a walker. // Weather permitting, // I would walk almost every day - two miles, sometimes three - determined that the knee injury and subsequent surgery that had derailed my running career two years prior would not affect my personal fitness or enjoyment of the outdoors. Although I missed the thrill and intensity of training for and participating in half-marathons, I had surprisingly come to enjoy walking a great deal. It had even become for me a form of daily meditation. There was something quite therapeutic about rising at dawn and going out into the still, cool early morning before the sun's warmth had evaporated the dew from the grass and the sounds of domestic activity had yet to make their way around the neighborhood.

3 2.34 **Listen to the recording, and mark on the transcript in Exercise 2 where the speaker pauses, as in the example. Listen again and underline the stressed words in each chunk. Practice reading the passage aloud to your partner.**

4 **Predict and mark where the pauses will occur in this passage with your partner.**

During the hike there were several things that I was unprepared for. In spite of the seemingly gradual slope of the trail, I was unprepared for the intensity of the workout. I was walking much slower but my heart rate was higher than it was when I walked on flat roads at twice the speed. Not only that but my muscles and my lungs were responding in a way that I found to be, in a word, exhilarating. Even with the poles I felt like I was getting a full body workout. I even had to engage my core muscles to navigate the uneven terrain.

2.35 **Listen and check. Practice reading the passage aloud with and without the recording.**

SPEAKING: ANECDOTE

You are going to tell a partner about a walk you have been on. It could be a major hike, a long trek, a brisk walk, or a short stroll, in an unusual or an everyday situation.

- Ask yourself the questions below.
- Think about *what* to say and *how* to say it.
- Tell your partner about the walk.

a Where and when did you go on the walk?
b Why did you go on the walk?
c Had you been on the same walk before?
d If it was a long walk, how did you plan it and what equipment did you take?
e Were you alone or with companions?
f What did you see, hear, feel, or smell on the walk?
g Did you meet anyone or stop on the way?
h How long did the walk last?
i How did you feel at the end of the walk?
j What did you do after you arrived at the end?

VOCABULARY

1 **Complete the sentences with *foot* or *feet*.**

a Hubert always gets itchy ______ in May and tries to talk Leonora into going on another trekking vacation with him. But this year Leonora put her ______ down and said she was staying home for a change, and that she wanted to put her ______ up and have a rest.

b The interview was going well, and Trevor thought he was on his way to getting the job of night cleaner at the law firm. But he really shot himself in the ______ when he said he only saw the job as a way of getting a ______ in the door, and that his ambition was to take over the company in five years' time.

c As far as Jessica was concerned, Tony was less-than-perfect husband material. They'd started off on the wrong ______ when he forgot her birthday, but Jessica forgave him, realizing he had ______ of clay like everyone else. To make things worse, when he took her dancing, she discovered to her horror that he had two left ______ . So now she's got cold ______ about the wedding.

d I really put my ______ in my mouth when I told Rhonda she should stop waiting on her children hand and ______ , and let them do things for themselves. She didn't like that at all. But honestly, they are nearly thirty now – it's time they learned to stand on their own two ______ .

2 **Work with your partner. Discuss the meanings of the expressions in Exercise 1. Use a dictionary to check, if necessary. Are there similar expressions in your language?**

3 **Work with your partner. Discuss the questions.**

a When do you like to **put your feet up**?
b Can you remember finding out that somebody you knew **had feet of clay**?
c Have you ever **shot yourself in the foot** in a work situation?
d Can you think of a time recently when you **put your foot down**?
e When should children **stand on their own two feet** financially, in your opinion?
f Can you remember a time when you were **waited on hand and foot**?
g Do you **have itchy feet** at the moment?
h Have you ever **gotten cold feet** about a vacation or change in your life?
i What is the best way of **getting a foot in the door** in a place you would like to work?
j Have you ever **put your foot in your mouth** in a social situation?
k Can you remember a situation in which you **started off on the wrong foot**?

LISTENING

1 **Do you like buying shoes? How many pairs do you own? What is your favorite pair of shoes and why? Tell a partner.**

2 2.36 **Listen to four people talking about their shoes on a TV show. Match their descriptions (1-4) with the pictures (a-d) on the right.**

Listen again and make notes on ...

- a why the shoes were bought.
- b when they are worn.
- c what they look like.

3 **Tell your partner about the shoes you are wearing today. Give as much information as possible.**

a

b

c

d

READING & SPEAKING

1 **Discuss with a partner the following questions about buying shoes.**

- a When is the best time to shop for shoes?
- b Why should you measure your feet every time you buy shoes?
- c How do you get the right size shoe when shopping online?

Read the article and check your answers.

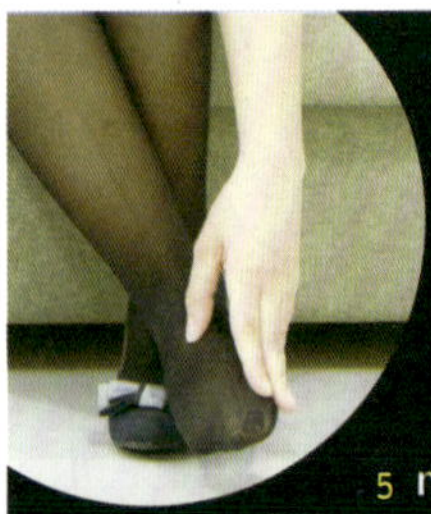

If the Shoe Fits ...!

Story in my life: I find this ravishing pair of heels in my closet, which I do not need, and which are only slightly too small and were way out of my price range. I bought them three years ago and they are still unscathed by pavement or asphalt. All told, I have forked out just as much on the shoes idling in my closet as I have on those that actually adorn my feet; I am quite embarrassed to admit. I am certain I will never overcome my irrational need to have far more shoes than I in fact use, but the very least I could do is buy shoes that fit! With that in mind, I offer a modest proposal on how to buy a properly fitting pair of shoes.

First and foremost, don't fool yourself into thinking that the sleek pair of stilettos that you slide out of just a bit and are a tad tight will feel good when you've been on your feet for hours. Shopping for shoes in the afternoon, when your feet are noticeably more swollen than at any other time of the day, is another step in the right direction. Wearing hosiery of the same thickness as you normally wear, and which you should have thrown in your bag before you left the house, is also a must; there is no excuse for using the never-washed try on pair of socks at the store that have been on untold hundreds of stinking feet.

Undoubtedly you know your shoe size, I am not trying to insult your intelligence, but over the years your shoe size changes and your two feet are probably not even the same size. That's why it's indispensable that you measure your feet every time you buy shoes, as even a tiny difference can lead to a significantly better fit.

It's also time to face up to the fact that not everyone has the same foot shape. Some feet are somewhat narrower, others wider; the disposition of the toes can differ as well, which means that as much as you love the silhouette of that cute pair of pumps, they are not for your cavewoman feet, something you'll get to know when you feel the blisters. You should also accept that some shoe brands, constructed on the mold of a lithe ballerina's foot, were never destined for your wardrobe.

Finally, do not buy shoes online, but if you really need to ignore my advice, try them on at a store before ordering them, in that way you'll be immensely reducing the odds of having to return them.

2 **Read the article again. Decide if the sentences are true or false.**

- a The writer has spent more on unused shoes than she has on shoes that she uses.
- b It is best to buy shoes in the afternoon when your foot is the smallest.
- c The author suggests that we may be dishonest with ourselves to justify buying a certain shoe.
- d According to the author, you should avoid buying certain brands.
- e A blister is the result of wearing an ill-fitting shoe.
- f The author affirms that it is fine to buy shoes online provided that you try them on first at the store.

3 **Work with your partner. Discuss the questions.**

- a Do you believe that you can tell someone's personality from their shoes?
- b What do you think your shoes say about you and your friends?

VOCABULARY & WRITING

1

3

5

2

4

6

sandals boots flip-flops mules pumps
sling-backs slip-ons slippers sneakers stilettos wedges

1 **Look at the different types of shoes in the box. Which are not normally worn by men? Which describe the shoes in the pictures?**

2 2.37 **Work with a partner. Listen to an interview with a psychologist. Discuss which of the shoes in the pictures (1-6) are being described. Which of the women on the right, Melanie, Saffron, Poppy, or Judith, do you think the shoes belong to? Why?**

3 **Look again at the shoes in the pictures. With your partner, write a description of the owner of one of these pairs of shoes. Read your description to another pair. Can they guess which shoes it refers to?**

GRAMMAR

1 **Read the sentences about shoes. Which of the expressions in bold refer to a) a large difference? b) a moderate difference? c) a small difference? d) no difference?**

- a The owner of these shoes is probably **a little** more flirtatious and feminine, and less domineering.
- b These shoes probably belong to someone who is **somewhat** older than the other women.
- c These shoes say, "I don't care about expensive designer fashions, there are so many other things that are **far** more interesting."
- d His shoes can say **just** as much about him as his carefully chosen car.
- e These shoes are **by far** the most extravagant ones I've ever bought.
- f The other shoes I tried on were **nowhere near** as comfortable as these.

2 **Which words or phrases from the box could replace those in bold in Exercise 1?**

a lot a tiny bit considerably definitely not easily
infinitely much noticeably slightly way

3 **Work with your partner. Write three sentences about a famous person. Use comparative structures and adjectives to compare him/her with other people.**

Read your description to another pair. Can they guess who it is?

4 **Grammar Extra 10, Part 2** page 150. Read the explanations and do Exercise 2.

Melanie, mother of two

Saffron, student

Poppy, talk-show host

Judith, retired

Comparative structures

The other shoes are **far** more comfortable than these.

These shoes are **nowhere near** as comfortable as the others.

These shoes are **somewhat** less comfortable.

These ones are **just** as comfortable as the others.

LANGUAGE FOR LIFE

1 **Work with a partner. Imagine your partner is tired. Try to persuade him/her to go out with you tonight.**

2 2.38-2.41 **Listen to four people trying to persuade someone to do something. For each conversation, note down what they are trying to persuade the other person to do and what the outcome is.**

Listen again and note down the reasons used to persuade the other person.

3 **Complete the extracts with useful phrases from the conversations in Exercise 2. Then listen again to check your answers.**

Trying to persuade someone

I disagree. I think it's (1) ______ making our voices heard.

Treat (2) ______ !

Oh, come on, nothing (3) ______ , nothing (4) ______ .

You might (5) ______ try.

Don't be (6) ______ !

You should cross that bridge (7) ______ . I think you should (8) ______ for it.

Expressing doubts or reservations

I don't really (1) ______ signing a petition.

What's (2) ______ spending so much money on shoes you're only going to wear once?

(3) ______ applying?

(4) ______ I get seasick?

Agreeing

OK. If (1) ______ think so.

Well, OK then, if (2) ______ happy. But I think it's (3) ______ time, frankly.

Well, maybe you're right. Maybe I should give it (4) ______ .

4 2.42 **Listen to another conversation. What is the woman trying to persuade her friend to do?**

5 **Listen again. Correct one of the words in the sentences so that they match the expressions used in the conversation.**

- a Come in, you know you want to!
- b No, absolutely not! It's out of the blue!
- c Come on, just with me!
- d Honestly, I'm not in the way.
- e You must be poking!
- f I'm still not sure I feel for it.
- g Come on, it'll make you good.
- h Oh, all right. You've twisted my leg.

Which are used a) to persuade? b) to refuse? c) to agree?

6 **Work with your partner. Write a conversation for one of these situations. A friend is trying to persuade another to ...**

- a go on an expensive vacation with them.
- b take up windsurfing or mountain climbing.
- c have a new haircut.
- d go to a costume party with them.

Read your conversation to another pair. Can they guess which situation it is?

Life Skills: Interpersonal Skills

Framing Opinions

Workplace confrontations take place for a number of reasons, some of which are unnecessary and should be avoided. Framing opinions properly is one way to prevent undue friction.

Some phrases we can use to frame our point of view are:

I feel like

I have the impression that

I'm sorry that you feel that way, but I think

It seems to me that

In my opinion,

- **Work with your partner and practice framing your point of view. Each student takes a side of the arguments below. Make your point non-aggressive by using framing phrases.**
  - One should never tell a lie.
  - Cell phones must be banned in schools.

MACMILLAN LIFE SKILLS

10 Writing Extra

REPORT

1 Read a report of students' travel habits. Match the headings (a–c) with the paragraphs (1–3).

a Recommendations
b Background
c Findings

1) ______
An investigation was carried out into the means of transportation currently used by students to travel into college. The purpose of the investigation was twofold: firstly, to establish how far existing public transportation arrangements are meeting the needs of college students; and secondly, in line with the college's Green Transportation Initiative, to consider how best to encourage students to travel to college by public transportation, by bicycle, or on foot, and how to minimize the use of cars.

2) ______
It was found that just over half the students (53%), the vast majority of whom lived within a 3km radius of the college, walked into college. However, a sizeable minority (31%) came by car, with 6% of these car-pooling with fellow students. Surprisingly, only 5% of those living outside the 3km radius used the bus, and only 11% cycled into college. The majority of students opting to use their cars cited the infrequency and unreliability of the local bus service as the main reason for this. When questioned about whether they would consider cycling, a number of respondents replied that they did not own a bicycle; further reservations centered around the perceived danger of cycling in local traffic, and the shortage of bicycle-storage facilities at the college.

3) ______
In light of the findings, the following measures are proposed:

- Negotiations should be initiated with local bus companies to increase the number and frequency of bus routes serving the college.
- The authorities should be encouraged to improve existing cycle paths, and increase the number of cycle lanes on roads into the college.
- Bicycle-storage facilities should be increased on college premises.
- Parking spaces should be reduced and a limited number of parking permits should be issued.
- The success of the measures should be monitored and evaluated a year after implementation.

2 Work with a partner. Discuss the questions.

a Why was the report written?
b In what way are these students' travel habits similar or different to those in your country?
c Do you agree with the recommendations?

3 Replace the highlighted words in the report with words in the box with a similar meaning.

asked conducted determine discovered distributed
focused on mentioned reduce started suggested

Underline uses of the passive in the report. Is it clear who wrote the report? Why? / Why not?

4 Match the following percentages with the quantity expressions in the box.

0.1% 1% 10% 25% 28% 35% 47% 90% 99%

a little under half a sizeable minority of a tiny percentage of
exactly a quarter of just over a third of one in ten
the overwhelming majority of the vast majority of virtually no

5 Work with your partner. Choose one of the topics below to ask the class about.

a going on regular walks
b walking for more than a kilometer a day
c walking to work or college
d going on trekking vacations
e power walking or jogging
f grocery shopping on foot
g taking a pet or children for a walk
h walking in the park

Prepare a list of questions. Interview other pairs. Then write a report using the headings in the report in Exercise 1.

11 Words

SPEAKING & LISTENING

1 **Work with a partner. Look at the pictures and read the tweets below. Do you agree with them?**

- **Grammar:** Avoiding repetition: substitution and ellipsis
- **Vocabulary:** New words
- **Language for Life:** Getting your point across

2 Work with your partner. Complete the sentences with the words in the box.

brunch   choice   facetious   feedback   fog   ma'am   peculiar   penguin   shampoo   smoke   weird

a ______ reads the same backwards or forwards.
b ______ comes from combining *breakfast* and *lunch*.
c Smog is formed by combining ______ and ______ .
d If you write ______ in capital letters, it reads the same upside down in the mirror.
e ______ contains all five vowels in alphabetical order.
f ______ contains the first six letters of the alphabet.
g ______ has been borrowed from Hindi and ______ has been borrowed from Welsh.
h Both ______ and ______ mean "strange." ______ originates from Old English and ______ from Latin.

3 Work in small groups. Discuss the questions.

a Can you remember the last new word you learned in English (excluding the words from Exercise 2)?
b Can you remember the last new word you learned in your own language? Is it a new word, borrowed from another language, or just new to you?
c Can you think of some English words that are used in your language?
d Can you think of three English words that people wouldn't have known 20 years ago?

Compare your answers with another group. How many of your words were the same?

4 ▶ 2.43-2.46 **Listen to some people talking about some of the questions in Exercise 3. Which questions (a-d) are they each discussing?**

Make a note of the words they talk about. Are any of them new to you? Did they mention any of the words you came up with in Exercise 3?

5 Look at the sentences. Which do you agree with more? How many people in the class feel the same as you?

a Our language is being weakened by the introduction of English words and expressions. I'd like to see all of them banned.
b I love what the internet is doing to our language. It's a global phenomenon making communication easier, as more and more words are the same in all languages.

VOCABULARY

1 **Look at the three comments from a lifestyle blog. What do you think they will be about?**

2 **Match the titles (a-c) with the comments from the blog (1-3).**

a Beware the Trolls!
b Binge-worthy?
c Gone fishin'

www.lifestyleblog.com

LIFESTYLE BLOG

Comment
11:36 am **Updated** August 2018

With so much entertainment to choose from, picking what to watch is no joke. From traditional cable to **streaming content** on various online platforms, it seems like the options are endless. Maybe this is why when we do come across something that really grabs our attention, we want to consume it all at once, and why **binge-watching** our favorite shows is now the norm, not the exception. A whole season in one night? Sure, why not?

Comment
2:45 pm **Updated** September 2018

Do you feel like you spend half your life closing **popups**? Is your inbox mostly **spam**? You're not alone. From cars to **froyo**, ads for anything and everything bombard us the moment we go online. What's creepier still, ads are now targeting users specifically based on their internet searches, **browser history**, and location. Even online news 'articles' are just **clickbait** half the time, trying to lure you in for a visit. Ah, the good old days, when you could just change the channel ...

Comment
8:32 am **Updated** November 2018

Being a teenager has never been easy, but these days they are under more pressure than ever. From **cyberbullying** to **catfishing**, online acts of meanness among teens are real and on the rise. So why do they do it? Maybe it's just **FOMO** – after all, the lives of social media stars always look perfect with their immaculate **selfies**. But don't assume meeting in **IRL** is any easier – you might just get **ghosted**.

3 **Match the paragraphs with the pictures (a–c). Which blog post would you like to know more about? Why?**

a

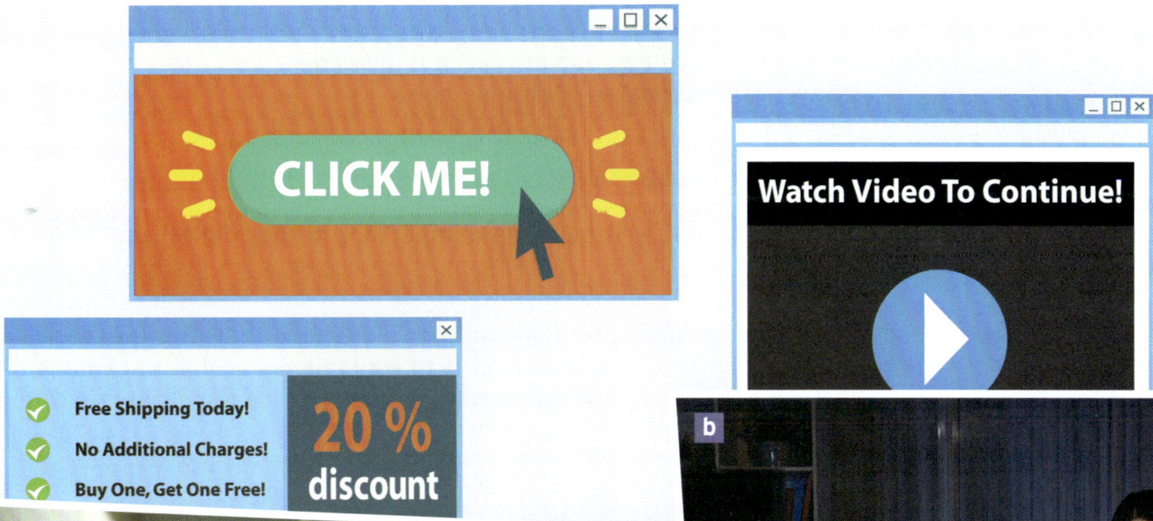

b

c

4 **Look at the words and phrases in bold in the paragraphs in Exercise 2. They are all relatively new to the English language. Divide them into three groups:**

a I know what it means.
b I've seen or heard it, but I'm not sure what it means.
c I've never seen or heard it before.

Compare your answers with a partner. Look at the words you put in groups *b* and *c*. Look again at the way they are used in the paragraphs. Can you guess their meaning from the context? Use the definitions from the glossary box to help you.

5 **Check your answers with your teacher or online. Which words or phrases are most relevant to your life and lifestyle? Why? Is there an equivalent in your language?**

Glossary

binge watch verb [T]: to watch multiple episodes of a program in a short amount of time

catfish verb [T]: to trick someone online by adopting a fake identity

clickbait noun [U]: a link on a website that is designed to catch people's attention and encourage them to click

cyberbully noun [C]: somebody who uses the internet to frighten or upset another person

froyo noun [C/U]: frozen yogurt

ghost verb [T]: to end a relationship with someone suddenly without any explanation

streaming adjective: describes getting video through the internet before the entire video has been downloaded

SPEAKING

1 **Work in small groups. Discuss which of these you write ...**

a all the time. b at least once a week. c once in a while. d never.

blog entries comments on websites emails instant messages (IM) letters status updates text messages

What else do you write on a regular basis?

2 **Look at the quotation. Do you agree that writing is more important in the "digital age" than it used to be? Why? / Why not?**

"As the world becomes increasingly digital, writing becomes more important. This is especially true for non-writers. If you work in an office, the majority of your communications are made with text by email or IM. Whether you like it or not, your ability to exchange ideas, collaborate with others, and ultimately succeed, hinges on the ability to write effectively."

READING & VOCABULARY

1 **Work with a partner and decide if you agree or disagree with the following statement: *People are worse writers now than they were 25 years ago.***

Think of five reasons to support your position and make notes.

2 **Read the article on page 119. Were any of your ideas in Exercise 1 mentioned in the article? Compare your answers with your partner.**

3 **Read the article again. Match the headings (a–g) with the paragraphs (1–7).**

a ☐ Generational comparison
b ☐ A novel form of expression
c ☐ Motivational factors
d ☐ Setting up a debate
e ☐ An educational proposal
f ☐ The influence of the dominant writing form
g ☐ The new use of a word

4 **Work with your partner. Discuss the questions.**

a Which of the two speakers do you agree with more? Why?
b Do you think that emoji could replace words? Why? / Why not?
c How do you think writing will change in the future?

5 **Look at the words and phrases highlighted in the article. Discuss their possible meanings with your partner. Then complete the glossary at the bottom of the article.**

6 **Complete the sentences with some of the words and phrases from the glossary. Make any necessary changes to the words and phrases.**

a If we really want to encourage students to improve their academic writing, we need to offer ______, not just threats.
b Outside of the world of ______, does it even really matter if students write in long, elegant sentences?
c I can present evidence which completely ______ all your arguments about how this is a 'new' problem.
d The claim that emoji are real words is ______ false.
e You say that emoji are a poor substitute for words. ______, they're not going anywhere anytime soon.
f ______ about the impact of technology on writing never tells the whole story.
g The new use of *because* as a preposition has even started to ______ political debates.

The Decline of Writing?

[1] We often get questions and comments (or complaints, more often) from our readers about the quality of writing in English these days. So, to find out what is really going on, we brought in two experts to weigh in on this matter: Dr Penny Harmer, a professor of classic literature, and Dr Michael Noble, a professor of linguistics. We asked them the following question: 'Is the quality of English writing really on the decline?' We have transcribed their debate, so you can judge for yourself.

Penny Harmer: Most definitely, and the evidence is all around us. Just ask any school teacher or university professor, or better yet, take a quick look online. The decline of writing is undeniable!

[2] **Michael Noble:** Well, hold on just a moment – there's a lot to unpack in that sweeping generalization you just made. You mentioned university professors, so let's start there, since we both work in academia. Of course, I see my fair share of poor writing, but what evidence is there that this is a new phenomenon? Older generations have complained about youth's writing for as long as writing has existed! In English, for example, the author William Langland complained that students couldn't 'write a decent letter' – and that was in 1386. Going even further back, there are records of complaints from teachers of Sumerian – the world's first written language!

Penny Harmer: Yes, yes, of course that's true, but that doesn't negate the fact that the current generation is unique. Ancient Sumerians didn't have the internet or smartphones after all, and their writing never had to compete with the influence of texting or emoji.

Michael Noble: Now, you're not going to try to claim that texts and emoji aren't authentic communication, are you? They are a completely legitimate form of conveying meaning – the very purpose of language.

[3] **Penny Harmer:** Meaning, yes, but only in very specific, informal genres. What irks me is when characteristics of these online genres seep into more formal text types. Students can't form complete sentences anymore since they are so accustomed to using abbreviations, fragments, and little smiley faces. What's worse, one dictionary, a supposed authority on language, named the 'face with tears of joy' emoji the 'word' of the year in 2015! That's patently absurd!

[4] **Michael Noble:** And why shouldn't they? Remember that people made these same arguments about email when it came out, saying that communication would suffer. If so, I haven't noticed! Emoji just add another element to convey feelings. I prefer to think of language as evolving rather than worsening, as it always has. Sure, texting and essays are two distinct forms of writing, I'll give you that. But why disparage texting? Neither is going away anytime soon and they both have their own merits. With that being the case, my recommendation is to increase training so that learners are aware of the differences. It would allow them to write equally well whatever the genre. And if you don't, I guarantee you they won't!

[5] **Penny Harmer:** How much texting training do young people need? The exposure to low-quality writing is already overwhelming, and no one reads classic literature anymore. Not to mention that, with tools like spell check, there is already little incentive to spell or use grammar correctly. Just the other day I had a student email me to say, "I didn't study last night because tired". I nearly fell out of my chair.

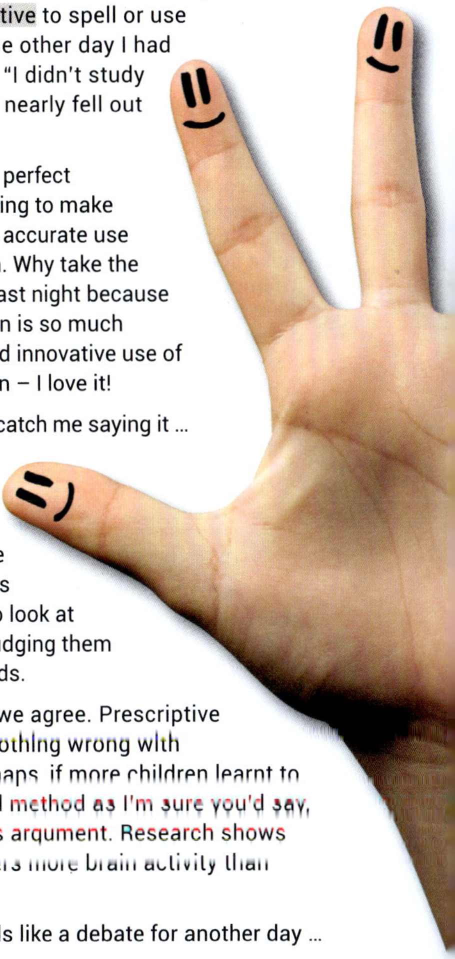

[6] **Michael Noble:** That is a perfect example of the point I'm trying to make – that use of because is an accurate use of because as a preposition. Why take the time to say, "I didn't study last night because I was tired" when his version is so much more concise. It's a new and innovative use of language that is catching on – I love it!

Penny Harmer: You'll never catch me saying it ...

Michael Noble: Be that as it may, your position seems to be very prescriptive – telling people how to write. I see myself as more descriptive – trying to look at how people write without judging them based on outdated standards.

[7] **Penny Harmer:** Finally, we agree. Prescriptive and proud of it – there's nothing wrong with upholding standards. Perhaps, if more children learnt to write by hand, an outdated method as I'm sure you'd say, we wouldn't be having this argument. Research shows that writing by hand triggers more brain activity than typing.

Michael Noble: That sounds like a debate for another day ...

Glossary

a ______ adverb: in a way that is so obvious that no one could disagree

b ______ phrase: a statement about all things of a particular kind, without considering all the necessary detailed information

c ______ phrasal verb [I]: to become involved in something

d ______ phrase: used for saying that even if something is true, it does not affect your opinion

e ______ noun [C/U]: emoticons used in electronic messages and on websites

f ______ verb [T]: to annoy someone

g ______ verb [T]: to make something have no effect

h ______ verb [I]: to enter or spread through something gradually

i ______ noun [C]: people, activities, and institutions connected with higher education

j ______ noun [C/U]: something that makes you want to do something or to work harder

k ______ verb [T]: to say unpleasant things about someone or something that show you have no respect for them

GRAMMAR

1 Work with a partner. Look at the extract from the article. What do the words in bold refer to?

Remember that people made these same arguments about email when **it** came out, saying that communication would suffer. If **so**, I haven't noticed! Emoji just add another element to convey feelings. I prefer to think of language as evolving rather than worsening, as **it** always has. Sure, texting and essays are two distinct forms of writing, I'll give you **that**. But why disparage texting? **Neither** is going away anytime soon and they both have **their** own merits. With **that** being the **case**, my recommendation is to increase training so that learners are aware of the differences. **It** would allow them to write equally well whatever the genre. And if you **don't**, I guarantee you they **won't**!

Avoiding repetition

Substitution

Think about **it** from their point of view.

The answer to **that** is obvious.

Do you want to improve your communication? If **so**, consider emoji.

Do so, and literature will soon disappear.

Ellipsis

Don't.

If **not**, I won't be able to teach them.

If they **don't**, I certainly **won't**!

2 Look at the tip for essay writing below. Substitute the sections in bold with a word or phrase from the box. You will not need to use all the words.

either way   it   its   that   their overuse   them   they   these   to do so

The use of short, staccato sentences is usually inappropriate in an academic essay. (1) **Short, staccato sentences** can also make your arguments seem too simplistic – or impossible to follow! (2) **Whether they make your writing too simplistic or impossible to follow**, it's important to show the links between your ideas. (3) **In order to show the links between your ideas**, use discourse markers such as *on the other hand, as a result,* and *in conclusion.* (4) **These discourse markers** can really help make your writing much clearer and easier to read. But beware of (5) **the overuse of discourse markers**! Too many discourse markers can make your writing heavy and clumsy. (6) **Discourse markers** can sometimes cloud the issue. So, remember, use (7) **discourse markers** carefully and sparingly when you write your essay.

3 Work with your partner. Look at the communication tips (a–d). Which words can you cut from the sections in bold without losing the meaning? Use full forms instead of contractions where necessary.

a Regardless of the genre, if you're going around in circles, it's probably because you're not really sure exactly what you want to say. **And if you don't know what you want to say, your readers definitely won't know what you're saying!**

b When writing online, you may feel that a point is important, and that you therefore want to write your message in all caps. **Don't write in all caps.** It's considered shouting.

c In your essays, do the paragraphs show where you take a breath and when you start out on a new idea? **If they don't show this, put them in.**

d Before posting a message on social media, make sure it's something that you don't mind the public seeing, **and make sure that you're ready for unexpected responses.**

2.47 **Listen and check. Which words were cut? Why were they cut?**

4 Work with your partner. Make the conversation as short as possible using substitution and ellipsis.

A: Do you do a lot of writing?
B: I used to do a lot of writing at school, but now I don't write at all.
A: What about writing text messages? Don't you ever write text messages?
B: Yes, of course, I write text messages every day! But I don't really think of writing text messages as writing. Do you think of it as writing?
A: No, I suppose I don't think of it as writing. But I do write a lot of emails at work. I think emails count as writing.
B: Yes, I guess that what you say is true. But I was thinking more about essays and reports ... now essays and reports are what I call real writing.

2.48 **Listen and check. Do you agree with the speakers? Why? / Why not?**

5 **Grammar Extra 11** page 152. Read the explanations and do Exercises 1 and 2.

SPEAKING

1 Work with a partner. Discuss the questions.

- **a** Do you think English spelling is difficult?
- **b** Which words do you occasionally misspell?
- **c** What changes do you think could be made to English to make spelling easier?

2 Look at this article, which was written by Mark Twain. Read it aloud with your partner.

Which of his suggestions do you approve of?

The American author Mark Twain was born in 1835 and is most famous for *The Adventures of Tom Sawyer* and *The Adventures of Huckleberry Finn*, both based on his own childhood.

A Plan for the Improvement of English Spelling by Mark Twain

In Year 1, that useless letter "c" would be dropped to be replased either by "k" or "s," and, likewise, "x" would no longer be part of the alphabet. The only kase in which "c" would be retained would be the "ch" formation, which will be dealt with later. Year 2 might reform "w" spelling, so that "which" and "one" would take the same konsonant, wile Year 3 might well abolish "y," replasing it with "i," and Iear 4 might fiks the "g/j" anomali wonse and for all.

Jenerally, then, the improvement would kontinue iear bai iear, with Iear 5 doing awai with useless double konsonants, and Iears 6–12 or so modifaiing vowlz and the rimeining voist and unvoist konsonants. Bai Iear 15 or sou, it wud fainali bi posibl tu meik ius ov thi ridandant letez "c," "y," and "x" – bai now jast a memori in the maindz ov ould doderez – tu riplais "ch," "sh," and "th" rispektivli. Fainali, xen, aafte sam 20 iers ov orxogrefkl riform, wi wud hev a lojikl, kohirnt speling in ius xrewawt xe Ingliy-spiking werld.

PRONUNCIATION

1 Mark Twain recognized that English spelling and pronunciation are often very different. Read the sentences and ~~cross out~~ the silent letters.

- **a** Knowing how to pronounce English words correctly is important, but there's no doubt that it is one of the hardest things to learn.
- **b** Keep your receipt if you want to return a purchase, otherwise there's no guarantee you'll get your money back.
- **c** I had a really bad case of pneumonia earlier this year. Even watching TV was tiring, so I spent most days just listening to the radio.
- **d** Psychiatrists can be very vague. They'll rarely give you a direct answer to a question.
- **e** During the flight the plane will climb to 10,000 meters above sea level.

2 The pronunciation of some place names can be difficult too. Look at these place names. How do you think they are pronounced?

- **a** Arkansas
- **b** Des Moines
- **c** Yosemite
- **d** Tucson
- **e** Greenwich Village
- **f** Boise

2.49 **Listen and check your answers.**

3 Work with your partner. Try reading this limerick.

There was a young girl from Knob Noster,
Whose parents thought they had loster.
From the fridge came a sigh,
"Let me out or I'll digh!"
But the problem was how to defroster.

4 2.50 **Listen and check. Correct the misspelled words with your partner.**

LANGUAGE FOR LIFE

1 2.51 **Listen to two people, Sue and Matt, talking about socializing online. Do they think it's a good thing to do? Why? / Why not?**

2 **Read the extract from the conversation. What exactly is Sue's point? Do you agree with her?**

Matt: So, are you saying that people who socialize online are all freaks and weirdos?

Sue: No, you know (1) that's not what I meant! (2) You're twisting my words. (3) All I said was that it can be a problem, you know, you don't know who you're talking to ... and they could be ... yes, I guess, they could be weirdos or something ... I mean, you never know ...

Matt: (4) So, what are you saying then? That we should all stop using chat rooms and networking sites and whatever?

Sue: No, (5) that's not what I'm saying ... and you know it ... (6) my point is that we need to be careful, that's all ... you know, don't give away too many personal details ... don't make yourself vulnerable ...

Matt: But surely it's much safer to talk to somebody at a distance than to talk to a stranger in a nightclub or a bar ...

Sue: (7) You're missing the point ... I'm not saying that it's dangerous to chat with people online ... (8) I'm just saying that you have to be really careful when it comes to arranging to meet them in real life ... you just don't know who they are, or what they want ...

Listen again and replace the highlighted phrases (1–8) with the actual useful phrases used in the conversation.

3 2.52 **Listen to the useful phrases again. Mark the main stress. Then practice saying them with the recording.**

- a I didn't say that!
- b You're deliberately misconstruing my words!
- c That's not what I meant!
- d You're twisting my words!
- e So, what are you implying?
- f That's not what I'm saying!
- g You're missing the point!

4 **Work in small groups. Respond to one of the statements below. Make sure you're getting your point across clearly and that your partners understand exactly what you're saying.**

- Social networks are great – they're the best way to keep in touch with friends and family.
- Face-to-face time with friends is really important.
- I'm getting tired of this always-on, always-connected lifestyle.

Life Skills: Communication

Exploring Words

1 **Work with a partner and answer the questions.**

- What do you do when you encounter a word you don't know in English?
- Do you ever use a dictionary? Why? / Why not? If so, do you prefer to use an online dictionary or a paper dictionary?
- What kind of information can you find in a dictionary?

2 **Look at the dictionary entry below for *erudite* from <www.macmillandictionary.com>. Match the parts of the entry (a–f) with their purpose (1–6).**

a **erudite** - definition and synonyms

b ADJECTIVE c FORMAL Pronunciation /ˈerəˌdaɪt/ d

e someone who is erudite has a lot of knowledge because they have read or studied a lot

Synonyms and related words

f Experienced and educated: *educated, learned, trained...*

Explore Thesaurus

1 register (level of formality)
2 words with similar meaning
3 phonetic transcription
4 head word
5 part of speech
6 definition

MACMILLAN LIFE SKILLS

3 **Choose one of the vocabulary items from this unit. Look it up and find out more information about it. Then, tell your partner what you have learned.**

11 Vocabulary Extra

ORIGINS OF NEW WORDS

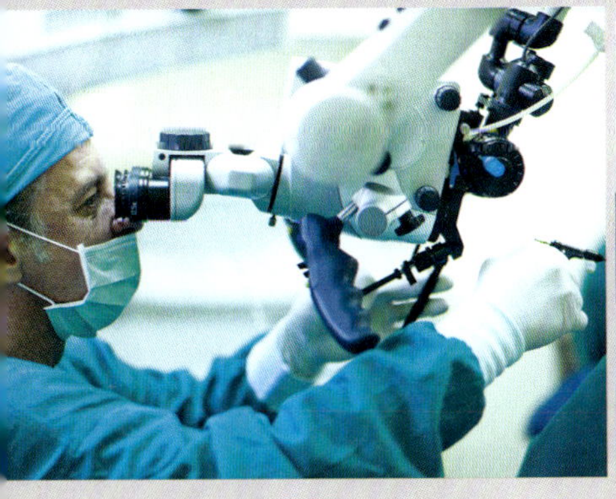 

1 Work with a partner. Look at the highlighted words. Can you explain exactly what they mean?

- **a** What kind of sandwich would you like for lunch?
- **b** There was an anti-terrorism demo downtown.
- **c** How good are you at guesstimating the calories on your plate?
- **d** If you don't know a word, Google™ it!
- **e** More and more people are having laser eye surgery.
- **f** Paparazzi were blamed for the celebrity's riding injuries.
- **g** Experts say tsunamis can travel at up to 500 km/h.
- **h** Hollywood's restaurants are full of wannabe actors waiting to be discovered.

2 Match each highlighted word from the sentences (a–h) in Exercise 1 with its origin (1–7). Two of the words have the same origin.

1. a word borrowed from another language
2. a noun which is the name of the person who invented it
3. a noun or brand name that is used as a verb
4. a verb phrase which has been made into an adjective
5. a combination of two words
6. the initial letters of a group of words
7. a shortened word

Check your answers in the box on the right.

3 Look at the words in the box. Do you know what they mean? Can you match them with the categories in the box on the right?

decaf Facebook™ (v) fuggedaboutit Kleenex™
kosher lol scuba stalkerazzi

2.53 **Listen to seven people talking about the words. Check your answers.**

4 Work with your partner. Discuss the questions.

- Do you ever Skype™, Facebook™, or YouTube™? If yes, how often?
- Do you think it's OK for an English-language student to use slang like *lol* and *fuggedaboutit*?
- Do you think there are too many borrowed English words in your language?

5 Check your own-language dictionary. How does it show information about sources of new vocabulary?

Sources of new vocabulary

- **Borrowing**
Many English words are "loanwords" from other languages, such as *paparazzi* (Italian) and *tsunami* (Japanese). Many are so familiar that we no longer think of them as borrowings – for example, *shampoo* (Hindi), *assassin* (Arabic).
- **Eponyms**
Eponyms are names of people, places, or companies that are associated with a particular product or thing, and that become used as general vocabulary items. Examples include *sandwich*, *sherry*, *watt*.
- **Conversion**
Conversion is the processs of changing the grammatical class of a word without changing its form. Conversion of nouns to verbs is particularly common in English – for example, *to word a message carefully*. More recently, nouns and brand names such as *Google*™, *email*, *text*, and *Skype*™ are also used as verbs.
- **Respelling**
Respellings often represent the way we pronounce certain words in informal situations – for example, *gonna* (*going to*), *pix* (*pics*, *pictures*). Sometimes they develop different meanings from the original versions – for example, the word *wannabe* is a respelling of the phrase *want to be*, but it is used as a noun meaning someone who wants to be famous or successful.
- **Blending**
A blend is a combination of parts of two words, usually the beginning of one word and the end of another – for example, *glocalization* (*global* + *localization*), *guesstimate* (*guess* + *estimate*), *netiquette* (*net* + *etiquette*).
- **Acronyms**
An acronym is an abbreviation in which a sequence of letters is pronounced as a word – for example, *AIDS* (*acquired immune deficiency syndrome*), *laser* (*light amplification by stimulated emission of radiation*).
- **Clipping**
In clipping, the beginning or ending of a word is cut off – for example, *demo* (*demonstration*), *rehab* (*rehabilitation*), *pro* (*professional*).

12 Conscience

SPEAKING & LISTENING

1 **Look at the pictures and answer the questions.**

a Which picture doesn't belong with the other three? Why?
b Which of the people would you be most likely to give money to? Why?
c Have you given money to anybody on the streets recently? If not, have you ever given money to anybody? If so, who did you give the money to, and when?

2 2.54-2.59 **Listen to six people talking about giving money to people on the streets. Match the speakers (1–6) with the people they're talking about in column *A*, and with their attitude towards street people in column *B*.**

	A		B
	beggars in general		the government should take action
	people who wash car windows	1	it's better to give something other than money
	street performers		you should only give money to charity, not beggars
1	homeless people		it's important to know where the money is going
	people who collect charity donations		it's OK if they do something to earn it
	charities in general		beggars are all lazy

3 **Listen again. Which speaker do you sympathize with most? Who do you sympathize with least? Why? Compare your answers with a partner.**

VOCABULARY

1 **Look at the words and phrases in the box. What's the difference between them? Which are a) neutral? b) potentially offensive? Which are a) more formal? b) more spoken or informal?**

bag lady   beggar   bum   hobo   homeless person   street performer
street person   street vendor   street windshield-washers   vagrant   wino

2 **Work in small groups. Discuss the questions.**

a Do you often see people asking for money on the streets in your town?
b Are they tolerated, or do the police tend to move them on?
c What do you think is the best way to help people who ask for money on the streets?

- **Grammar:** Special uses of the simple past
- **Vocabulary:** Describing street people. Verb/Noun collocations. Expressions with *conscience*
- **Language for Life:** Apologizing

GRAMMAR

Special uses of the simple past

It's time we did something.

I'd rather they did something.

Suppose you were in that position.

Imagine you had no money.

1 **Complete the sentences from the recording in Speaking & Listening, Exercise 2 on page 124, using an appropriate form of the verb in parentheses.**

a I'd rather they actually _____ (do) something to earn the money.
b I think it's about time the government _____ (do) something about it, because it really is annoying.

2.60 **Listen and check. Which tense is used? Why?**

2 **Look at the expressions and sentences in bold below. Do they all refer to an action in the past? Would you use a past form in these sentences in your language?**

a **Suppose I gave him a few dollars**, what then? Would he use it to buy food, do you think?
b **Imagine you had no home and no friends or family**. What would you do?
c **It's about time we started thinking about other people** and not only about ourselves.
d **It's time you asked somebody for help.**
e **I'd rather you didn't tell anybody**. I don't want my family to know I'm begging.
f **I didn't tell anybody I'd seen her**. I didn't want to make things worse for her.

3 **Complete each sentence with a verb in the appropriate form.**

a It's about time people _____ expecting others to look after them.
b It's about time we _____ giving more generously to charity.
c Imagine what we could do if we all _____ a little every day.
d I'd rather people _____ something concrete to help, instead of handing out money to ease their consciences.
e Suppose I _____ one of them a bed for the night. Would that solve the problem?
f I'd rather local government _____ money on building new youth clubs or improving leisure facilities for young people than redeveloping old buildings.

Which of the sentences above do you agree with? Compare your answer with a partner.

4 **Complete the punch lines for the cartoons using *It's about time* and *I'd rather*.**

_____ a shave.

_____ speak with your mouth full.

5 **Grammar Extra 12** page 152. Read the explanations and do Exercises 1 and 2.

READING

1 **Quickly read the first section of a magazine article. What is the connection between fashion and homelessness?**

Dressed *for* Success

You've probably heard the idiom "*Dress for the job you want, not the job you have*". Well, it turns out that current research backs up this saying. In recent studies, it was shown that people wearing more formal work clothing were seen as better at negotiating and possessing more leadership skills.

Now imagine yourself in this unenviable Catch 22: You don't have money, so you need to get a job. For the job interview you need to look professional. To look professional, you need to have money. But you don't have money, so you need to ...

Fortunately, there are organizations trying to address this problem to break this vicious cycle. Their goal is to help empower low-income and homeless people in their communities. What's their method? One suit at a time.

2 **Work with a partner. You are going to find out more about dressing homeless people for success. Student A: look at Article A on page 128. Student B: look at Article B on page 141. Answer the questions.**

a In what ways do organizations like *Look the Part* help homeless and low-income people?
b What are some of the issues homeless people encounter when seeking employment?

Tell your partner about your article and compare your answers.

3 **Work with your partner. Decide whether the information in the statements (a-f) is found in Text A only (A), Text B only (B), both texts (BOTH), or neither text (N). Underline the passages in the articles that support your answer.**

a *Look the Part* helps people improve their résumés.
b *First Impressions* is endorsed by a well-known celebrity.
c The people receiving help are 50% more likely to be successful in a job interview.
d The organizations described do not make money from their operations.
e Clothing donations come from a variety of sources.
f The general population is becoming more aware of these organizations.

4 **Think of two ways to complete the sentence according to one or both of the articles. One sentence must be true, the other must be false. Show your sentences to your partner. Can they choose the correct option?**

Organizations like Look the Part ...
1
2

5 **Work with your partner. Create a slogan to raise the profile of one of the organizations from the articles. Explain what the organization does and what it aims to do. Compare your slogan with the rest of the class. Vote on the best one.**

Slogan

a short phrase that is easy to remember and is used to advertise something or to express the beliefs of a political party or other group

TEXT A

Like many homeless people in America, Derek Foster's story is not one of crime or bad choices. Instead, he was a casualty of the economic recession.

"One day my company laid off half its employees. Soon I was behind on my rent, and before I knew it I'd lost my apartment."

To make matters worse, Derek could not secure employment and thinks he knows why.

"I would show up in my cleanest pants and shirt, but I knew I didn't represent myself well – the other applicants all looked so much more professional. It really affected my self-esteem."

Luckily, through a local agency, Derek got in touch with *Look the Part*, a non-profit organization dedicated to helping homeless people join the workforce. Their motto: *Look the part*.

"They were phenomenal, giving me a complete makeover inside and out. Not only did they get me a nice suit, but they gave me a haircut too. Then, they helped with my résumé, and we practiced mock interviews. I was more confident than ever, and I nailed my next interview. I've been working ever since, and I couldn't be more grateful."

Unfortunately, the demand for services like those provided by *Look the Part* far outweighs their current capabilities. And even though there are other similar organizations, like *JobReady* and *First Impressions*, there are many people still struggling to find employment.

VOCABULARY

1 Match the verbs (a-f) with the nouns to make collocations.

a address	yourself
b boost	a problem
c pursue	employment
d represent	an education
e reunite	families
f secure	self esteem

2 Complete the sentences with the collocations from Exercise 1. You may need to make some changes.

a Those suffering homelessness are forced to _____ numerous _____ when looking for a job, including discrimination based on their appearance or lack of a formal address.

b Employers often judge job applicants based on superficial aspects like clothing and grooming since they are an indication of how you _____ _____ .

c For many of the program participants, their difficulties are compounded by the fact that they never had an opportunity to _____ an _____ beyond high school.

d The initial aim of organizations like *Look the Part* or *First Impressions* is to help people _____ _____ and financial stability, but this is just one of their goals.

e Some of the participants in the programs _____ with their _____ after finding stable jobs and living conditions.

f In addition, changing a person's appearance can _____ _____, and the positive effects of confidence cannot be overlooked.

3 Rewrite the sentences in Exercise 2 with a similar meaning, using the verbs given below. Make any other changes that are necessary.

a deal

Those suffering homelessness are forced to deal with numerous problems when looking for a job, including discrimination based on their lack of an address or appearance.

b see
c take
d get
e get back
f feel better

Which version is more formal? Which verbs were used in the articles?

4 Work in small groups. Order the following according to their importance for living a happy and fulfilled life, in your opinion.

- a good education
- a good job
- getting along with your family
- good self-esteem

Do you think any of the four can exist without the other three?

READING & SPEAKING

1 **Work with a partner. Take the quiz. Keep a note of your answers.**

Guilt-free Shopping?

How you shop says a lot about your personality. Take our quiz and find you if you're a 'conscious consumer' or a guilty shopper!

1 ***You're planning a special meal for your family and want everything to be perfect. When you get to the grocery store you …***

a) avoid any products that aren't organic or in-season, and buy exclusively from local suppliers. Maybe you'll even cook a vegan meal.

b) choose the healthier, local options if they aren't too expensive, but don't worry about it too much. No one will be able to tell!

c) buy whatever ingredients you think look yummiest. It's the taste that counts!

2 ***You've been invited to a friend's wedding, but you don't have anything formal to wear.***

a) You see if you can borrow something, or maybe you can pick up some secondhand clothing. Why waste money on stuff you'll hardly ever wear?

b) You buy one or two items to combine with what you already own. And if there's a sale at your local independent store, so much the better.

c) It's a special occasion and you need to look your finest. Time to break the bank and get a whole new designer outfit!

3 ***It's your young niece's birthday and you're out shopping for a present.***

a) It's not what she asked for, but a homemade, educational toy would really show how much you care.

b) She's probably got enough toys, so you offer to take her to a movie of her choice and all the popcorn she can eat.

c) You know she'd love that fighting robot, and you'd get to be the cool uncle/aunt. Sure, it's made of cheap plastic from who knows where, but isn't everything nowadays?

4 ***You're all out of shampoo and head to the local store. There are so many options, so you …***

a) carefully read the back of the bottles, looking at ingredients and whether it was tested on animals. You even check the internet to be sure.

b) avoid a few brands that you have heard bad things about, then choose one on sale that looks pretty natural.

c) scan the names and prices and grab one that you recognize. Hey, their TV ads were hilarious!

2 **Turn to page 141 and check your answers with the quiz results. Discuss with your partner what kind of person you think would always give the *a*, *b*, and *c* answers. What does the quiz say about you?**

LISTENING

1 2.61 **Listen to a short conversation between Jade and Kiera. What is the link between the four pictures (a–d)?**

a

b

c

d

Jade

Kiera

2 **Work with a partner. Answer the questions.**

- a What does Jade feel guilty about?
- b What is she going to do to ease her conscience?
- c What would you do in her position?

3 **Look at the extracts (a–e) from the conversation in Exercise 1. When the speakers say them in the recording, they drop one or two of the words. Which words do they drop?**

- a How are you doing?
- b I'm fine. How are you?
- c Do you want to come?
- d Do you know my cousin Beth?
- e I almost forgot to tell you ...

Listen again and check.

4 **Who do you identify with more, Jade or Kiera? Why?**

VOCABULARY

1 **Complete the sentences with the expressions with *conscience* in the box.**

a clear conscience   eased my conscience   in good conscience   a guilty conscience   on his conscience

- a It was a tragic accident. He'll have it ______ for the rest of his life.
- b I was able to leave with ______ , happy that I'd done all I could to help.
- c He suffered from ______ for months after he left his wife and family.
- d I ______ by telling my boss about the mistake I'd made.
- e Can you, ______ , take their money when you know how much they need every penny?

2 **Which of these things would give you a guilty conscience? Add another three things to the list.**

- throwing away something that could be recycled
- littering in the park
- spending money on luxury items
- eating too much chocolate
- forgetting someone's birthday
- not doing your homework
- losing your temper with someone
- not keeping a promise
- keeping people waiting
- forgetting to water the plants

Compare your answers with your partner. Which three things make you feel the guiltiest? What would you do to ease your conscience in each case?

3 **Can you think of a time when you felt guilty about doing any of these things? What did you do to make amends?**

LANGUAGE FOR LIFE

1 2.62-2.67 **Listen to six short conversations (1–6). What are the people apologizing for? Who sounds the most apologetic?**

2 **Listen again and complete the useful phrases.**

a Oh, I'm _____ , it totally _____ !
b I think I _____ .
c _____ ! I had _____ you were so touchy today!
d I'm _____ sorry.
e I really, really _____ . ... But it _____ again.
f We _____ that tonight's concert has been canceled.

3 **Listen again. Notice the use of intonation and voice range. Practice repeating the useful phrases in Exercise 2 with the same feeling.**

4 **Match the apologies (a–e) in Exercise 2 with the responses (1–5). Which person feels most upset about what's happened?**

1 Yeah, well, it better not!
2 Yeah, well, don't waste any time!
3 Yes – this time!
4 That's all right. Don't worry about it. It's an easy mistake to make.
5 Can we just drop it, please?

What do you think the relationship is between the two people in each of the conversations (1–5)? Who do you think is making the apology in the last conversation (6)?

5 **Work with a partner. Look at the situations and decide what you would say in each. How angry do you think the other person would be?**

a you borrowed someone's bicycle and damaged it
b you lost your friend's memory stick containing an important file
c you spilled a drink on a stranger
d you crashed into the back of someone's car

Choose one of the situations and act it out between you.

6 2.68 **Listen to people saying *sorry*. Match each *sorry* (1–6) with its use (a–f).**

a apologizing for doing something wrong
b breaking bad news
c offering commiserations
d asking someone to move
e asking someone to repeat what they said
f attracting someone's attention

What do you say sorry for in your language? Would you use the same expression for all six uses (a–f)?

Life Skills: Social Responsibility

Individual Social Responsiblity

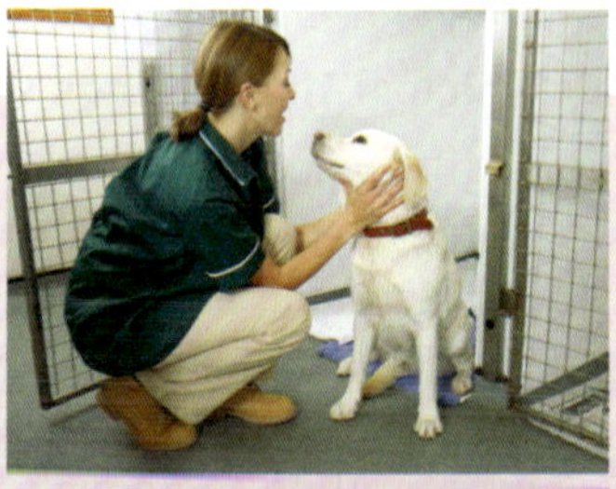

1 **What does the term *social responsibility* mean to you? Look at the pictures for examples of social responsibility. Discuss your ideas with your partner and write a definition in one sentence.**

Now, check your answers with the definition on page 141. Is it similar or different to your definition?

2 **Work in a group. Discuss the different options below for being more individually socially responsible. Which would you most like to do?**

- volunteering at an animal shelter
- donating blood at a hospital
- giving talks or tutoring children at a local school
- participating in local elections
- donating money to a local charity
- encouraging family and friends to recycle
-
-
-

Add three more options that are available to you in your local community.

MACMILLAN LIFE SKILLS

12 Writing Extra

INQUIRY EMAILS

1 2.69 **Listen to a conversation between two friends. What is Kelly interested in doing? What suggestion does Laura have?**

2 **Read the inquiry email Kelly sent to the animal shelter to find out more information. What impression do you think the email made when the animal shelter staff received it?**

To: contact@greenfieldshelter.org
Subject: hello!

Hi guys,
I was talking to my friend the other day and she thought you could use my help with the dogs. Do you ever get volunteers? I love dogs, so I thought we'd be a great fit. Anyways, send me an email when you get a chance and let me know when I can start working with you. I just need to know where you are exactly and what kind of stuff I'd be doing. About that, I should probably tell you - walking and feeding dogs is great, but I'm really not into giving them baths or anything like that.
See you soon!

Read the email again. What were the three main mistakes Kelly made?

3 **Look at this alternative email. What impression would this email give to the animal shelter staff? Why?**

To: contact@greenfieldshelter.org
Subject: Inquiry about volunteering

Dear Greenfield Animal Shelter,
My name is Kelly Urbina and I am writing to inquire about the possibility of volunteering with your organization. I am an avid dog lover with two of my own and a long-time resident of Greenfield. At present, I am eager to help other dogs in our local community and I would appreciate it if you could let me know if you are currently accepting volunteers. If you are, any information you have about the typical duties and schedules would be very helpful. I am available to talk at your convenience and I look forward to potentially meeting your staff in the near future.
Kind regards,

Kelly

Read the email again. Underline the passages where Kelly says:

a the reason I am contacting you is
b can you please tell me
c whenever is a good time for you
d I am excited about the chance of

4 **Look at an advertisement posted in the local library. What kind of person might respond to this ad? Is this something you would be interested in?**

TUTORS WANTED!

Currently, we are looking for tutors to take part in our after-school mentorship program. Our mission is to strengthen the community by connecting teenagers and volunteers, helping the youth achieve their academic goals. If you have expertise in a high-school subject, please email us to find out more about this exciting opportunity.

CONTACT: TUTORS@AIO.COM OR 17 5467 89000

5 **Work with a partner. Discuss what information about the program you would like and respond to the email.**

6 **Read through your email and make sure you have addressed the following points.**

- introduced yourself and why you are writing
- briefly described why you are interested in tutoring and are a suitable candidate
- asked questions to find out more information about the program
- described how you can be contacted

Review D

▶ Grammar Extra pages 151–153

GRAMMAR

1 Underline the correct alternative.

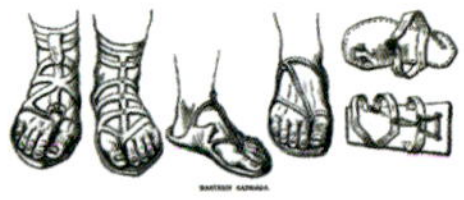

The first shoes worn by humans were a type of sandal. Sandals (1) **wore / were worn** in most early civilizations. The oldest sandals (2) **found / were found** in the south-west of the USA. These sandals (3) **date / are dated** back approximately 8,000 years. A few early cultures also (4) **had / were had** shoes. In Mesopotamia, more than 3,000 years ago, a type of soft shoe (5) **used / was used** by the mountain people who (6) **lived / were lived** on the border of Iran. The soft shoe (7) **made / was made** of wraparound leather, similar to a moccasin. Until relatively recently no difference (8) **existed / was existed** between left and right shoes.

2 **Write the reduced passive clauses in bold as full relative clauses.**

a These highly practical and resistant shoes, **designed originally for use on boats**, are now the number one preferred beachwear for all ages.

b This type of shoe, **supposedly made to be worn on the beach**, is now seen everywhere.

c This sturdy footwear, **previously seen mainly on fishermen or farmers**, has now become the height of fashion.

Match the sentences above with the pictures (1–3).

1

2

3

3 **Work with a partner. Write sentences comparing the shoes in the pictures in Exercise 2 with the ones you are wearing now. Use all the comparative structures in the box at least once.**

a little more | by far | considerably | infinitely | nothing like | nowhere near as | somewhat | slightly

4 **Make the article as short as possible by replacing or dropping any unnecessary words and phrases.**

Crowdsourcing: what is crowdsourcing? Who takes part in crowdsourcing? Well, everyone and anyone can take part. Everyone and anyone taking part in crowdsourcing is part of the basic concept. The term "crowdsourcing" was first used in 2006. The term describes a process by which a company broadcasts a business problem online and issues an open call for solutions. These solutions come from any person and every person who is online. The crowd offers solutions to the problem which was broadcast by the company, and they also sort through the solutions and find the best solutions. And the company doesn't have to pay a penny for the service!

5 **Work with your partner. Write the verbs in parentheses in the appropriate form.**

a I'd _____ (prefer) that you didn't tell anyone.

b It's about time you _____ (face) your responsibilities.

c I'd rather _____ (tell) him myself.

d If I _____ (not/know) you so well, I'd think you were hiding something from me.

e If only he _____ (know) how she felt about him.

Look at the sentences again. Who do you think is talking, and who are they talking to? What do you imagine the situation is?

VOCABULARY

1 **Work with a partner. Complete each sentence with a word from the box. More than one answer is possible at times.**

energy-efficient locally grown
organic recycled renewable
solar-powered sustainable

a All official forms are printed on ______ paper whenever possible.
b The local restaurants often offer ______ meat on their menus.
c There's a lot of ______ produce available in stores.
d Our building has ______ hot water.
e The county has started an initiative to help householders buy ______ kitchen appliances.
f The senator is a strong believer in ______ agriculture.
g The government is investing money in creating reliable ______ energy sources.

Are any of these statements true for your country?

2 **Match the expressions in the box with the definitions.**

be waited on hand and foot
get a foot in the door get cold feet
have itchy feet put your foot down
put your foot in your mouth
put your feet up shoot yourself in the foot

a accidentally annoy or embarrass someone
b sit down and relax
c firmly refuse to do something
d say or do something stupid that gets you into trouble
e get a chance to start working somewhere
f have everything done for you
g want to travel or make a change in your life
h suddenly feel uncertain about a plan

Have any of these things happened to you recently? Tell your partner about it.

3 **Complete the expressions in the text.**

Not everyone suffers during a credit (1) c______. In fact, some companies have found their profits soaring in the so-called lipstick (2) e______, where people are spending money on affordable treats instead of indulging in conspicuous (3) c______.
The art of writing seems to have made a comeback, albeit in the shape of (4) l______ casting and (5) m______blogging. Everyone can be a writer now, publishing their thoughts and deeds in (6) s______ updates on any number of social networks.
I'm completely fed up with this (7) a______-on, (8) a______-connected lifestyle. I'm sorely tempted to turn everything off, indulge in a bit of (9) d______ down time, and try to readjust my (10) joy to s______ ratio!

4 **Match the two halves of the sentences.**

a He traveled abroad to pursue
b After many long years she was finally reunited
c She worked hard to address
d Winning such a prestigious prize certainly helped boost
e He worked for years in badly paid jobs before he secured

1 a career in acting.
2 her confidence and self-esteem.
3 her drug problem and eventually overcame it.
4 his first professional movie role.
5 with her family.

PRONUNCIATION

1 **Say the words and add them to the table.**

conspicuous development emissions
energy facetious feminine flirtatious
honestly information misconstruing
punctuation renewable repetition
settlement stilettos sustainable

A: □□□	B: □□□	C: □□□□	D: □□□□
		conspicuous	

2 **Underline the stressed syllables.**

2.70 **Listen, check, and repeat.**

Additional Material

Unit 1 Speaking & Listening (page 12)

Read the information and act out a telephone conversation.

Group A

Suzi

Last night, you and your boyfriend decided to go to the movie theater tonight to see a movie you both really wanted to see. Tonight is the last night it's showing. He's already canceled once because of work. You're not too sure about your relationship right now. You think there must be something worrying him, but he refuses to talk about it. You're going to call your boyfriend to make arrangements to meet up. Think about what you're going to say to him and the language you're going to use.

Group B

Brian

You and your girlfriend had talked about going to see a movie tonight, but you've been having a hard time at work lately and you just want to stay home alone. You and your girlfriend can go out another time when you're not so tired. It's not that you don't want to see her, it's just that you know you wouldn't be good company tonight. Your girlfriend will be calling you soon. Think about what you're going to say to her and the language you're going to use.

Unit 2 Speaking (page 18)

Answers

a refried beans: Max
b cauliflower: Julia
c a bar of dark chocolate: Janet
d nuts: Brad

Unit 2 Listening (page 24)

Anne: Thailand
Kim: Japan
Bill: Hungary
Steve: Mexico

Unit 2 Reading (page 20)

Group B

Read text B and make notes about what changed in terms of ...

a the interior of the restaurant.
b the staff and customers.
c the menu and food.

TEXT B

I entered with trepidation. Whereas the ambience before had exuded class and sophistication, the new décor screamed poor taste. Paper tablecloths hid plastic tables, Christmas lights were strung from the ceiling, and in the corner had been set up a makeshift DJ booth. There were certainly more people, mostly young tourists by the look of it, at ease in the scruffy hostel-like atmosphere. I made my way to the counter where a young woman was taking orders and chatting to customers.

She must have noticed that I seemed uneasy, and asked if I'd been here before. I explained that I had, but many years prior, and was surprised by the difference. She laughed kindly and agreed that the restaurant had changed, in large part due to the internet and young backpacking tourists. They hadn't been able to keep up with competitors and decided to change tack. It turns out she was the daughter of the previous owner and still remembered the 'old days' as she called them, much to my chagrin.

By this point I was starving, so decided to stay for the meal. I asked if I could eat on the same balcony, but it was no longer open to the public. So I selected what seemed like the quietest corner and perused the menu. Gone was the gourmet Cuban cuisine, replaced with a selection of 'international' favorites you could find at most American diners. I opted for the Cubano sandwich, plantain chips, and a lemonade – the most Cuban items I could find on the menu. I won't describe it in much detail here as it really was unremarkable – fine for what it was, but certainly not worth the pounding headache ringing in my ears.

I decided to skip the dessert and went to pay the bill, shocked to find that the cost was more than my entire feast on my last visit. Luckily, they now take credit cards, so I could at least cover the bill. I quickly thanked my host and made a hurried exit to find a cab. Sitting in the back seat on the ride home, I felt a deep sense of nostalgia; I wondered if it was just me getting old, or whether truly unique dining experiences were vanishing in this age of online connectivity.

Unit 2 Vocabulary (page 21)

Group B

Students from Group B: prepare to teach four of the words and expressions in the box from your part of the review to a student from Group A.

trepidation exuded décor scruffy keep up with change tack chagrin nostalgia

a Read text B again and find the words.
b Discuss their meanings with your partner. Think about the best way to explain them.

Unit 3 Grammar (page 29)

Cities Are Top Choice

According to a survey published in the press today, it would appear that most people under the age of thirty would much prefer to live in a large city if given the choice. By far the most important factor given in their answers would seem to be the fact that it is far easier to find work in larger cities. However, the results show that there is no doubt that the range of leisure facilities is also an important factor in the decision to leave families and homes in rural areas.

Unit 3 Reading (page 31)

The texts describe four cities from the following list: Bangkok, Buenos Aires, Cape Town, Doha, Edinburgh, London, Madrid, New York, Prague, Tokyo.

Unit 3 Reading & Vocabulary (page 34)

Student A

1 **Below are four words from the article. Check their meanings in a dictionary if necessary and explain the words to your partner. Your partner must listen and identify the words from the article.**
a throngs b vie c marquee d converge

2 **When you are finished, listen to your partner's description of four more words from the article and identify the words being described.**

Unit 4 Vocabulary (page 43)

An Urban Myth

The Flat Tire

Two college friends decided to go skiing for the weekend, but planned to be back on campus in time to study for an important test on Monday morning. However, they were having such a good time on the slopes that they knew that they would have to come up with a good excuse for not being prepared for the test. Therefore, they decided to tell their professor that they had set off with plenty of time to get back and do some studying, but that they had gotten a flat tire on the way back and therefore deserved to take the test at a rescheduled time.

When he heard the story, the professor agreed that it really was just bad luck, and suggested that they took a few days to study and take the test at the end of the week. The students, of course, were delighted. At the appointed time, the professor greeted them and placed them in two separate rooms to take the test.

The few questions on the first page were worth only 10% of the overall grade and were very easy. Each student grew progressively more confident as they worked their way through the questions, sure that they had gotten away with fooling their professor. However, when they turned to the second page, they discovered that really they hadn't. The only question on the page, worth 90% of the test, read: "Which tire?"

Unit 3 Reading & Vocabulary (page 34)

Student B

1 **Below are four words from the article. Check their meanings in a dictionary if necessary, and explain the words to your partner. Your partner must listen and identify the words from the article.**
a traverse b encompass c mimic d jam-packed

2 **Your partner will explain four more words from the article. You must listen and identify the words being described. When your partner is finished, explain your four words for your partner to identify.**

Unit 4 Listening & Speaking (page 47)

Student A

Joke 1

A man's walking down the street and he sees this other guy with a big dog, and he says to him, "Does your dog bite?"

The man with the dog says, "No, my dog doesn't bite." So the man pats the dog and gets his hand bitten off.

"I thought you said your dog didn't bite," says the first man. "That's not my dog," says the other one.

Unit 5 Reading & Vocabulary (page 50)

Mostly As

You take a careful approach to budgeting and like to keep track of your income and outgoings. You tend to live within your means, planning ahead and clearing your debts as soon as you can. You avoid overpaying for your purchases and are not waylaid by special offers - but equally you do allow yourself to indulge in the occasional treat or extravagance.

Mostly Bs

Your approach to spending is frugal in the extreme, and you economize and cut corners where you can - your friends might even accuse you of being tight-fisted. You have an eye for a bargain, and prefer window-shopping to the real thing. But does your thrifty attitude mean you could be missing out on friendships and the fun side of life?

Mostly Cs

You like to live life to the full regardless of the cost, and your money often burns a hole in your pocket. You are generous with your money and enjoy life's luxuries. However, your laid-back attitude towards spending and credit can land you in trouble, and you may need to take a careful look at your finances if you want to avoid always being overdrawn and in debt.

Unit 5 Language for Life (page 58)

Student A

1 You are a customer at a street market. You see a jacket that you would like to buy. There is a small mark on the sleeve and one of the buttons is missing. Try to negotiate a discount - ideally 20%.

2 You would like to borrow a friend's car to take your elderly aunt, who has difficulty walking, to the airport. There are no buses or trains as it is an early flight. Try to persuade your friend to lend it.

Unit 6 Speaking (page 60)

Answers

a False: the average male brain weighs 1.4 kg and the average female brain weighs 1.3 kg.
b True
c False: 80% of the average human brain is water.
d False: the brain is pinkish-gray on the surface and white inside.
e True
f False: we use 100% of our brains in everyday life.
g True
h False: the brain is very active during sleep, but the activity is of a different type from waking activity.
i False: we yawn more when the brain is being stimulated to allow more oxygen to the brain.
j True

Unit 4 Listening & Speaking (page 47)

Student B

Joke 2

A couple is going out for the evening. They get dressed and put the cat out for the night. The taxi arrives, and as they leave the house, the cat races back in. They don't want the cat shut in the house, so the wife goes out to the taxi while the husband goes upstairs to find the cat. The wife, not wanting it known that the house will be empty, says to the taxi driver, "He's just going upstairs to say goodbye to my mother." Then the husband gets into the taxi. "Sorry I took so long," he says. "Silly thing was hiding under the bed!"

Unit 5 Language for Life (page 58)

Student B

1 You are a market trader. You are prepared to offer a very small discount for goods but only if you have to - ideally no more than 20%.
2 You have a car. The last time a friend borrowed it, it got scratched, so you would really prefer not to lend it again.

Unit 6 Reading & Speaking (page 61)

1 one point for each piece of information
2 1 point - clothes 2 points - clothes and colors 3 points - clothes, colors, shoes, and accessories
3 10
4 2 circles
5

5	0	2	2
3	3	2	1
1	3	0	5
0	3	5	1

6 fewer than five words = 0; 5-10 words = 1; 11-14 words = 2; 15 words = 5

Unit 7 Language for Life (page 80)

Student A

You boss has offered you a promotion. The job will mean longer hours and lots of traveling, but it will also mean a generous raise. You have a young family and you need the extra money, but you don't want to spend so much time away from home.

Unit 8 Listening & Grammar (page 83)

During a court case held in Barbados, a judge learned a valuable lesson about the power of the spoken word. A Barbadian man stood in the witness stand, accused of shoplifting. Defending him was a Barbadian attorney. The attorney asked the judge towards the end of the trial whether he could speak to the jury in Bajan, the main spoken language of the island. Not wishing to appear biased towards English, the judge agreed. Shortly afterwards, a verdict of not guilty was returned. What puzzled the judge was the verdict, as the defendant was obviously guilty. Not being able to speak Bajan, the judge hadn't understood what the attorney had said, which was: "The prosecutor is British, the prosecution counsel is British, the judge is British. But the prisoner is a Barbadian, I am Barbadian, and you are Barbadians. Do your duty."

Unit 8 Speaking & Listening (page 84)

Case 1
The driver was driving within the established speed limit and was not guilty of violating any driving offenses. As such, he could not be made liable for the injuries to the pedestrian. However, his car was insured against accidental injuries to third parties, and the driver's insurance company paid the pedestrian $5,000 in damages for the injuries incurred (a broken wrist and ribs). As the car was covered under a fully comprehensive insurance policy, the insurance company also paid for the damages to the car. The insurance company sought to take the child's parents to court to sue them for the damages to both car and pedestrian, but the court ruled that the parents could not be held liable for their child crossing the road, as they had done everything in their power to try to stop her.

Case 2
The court found the soccer player not guilty of deliberately seeking to injure his opponent, and although he had committed a foul, he had not premeditated an assault on his opponent. However, the club's insurance company was forced to pay damages for loss of earnings while the player was recovering from his injuries.

Unit 9 Reading & Speaking (page 92)

Mostly As
You are definitely an early bird, or a morning person. You are alert and at your peak first thing in the morning, and go steadily downhill after that. You accomplish your best work in the morning, so try to do important tasks then and leave the afternoon and evening for winding down and relaxing.

Mostly Bs
Like most people, you are neither a night owl nor an early bird, but somewhere in-between. This means you can fit in with most schedules and can accommodate the occasional early morning or late night with little disruption to your body clock.

Mostly Cs
You are definitely a night owl, or an evening person. You tend to spend the first part of the day waking up and really come to life in the evening. Getting up and fitting in with most work schedules can be a challenge, but you are able to enjoy and make the most of all the available nightlife.

Unit 10 Grammar (page 107)

Student A

Read the information about a historic site under threat. Write a brief report using passive structures, answering these questions: a) What is the problem? b) What is being done? c) What has been done? d) What should be done in the future?

Lascaux caves, Dordogne, France
Bacterial and fungal infection threaten prehistoric paintings. Caves now closed to tourists. Authorities monitoring the situation. Preserving the paintings is necessary.

Unit 7 Language for Life (page 80)

Student B

Your neighbor has invited you to go on vacation with his family to the Caribbean for a month. He will pay all your expenses, but he has five small children and you will be expected to help take care of them. You'd love to go to the Caribbean, but you're worried you may end up being stuck with the kids all day.

Unit 10 Grammar (page 107)

Student B

Read the information about a historic site under threat. Write a brief report using passive structures, answering these questions:

a What is the problem?
b What is being done?
c What has been done?
d What should be done in the future?

Wadi Mathendous rock art, Libya

Tourism and vibrations from oil-drilling threaten ancient cliff carvings. Prehistoric people drew animals and other symbols on the dry river bed. Tourists climb on the rocks, defacing the pictures. The oil-drilling must stop.

Unit 12 Reading (page 127)

Text B

Homelessness and Unemployment

In one of the world's richest nations, the United States, the problem of homelessness is an all-too-real problem. As of 2016 …

- over 500,000 people are homeless, living on the streets, in cars, or in shelters.
- more than 200,000 homeless people are in families, including young children.
- the unemployment rate in the US is around 5%, but often one job is not enough to afford a place to live.
- approximately 50,000 homeless people are veterans.
- 50% percent of the homeless population is over the age of 50.

Tackling this situation head-on are organizations like *Look the Part*, *JobReady*, and *First Impressions*, who are taking concrete steps to help low-income Americans find employment. Through donations from the public, businesses, and manufacturers, these NPOs gather business attire which can help the needy who are interviewing for jobs.

In addition, other complementary work-readiness training and services are offered, for example image consultancy, interview coaching, and life-skills coaching. Often, the real issue is not simply a matter of nicer clothing, but is rooted in struggles with self-esteem, confidence, and a lack of job training. The ultimate goal, then, is not a quick fix donation of a few shirts and ties, but rather, to support hard-working individuals to become self-sufficient. Currently, thanks in part to social media and celebrity endorsements, the visibility of these organizations has been on the rise. For *JobReady*, a former NFL quarterback donated his own suits, and for *Career Gear*, a popular actress even helped one young man choose his new suit.

Unit 12 Reading & Speaking (page 130)

Mostly As

You're the very definition of a conscious shopper! You care about the quality of products and how your purchasing affects the world. Some people might think you're too picky, but you are happy with your guilt-free shopping.

Mostly Bs

You really are pragmatic! You find a balance between your own needs and comfort, and trying to shop ethically. You won't please everyone this way, but you keep an open mind and you're doing your best.

Mostly Cs

You're a real shopper and proud of it! You also care deeply about your family and friends. Critics say you need to think more about the big picture when you shop, but you're just trying to enjoy all the pleasures that life has to offer.

Unit 12 Life Skills (page 132)

Social responsibility: Social responsibility is the idea that everyone, individuals as well as businesses, have an obligation to act in a way that benefits society and not just themselves.

Grammar Extra

Unit 1 Position of adverbials. Aspect

Part 1: Position of adverbials

An adverbial can be a word (*sometimes*, *actually*) or a phrase (*in due course*, *on TV*). Adverbials are generally used to provide additional information about a verb, an adjective, or the sentence as a whole.

Adverbs of frequency are usually used between the auxiliary verb (when there is one) and the main verb: *We don't **always** make up after a fight*.

Adverbs which express possibility and probability are normally used between the auxiliary and the main verb in the affirmative: *We'll **probably** see you tomorrow*. But they are often positioned before the auxiliary in the negative: *We **probably** won't see you tomorrow*.

Adverbs of manner and **indefinite time** can also be used between the auxiliary and main verbs: *We **quickly** finished our lunch*. / *We'll **finally** meet the deadline!*

Adverbs such as *apparently*, *presumably*, *frankly*, which comment on the sentence as a whole, usually go at the beginning of the sentence: ***Frankly**, I've had enough of the situation*. But they can also be used at the end: *I've had enough of the situation, **frankly***.

Changes in position and meaning: most adverbials are very flexible and can be used in any of the three positions. However, sometimes a change in position can change the meaning of a sentence: *Maria **only** speaks Spanish*. (she doesn't speak any other languages) as opposed to ***Only** Maria speaks Spanish*. (nobody else speaks Spanish)

▶ **Now do Exercise 1.**

Part 2: Aspect

The perfect aspect

Perfect verb forms are used to look back at an action, or series of actions, that took place (or will take place) before a given point in time: ***He hasn't spoken** to her for three days*.

The progressive aspect

Progressive forms are used to describe an action, or series of actions, in progress at (or around) a given point in time: ***She was attending** an important meeting when I called, so I couldn't talk to her*.

The perfect progressive aspect

The two aspects can be combined to form perfect progressive forms. Perfect progressive forms generally emphasize the length of time an action has been in progress, or the fact that it has only recently stopped. ***He'd been waiting** a long time and he was getting very frustrated. Wasn't anybody going to help him?*

▶ **Now do Exercise 2.**

Unit 2 Noun phrases. Describing nouns and order of adjectives. Fronting

Part 1: Noun phrases. Describing nouns and order of adjectives

In addition to the noun, a noun phrase may contain a determiner and extra details describing the noun:

Determiner	Pre-modification	Head	Post-modification
articles possessive adjectives quantifiers, etc.	adjectives nouns compound nouns	main noun	prepositional phrases relative clauses reduced relative clauses
A cup of *The*	*black espresso* *Lebanese*	*coffee* *restaurant*	*with two or three sugars.* *your cousin recommended.*

When there are two or more adjectives before the noun, they usually follow a certain pattern. Opinion adjectives always come before adjectives that describe facts. Other adjectives follow the order below.

size	other qualities	age	shape, pattern, color	origin	material	type

For example, *delicious fresh black Italian espresso coffee*

▶ **Now do Exercise 1.**

Part 2: Fronting

Fronting = to start a sentence with something other than the subject and the verb. Fronting is often used in journalism and literature for dramatic effect or emphasis: ***Here comes** John ...*

Inversion: when you bring an object, complement, or adverb to the beginning of the sentence, you often reverse the order of the subject and the verb: *Damien **was his name***.

Fronting questions: when you front a reported question there is no inversion: *What they were doing there, we did not know*. The fronted question follows the normal word order pattern for indirect questions (question word, subject, verb): *Why he had come, I could only guess*. Notice the use of the comma after the fronted question.

▶ **Now do Exercise 2.**

Unit 1 Exercises

1 **Put the phrases in the correct order to form sentences. More than one order is possible. Choose the one you think sounds most natural.**

a I / watch TV / always / before going to bed / for half an hour
b I / worked late / last week / every night / at the office
c I / love reading a good book / more than anything else / frankly
d I / won't do anything special / probably / tonight
e I / wish I had more time / on weekends / sometimes / to do fun things
f I / dislike loud music / particularly / in public places
g I'll / have time / to play more sports / probably / once I finish my exams
h I / know I / I'm / eat / in a hurry / always / too quickly / but

Are these sentences true for you? If not, change them so that they are. Then compare your sentences with a partner.

2 **Complete the short conversations with the correct form of the verb in parentheses.**

a A: Where ______ (1 you/be)? I______ (2 wait) here for hours!
B: Don't exaggerate! I bet you ______ (3 just/arrive). Jack said he talked to you half an hour ago and that you ______ (4 just/get) off the bus!

b A: How long ______ (5 you/live) in this apartment? It ______ (6 must/be) a long time.
B: Yes, this time next week, we ______ (7 be) here for five years.
A: And when ______ (8 you/move) out?
B: At the end of the month. We ______ (9 move) into the new apartment on July 1. We'll be sad to go.

Practice reading the exchanges with your partner.

Unit 2 Exercises

1 **Write the sentences in the correct order.**

a rust / bike / A / old / covered / in / battered
b great / soundtrack / thriller / An / with / a / action-packed
c a / man / story / no / home / with / about / A / moving
d high-heeled / wear / black / to / work / I / A / shoes / pair / of
e world / sandwich / bar / coffee / best / Italian / An / the / that / espresso / makes / in / the
f Asian / dishes / new / serving / a / restaurant / range / seafood / of / A / wide

Now write three complex noun phrases describing a) one of your favorite possessions, b) a book or movie you've enjoyed, or c) a place where you've eaten recently.

Compare your sentences with your partner. Do you have similar tastes?

2 **Rewrite the sentences starting with the words in bold.**

a The curtains came **down** on her last act.
____

b Her long blond locks were **gone**.
____

c There was a special light **in** her eyes.
____

d Her youthful beauty was **still** intact.
____

e Applause rang **loudly** through the theater.
____

f There was **nobody else** on the stage with her as she took her last bow.
____

g Nobody knew **what** would become of her now.
____

Look at the sentences again. They all come from the same text. What kind of text is it? What is the event being described in the text?

Unit 3 Hedging. Inversion after negative and limiting adverbials

Part 1: Hedging

Hedging = to avoid answering a question or making a statement, in a direct way. You can use a range of expressions to do this:

- **Verbs**
  Use verbs such as *seem*, *appear*, *suggest*.
  *It **appears** that people are happier in the city.*
  To further distance yourself from the answer or statement, use *would*.
  *It **would** appear that people are happier in the city.*
- **Passive**
  Use the passive with verbs such as *think*, *recognize*, *believe*, *report*, and *know* to show that an opinion is not necessarily your own.
  *It is widely **recognized** that ... It has been **reported** that ...*
- **Noun phrases**
  Use noun phrases to explain your attitude towards the reliability of a statement.
  Strong evidence: *there is little/no doubt, there is little/no discussion*
  Fairly strong evidence: *there is some evidence / there is some discussion / there is some doubt*
  Unreliable statement: *there is little/no evidence*

▶ **Now do Exercise 1.**

Part 2: Inversion after negative and limiting adverbials

Sometimes a negative or limiting adverbial is placed at the beginning of a sentence to create emphasis.
This effect is most frequently found in writing and is considered both formal and literary.

Negative adverbials

Adverbial phrases which contain words such as *no*, *not*, *never*, *no sooner*, *not until*, *never before*

Limiting adverbials

Adverbials such as *seldom*, *rarely*, *hardly*, *barely*, *little*, or adverbial phrases that contain the word *only*:
***only after** I had taken the test, **only** by bribing the officer ...*

Inversion

When these adverbials are used at the beginning of a sentence, the subject and auxiliary verb are inverted: *Never **have I** seen anything quite so breathtaking*. The same happens with the verb *be*: *Not only **is it** one of the oldest cities, it is also one of the most beautiful*. In the simple present and simple past, use *do/does* or *did*. *Rarely **do** we visit that part of town.*

▶ **Now do Exercise 2.**

Unit 4 The future as seen from the past. Discourse markers in writing

Part 1: The future as seen from the past

You can use a range of structures and expressions to talk about the future as seen from the past. You can talk about:

- **events that took place** using *would*, or *was/were to*: *Who could have guessed that he'**d** become President one day? / Those **were to** become the happiest years of his life.*
- **events that did not take place** using *was/were* + perfect infinitive: *They **were to** have gone to Mexico, but they had to change their plans at the last minute.*
- **future plans in the past** using *was/were going to*, *was/were planning to*, *had been hoping to*, *had been thinking of*: *He **had been hoping to** go to college, but he failed all his exams.*
- **imminent events in the past** using *was/were due to*/*(just) about to*, *on the point/verge of*: *I **was about to** leave. / He **was on the point** / **verge** of giving up.*

▶ **Now do Exercise 1.**

Part 2: Discourse markers in writing

You use discourse markers to show how ideas relate to each other and to show our attitude towards those ideas.
*I love silly jokes, **particularly** those involving slapstick, **such as** pies in faces.*
Here are some common uses with examples of common discourse markers:

- giving examples: *for example*, *for instance*, *e.g.*, *say*, *such as*, *including*
- emphasizing one example: *in particular*, *particularly*
- specifying who or what exactly you're talking about: *namely*, *viz.*, *i.e.*
- clarifying what you want to say: *that is to say*, *in other words*, *strictly speaking*, *to put it another way*
- adding information: *too*, *in addition*, *not to say*, *as well as*, *moreover*
- qualifying a statement: *or at any rate*, *or even*, *or at least*
- contrasting two things or ideas: *on the other hand*, *by contrast*, *however*, *nevertheless*
- emphasizing a similarity: *likewise*, *similarly*
- introducing a question: *so*, *then* (when word position changes).

Notes

Too, when used as a discourse marker, is never used at the beginning of a sentence.

▶ **Now do Exercise 2.**

Unit 3 Exercises

1 **Underline the most appropriate alternative, in your opinion.**

a **It is widely agreed / There is little evidence to show** that younger people prefer to live in cities.

b **There is no doubt / It would seem** that there are better job opportunities in large cities.

c **It is generally recognized that / There is some discussion about whether** small communities offer better services to senior citizens.

d **Research suggests that / There is some doubt about whether** most people would prefer to work from home rather than travel to an office every day.

e **It has been reported / It is not believed** that most young graduates would be happy to move abroad to find work.

f **There is no doubt / Some experts suggest** that the future of work lies with the internet.

Compare your answers with a partner. Do you agree? Why? / Why not?

2 **There is one mistake in each sentence. Find and correct the mistakes.**

a Never before I had felt so happy.

b Not until had we reached the top did we realize how far we had come.

c Only once the show was over we could relax and enjoy ourselves.

d Only after some years I understood how important that experience had been for me.

e Not only did I want to do it again, did I want to do it as soon as possible!

f Barely had I arrived when happened the strangest thing.

Look at the sentences again. Choose two of them that relate to an experience you have had in your life. Tell your partner about the experience.

Unit 4 Exercises

1 **Match the sentence beginnings (a-f) with the sentence endings (1-6).**

a I was about to go out

b We all knew that

c He had planned to

d She was to have left today, but

e They weren't going to go, but

f They started out as a small-town band, but

1 would go on to become one of the best musical groups of all time.

2 then we managed to persuade them.

3 she decided to extend her stay.

4 retire to the country.

5 he wouldn't be coming back.

6 when the telephone rang.

Underline all the verb forms that refer to the future as seen from the past. Rewrite the sentences using an alternative form.

2 **Complete the sentences using the discourse markers in the box. You do not need to use all the discourse markers.**

in addition	including	in particular	not to say	or at least	so	that is to say

a The class provides an introduction to Spanish culture, and ______ to flamenco and Spanish guitar music.

b The show was based on old-fashioned slapstick humor, ______ , people falling over and throwing pies in each other's faces.

c The show went on for far too long, ______ that seemed to be the general feeling among the audience.

d I thought his jokes were very macho, ______ sexist, and generally in very bad taste.

e The story was weak and the animation was dated. ______ why was it such a success?

f There were a number of guest stars, ______ sports stars and TV celebrities, who all drew a loud cheer from the audience.

Think of a show, live or on TV, that you have seen recently. Write a very brief review describing the show and your general opinion of it. Use some of the discourse markers in the grammar reference section.

Unit 5 Prepositions in relative clauses. Articles

Part 1: Prepositions in relative clauses

Prepositions in defining relative clauses

Prepositions normally come at the end of a defining relative clause in informal written and spoken styles: *The woman that/who you were talking* ***to***.

In more formal styles they come before the relative pronoun. *Who* is replaced by *whom*. Do not use *that* after a preposition.

⚠ *The woman* ***to*** *whom you were talking.* (NOT ~~*The woman* ***to that*** *you were talking.*~~)

Of **in non-defining relative clauses**

You can modify the relative pronoun in non-defining relative clauses using quantifiers and determiners such as *many*, *all*, *most* + *of*. When talking about people, the relative pronoun *who* changes to *whom*: *The audience,* ***many of whom*** *had seen the movie before, all stood up and applauded.*

The relative pronoun *which* stays the same: *He offered me a pile of books, many of* ***which*** *were battered and torn.*

Remember that you cannot use the relative pronoun *that* in non-defining relative clauses:

⚠ NOT ~~*He offered me a pile of books,* ***many of that*** *were battered and torn.*~~

▶ **Now do Exercise 1.**

Part 2: Articles

a/an, some, the**: general rules of use**

If something is unknown to the speaker, the listener, or both, use *a/an*, *some*, or no article. Use *a/an* with singular countable nouns.

Use *some* or no article with uncountable nouns and plural countable nouns: *I need (****some****) accommodations, for example a room in an apartment with (****some****) students.*

If something is known to both the speaker and listener, use *the*: ***The*** *apartment I saw yesterday was really nice.*

If you are talking about something in general terms, use *a/an*, *some*, or no article: *I love spaghetti.* If you are talking about a specific person or thing, use *the*: *I loved* ***the*** *spaghetti we had last night.* When there is only one, use *the*: ***the*** *world,* ***the*** *North,* ***the*** *economy*

Definite article *the*: some special cases:

- use with an adjective to talk about a group of people: ***the*** *rich,* ***the*** *British*
- use with household chores: ***the*** *cooking,* ***the*** *cleaning,* ***the*** *shopping*

No article: do not use *the*:

- to talk about meals as part of a routine: *What do you have for breakfast?*
- to talk about transportation with *by*: *I usually go* ***by*** *car.*
- with *last* or *next* in time expressions referring to the immediate past or future: *I slept well last night.*
- with points of the compass used as adverbs: *He traveled north.*

▶ **Now do Exercise 2.**

Unit 6 Verbs of the senses. Participle clauses

Part 1: Verbs of the senses

You can talk about your senses in two ways:

- to refer to abilities or sensations (stative)
- to refer to voluntary actions (dynamic)

These verbs can be used with both a stative and a dynamic meaning: *see, hear, feel, sense, smell, taste, look.* These verbs are always dynamic: *listen, touch.*

can, could, **and** ***be able to***

Stative verbs of the senses are often used with *can, could,* or *be able to*: *I would love* ***to be able to hear*** *as well as I* ***could*** *when I was younger.*

Progressive forms

⚠ Verbs of the senses with stative meanings are not usually used in progressive forms. *I can see the car over there.* (NOT ~~***I'm seeing*** *the car over there.*~~)

Meaning changes

When you use *see, hear, feel, sense, smell,* or *taste* in progressive forms, the meaning often changes: *I can't see that sign very well. What does it say?* (see referring to the sight) *I'm seeing the doctor tomorrow about my back.* (see = meet) *I think I can taste salt in this.* (*taste* referring to sense of taste) *They're tasting the dessert to see if they like it.* (*taste* = test)

Progressive forms can also be used to talk about temporary states: *I'm feeling good. / I'm hearing the music.*

▶ **Now do Exercise 1.**

Part 2: Participle clauses

Participle clauses do not include a subject. They are used to avoid repetition and shorten complex sentences. They are commonly found in written texts such as reports and essays.

Present participle clauses

The present participle substitutes for the subject and a different form of the verb:
Because he was a little shy ... ➜ *Being a litte shy ...*

Past participle clauses

The past participle is substituted for the subject and the verb *be*:
James was woken by a noise, so he ... ➜ *Woken by a noise, James ...*

Perfect participle clauses

The perfect participle substitutes for the subject and a verb in a perfect form:
Because she hadn't understood the question, ... ➜ *Not having understood the question, ...*

Position of ***not***

Not always comes at the beginning of the participle clause: ***Not*** *knowing what else to do, I called the police.*

▶ **Now do Exercise 2.**

Unit 5 Exercises

1 Add the prepositions in parentheses to the sentences.

- **a** Is that the book you were telling me yesterday? (about)
- **b** Who was that strange person that you were talking on the bus? (to)
- **c** What's the name of that restaurant that we went with Rob? (to)
- **d** I have lots of pretty dresses, many which I rarely wear. (of)
- **e** This is the woman whom I work. (with)
- **f** I spoke to a number of different people, many whom I had never met before. (of)

Which three sentences or questions are more formal in style? Rewrite these sentences in a more informal style.

2 Complete the sentences with *a*, *some*, *the*, or – (no article).

- **a** I usually do ______ grocery shopping on my way home from ______ work.
- **b** I go to ______ small store around ______ corner from my house.
- **c** I buy ______ fresh fruit and vegetables and ______ bread.
- **d** On Saturdays, in ______ morning, I go to ______ farmers market in ______ town square.
- **e** There's ______ great fish stall there and I usually buy ______ fish and ______ shellfish. Not too much. I'm usually only cooking for one!
- **f** If I have ______ guests coming over for ______ dinner, I'll buy ______ soda and spend ______ money on something special at ______ bakery.
- **g** I love ______ shopping for ______ food. It's much more fun than ______ shopping for ______ clothes.
- **h** Of course, I still love going to ______ mall with ______ friend to do ______ window-shopping.

Do you feel the same about food shopping? Compare your ideas with a partner.

Unit 6 Exercises

1 Underline the correct alternative. In one sentence both options are possible.

- **a** I think my eyesight is failing. **I can't see** / **I'm not seeing** as well as I used to.
- **b** A: **Can I hear** / **Am I hearing** things, or is there a pig in your bathroom?
  B: No! It's the fan. It makes a strange noise.
- **c** Hey, Greg, **can you taste** / **are you tasting** this for me? I'm not sure if I need to add more salt.
- **d** I sat in the backyard **hearing** / **listening to** the birds singing in the trees.
- **e** Are you on YouTube™? What are you **seeing** / **watching**? Anything interesting?
- **f** We used to live above a café. We **could always smell** / **were always smelling** fresh bread and coffee in the morning. Delicious!
- **g** I **could hear** / **'ve heard** some strange things about the new boss. Are they true?
- **h** I don't know what it is between those two, but I **can sense** / **'m sensing** a lot of tension.

Work with your partner. Compare your answers. Explain why you chose each option.

2 Look at the transformations. There's a mistake in each one. Find the mistake and correct it.

- **a** Because I'm so shy, I hate going to parties where I don't know anybody.
  Because being shy, I hate going to parties where I don't know anybody.
- **b** Now that I've finished college, I'm looking for a job.
  Finishing college, I'm now looking for a job.
- **c** I was impressed by the publicity, so I signed up for this course.
  Impressing by the publicity, I signed up for this course.
- **d** I was brought up to be independent, so I hate having to follow orders.
  Having brought up to be independent, I hate having to follow orders.
- **e** I find it difficult to understand grammar, so I make lots of mistakes.
  Finding difficult to understand grammar, I make lots of mistakes.

Are any of these sentences true for you? Compare your answers with your partner.

Unit 7 Complex sentences. Speculating about the future

Part 1: Complex sentences

Simple sentences only contain one clause: *I called Tom.*

A complex sentence contains two or more clauses: (1) *I called Tom* (2) *because I was bored.* (1) *Feeling bored,* (2) *I called Tom,* (3) *who was still at work.*

Complex sentences are used to show the link between ideas and events and to avoid unnecessary repetition. The main clause describes the main or central event: *I called Tom.* A main clause is similar to a sentence; it typically contains a subject and a verb. The other clauses are subordinate clauses and add information about the main event: *Feeling bored, I called Tom, who was still at work.*

Linkers are often used to introduce subordinate clauses. *I called you **because** I wanted to talk about the project.* Relative pronouns are also used: ... *the project **that** starts next week.* Subject pronouns, auxiliaries, and main verbs can often be dropped in subordinate clauses: *I called you to talk about the new project.*

Participle clauses are often used to combine sentences and avoid repetition. They are particularly common in more formal written styles: ***Needing** to talk to someone, I picked up the telephone.*

▶ **Now do Exercise 1.**

Part 2: Speculating about the future

Modal verbs

will = you are confident that something will happen: *Time travel **will** one day be possible.*

may/might = there is a possibility, but you're not 100% sure: *Time travel **may/might** one day be possible.*

could = it's logically or physically possible, but you are not saying that it will definitely happen: *It **could** happen one day.*

should / ought to = you think it is logical/ reasonable to expect that something will happen, although there may be unforeseen setbacks: *It **should** happen fairly soon if our projections are correct.*

Adverbs with *will* and *won't*

You can use adverbs such as *certainly, almost certainly, definitely, easily, probably* with *will* and *won't* to clarify or modify your speculations: *We will **probably** have colonized the moon before the end of the century.* The adverbs usually come between *will* and the main verb but before *won't*: *We **certainly** won't have developed a way to travel through time.*

Adverbs with *may, might,* and *could*

You can use the adverbs *possibly / (very) well / easily* with *may, might,* and *could*: *Our grandchildren **may / might / could well** travel to the moon.*

Phrases: the following phrases can also be used to speculate about the future: *be sure to / bound to* = you're confident that something will happen: *They're **bound to** find a clean alternative to oil.*

be (highly) likely to/ that = you're fairly confident but not 100% sure: *It's **likely to** happen in the next twenty years.*

be (highly) unlikely to/that = you're fairly confident something will not happen: *It's **highly unlikely** that people will ever live on the moon.*

Note: use *to* + infinitive after *likely/unlikely* when the subject of the verb is the same: *We're likely **to be** late.* Use *that* when the subject is different: *It's likely **that we'll** be late.*

▶ **Now do Exercise 2.**

Unit 8 Paraphrasing. Using modals to talk about the past

Part 1: Paraphrasing

The normal word order in a sentence in English is: subject + verb + object + adverb. *They called the police at once.* However, this order is often varied to add emphasis or avoid repetition. You can change the order in a number of ways:

- Using the passive: *The police **were called** at once.* You use the passive to bring the object of an action to the beginning of the sentence.
- Using participle clauses: *They called the police as soon as they heard the bang.* ➜ ***Hearing** a bang, they called the police.* You often use participle clauses to highlight relationships of cause and effect, or the sequence of events.
- Varying the position of adverbials: ***As soon as** they heard the bang, they called the police.*
- Using cleft sentences: we use clauses with *it* or *what* + *be* to focus attention on the information that follows: ***It was** the bang that made them call the police.* ***What** made them call the police **was** the bang.*

▶ **Now do Exercise 1.**

Part 2: Using modals to talk about the past

Modal + infinitive: Use *would* to talk about (1) past habitual actions: *We **would drive** to town every Sunday.* (2) to explain that someone refused to do something: *They just **wouldn't accept** no as an answer.*

Use *could* as the past form of *can* to talk about abilities, possibilities, and permission: *I **couldn't** believe my eyes. / We **could** do whatever we liked.*

Modal + *have* + past participle: Use *should / ought to have* to suggest that a past action was not good or advisable: *You **shouldn't have signed** it.* = I don't think it was a good idea to sign it.

Use *may/might/could have* to speculate about possible past actions: *They **might have made** a mistake.* = I don't know, I'm just suggesting a possible explanation.

Use *would have* to give an opinion about past events: *They **wouldn't have said** something that rude, surely.* = I don't believe they could say something like that.

Use *couldn't have* to say that you think a past event was impossible: *He **couldn't have forgotten**.* = He never forgets appointments.

Use *must have* to say that it is sure to have happened: *He **must have got caught** in traffic.* = It's the only explanation.

⚠ Note that you don't use *can have* or *mustn't have*: *He may/might/could/must have forgotten.* ✔ (NOT ~~*He can have forgotten.*~~) *She can't have liked it.* (NOT ~~*She mustn't have liked it.*~~)

▶ **Now do Exercise 2.**

Unit 7 Exercises

1 **Combine the three simple sentences to make one complex sentence. Use the words in parentheses. Do not reuse the words that are ~~crossed out~~.**

a I needed a new phone. Someone had stolen mine. I went to the mall to buy a new one. (needing, because) ____________________

b There was a high-tech model. It had some great new features. One of the features was a built-in navigation system. (that, such as, ~~it~~)

____

c I thought about it for some time. I decided it was too expensive. I bought a simpler model. (having, so) ____________________

d I thought about it again. I realized I just needed a straightforward phone. I use my phone to make calls and send text messages. (thinking, ~~I use~~) ____________________

e I'm happy with my purchase. It's smaller and lighter. It looks really good! (because, being, ~~it's~~) ____________________

Write two complex sentences describing the last time you bought a phone or other electronic gadget.

2 **Underline the correct alternative.**

a I **may** / **won't** well have to do some work over the weekend.

b I probably **won't** / **might not** be taking another vacation until next year.

c I think I **could** / **should** be able to get this exercise done fairly quickly.

d It's highly unlikely **to be** / **that I'll be** going out tonight.

e **I'm bound to** / **It's unlikely to** get a new job before the end of the year.

f I **certainly won't** / **won't certainly** be studying English by this time next year.

Are these sentences true for you? If not, change them and then compare your new sentences with a partner.

Unit 8 Exercises

1 **Complete each sentence so that it means the same as the one above it.**

a Grammar is the most difficult aspect of learning a language.
It's ____________________ .

b Grammarians often make grammar rules appear more difficult than they really are.
Grammar rules are ____________________ .

c Grammar is best learned by using and being exposed to the language.
The best way ____________________ .

d I learned my first language through exposure, so I think it's the best way to learn a language.
Having ____________________ .

e Studying grammar rules and doing grammar exercises is a waste of time.
It's a ____________________ .

f I think it's important to study the rules of the language because it helps me learn more efficiently.
What helps me ____________________ .

Do you agree with these statements? Discuss them with your partner.

2 **Put the words in the correct order to make sentences.**

a must / He / have / forgotten / keys / his / or / something

b window / The / may / purpose / have / left / on / open / been

c climbing / out / actually / front / The / have / stuck / got / he's / door / could / and

d can't / wanted / He / do / it / have / to

e into / my / lost / keys / I / my / get / apartment / once / couldn't / and / back

f the / doormat / under / When / I / we / leave / key / young / was / would / the

Which sentences refer to the picture? Which of these sentences do you think are most probable? Can you think of any other explanations? Look at the sentences that don't refer to the picture. Are they true for you? Compare your answers with your partner.

Unit 9 Concessive clauses and adverbials. Regrets and past conditionals

Part 1: Concessive clauses and adverbials

You use concessive clauses and adverbials to contrast two situations or to show that an action or event is unexpected or surprising: *Although I slept for ten hours, I was still tired the next day.*

You can use linkers such as *even though* and *although* to introduce a concessive clause. Use a comma after the concessive clause: ***Even though*** *I had slept well, ... /* ***Although*** *I'm usually a good sleeper, ...*

You can use *even so*, *yet*, *however*, and *saying that* at the beginning of a sentence. Use a comma after the linker: *I usually sleep very well. However, last night was an exception.*

However and *though* can both be used at the end of a sentence:
I slept well. I was still tired in the morning, ***though/ however.***

Use *despite* and *in spite of* with a gerund or noun: ***Despite having*** *slept for ten hours, I was still tired. /* ***In spite of*** *the comfortable bed, I still couldn't sleep.*

You can also use adverbial phrases such as *try as I might*, *strange as it may seem*, *hard as I tried* to highlight the contrast with the main clause. Use a comma to separate the phrases from the main clause: ***Try as I might,*** *I just couldn't get to sleep.*

▶ **Now do Exercise 1.**

Part 2: Regrets and past conditionals

You can use sentences with *I wish*, *if*, and *if only* to talk about regrets: ***I wish*** */* ***If only*** *I'd said goodbye. /* ***If I'd*** *gone to the party, I'd have been able to say goodbye.*

Use the past perfect or *could have* + past participle with *wish* and *if only*:
(1) ***I wish I'd gone*** *to the party*. (2) ***I wish I could have gone*** *to the party*.
(1) *I'd gone* tells us you didn't go. (2) *I could have gone* tells us that for some reason you were unable to go.

If* and conditional sentences:** use *if* + past perfect (simple or progressive) to talk about a past situation: ***If I hadn't been working *late ... /* ***If the car hadn't broken down*** ... Use a modal (*would*, *could*, *might*, *should*, *ought to*) + *have* + past participle to describe the desired past action: ***I would/could have gone*** *to the party*. Use a modal + infinitive to talk about a desired (but impossible) present result: ***I wouldn't*** */* ***might not feel*** *so bad*.

Substituting for *if*: (1) drop *if* and invert the subject and the auxiliary verb: ***Had I*** *gone to the party ...* (2) Use *but for* with a noun (noun + gerund): ***But for the car*** *breaking down ... /* ***But for*** that last-minute job ...

Regret: whether you use *regret* + verb + *ing* or *regret* + *having* + past participle, the meaning is the same: ***I regret not going*** *to the party. /* ***I regret not having gone*** *to the party*. You can use similar structures with *I'd have liked*: ***I'd have liked*** *to go /* ***I'd have liked*** *to have gone*. The two structures mean the same.

Other phrases: *it's a pity*, *it's a shame*, *that's too bad*. With these phrases you use the simple past: *It's a pity/ shame I* ***didn't*** */* ***couldn't*** */* ***wasn't able to*** *go to the party*.

▶ **Now do Exercise 2.**

Unit 10 Passive structures. Comparative structures

Part 1: Passive structures

You use the passive: a) when you want to focus attention on the object of an action and establish the topic of a sentence; b) when the agent of the verb is not known, generic, or obvious; c) to refer back to the previous sentence in a text. Passives structures are more common in formal written styles, such as news reports. Active sentences are more common in informal speech.

Focusing attention: the subject of the passive sentence is the topic of the sentence; this is what we are talking about: ***The prehistoric ruins of Jarlshof*** *are being threatened by storms and rising sea levels*.

Unknown agent: when you do not know who performed an action, or when the agent of the action is generic and/ or obvious (for example, *people*, *the police*), a passive structure is usually used: *The settlement was built 9,000 years ago* is preferred to *People built the settlement 9,000 years ago*.

Referring back: the passive structure is often used in order to refer back to the topic at the end of the previous sentence in a text: *Experts* ***are alarmed*** *by this loss. The situation* ***is being monitored*** *by an organization called SCAPE. SCAPE* ***was set up*** *to protect ancient shoreline sites*.

▶ **Now do Exercise 1.**

Part 2: Comparative structures

Modifying comparative structures

Use these modifiers with comparative structures to show ...

- a large difference: *far*, *a lot*, *considerably*, *infinitely*, *much*, *way*: *He's* ***way*** *more intelligent than me*.
- a moderate difference: *somewhat**, *noticeably**: *a* ***noticeably*** *bigger house than ours*
  *both of these modifiers are fairly formal in style
- a small difference: *a tiny bit*, *a little*, *slightly*: *It's just* ***slightly*** *smaller than the last one*.
- no difference: *no*: *It's* ***no*** *faster than going by bus*.

Use these modifiers with structures with *as ... as ...* to show:

- a large difference: *nowhere near*, *definitely not*, *not nearly*: *He's* ***nowhere near*** *as tall as his father*.
- a small difference: *almost*, *nearly*: *She's* ***almost*** *as good as her sister*.
- no difference: *just*: *He's* ***just*** *as bad as ever*.

You can also use modifiers to intensify superlative structures: *She is* ***by far*** */* ***easily*** *the best teacher*.

▶ **Now do Exercise 2.**

Unit 9 Exercises

1 **Link the two sentences using the words and phrases given. Make any necessary changes.**

1 I'm usually a really heavy sleeper. That night every single noise and movement seemed to wake me up.
   a although
   b even so
   c despite
2 They reassured me and offered me good advice. But I was still worried about the situation and couldn't sleep a wink.
   a in spite of
   b try as I might
   c even so
3 I went to bed tired and depressed. I woke up refreshed and ready to face the day.
   a even though
   b however
   c yet

2 **Complete the sentences with an appropriate form of the verb in parentheses.**

a If only ______ (I/stay) a little longer that night, I ______ (find out) what happened to John and his friends.
b If things ______ (go) a little bit differently that day, I ______ (not be) in the mess I'm in now!
c I wish ______ (pay) more attention to my parents' advice when I ______ (be) younger.
d He wished he ______ (take part) in the competition, but his parents wouldn't let him.
e If they ______ (not/talk) to each other at the time, they ______ (hear) what the police officer said.
f ______ (I/tell) him about it sooner, he could have done something about it.
g I really regret ______ (stay) home now. It sounds like I missed a great party!
h I'd really have liked ______ (see) the movie last night. Was it good?
i It's a shame you ______ (not/meet) Laura. I think you would have liked her.

Unit 10 Exercises

1 **Read the article and rewrite the phrases in bold as passive structures. Add *by* + agent where necessary.**

First meeting imminent

(1) **Government officials were still finalizing plans** last night for the first face-to-face meeting with intelligent life from outer space. (2) **They first established contact** over three years ago, but (3) **they only made the information public** once (4) **a team of international experts had confirmed** without a shadow of a doubt that Gaters are indeed friendly.

(5) **The ETF (Earth Task Force) are issuing daily bulletins** on the state of communication with Gat, the Gaters' home planet. (6) **They have reported** that Gaters have been trying to make contact with us for over 25 years, but their messages of peace and goodwill had fallen on deaf ears.

(7) **Government officials are still to confirm the exact location and date of the meeting**, but (8) **we are expecting a visit** could take place anytime from June 27 onwards. There has been much speculation concerning the Gaters' physical appearance. However, (9) **the authorities have not released any information on this point**.

1 Plans ______ .
2 Contact ______ .
3 The information ______ .
4 It ______ .
5 Daily bulletins ______ .
6 It ______ .
7 The exact location ______ .
8 A visit ______ .
9 No information ______ .

2 **Add the words and phrases in the box to the sentences.**

as   by far   considerably   just   less   more   no   slightly

a He's more patient than I ever gave him credit for.
b There really isn't much difference between the two of them; I suppose this one is just more attractive.
c She's better than the last one, as far as I can make out. Just as pompous, just as full of herself.
d I'd say that this year's vacation was as good as last year's, wouldn't you?
e This is the worst movie I've ever seen!
f I don't know, it's no different from his other movies; just as outrageous, just violent.
g I think your job is far stressful compared to Randy's. You don't know how lucky you are!
h This novel is far challenging in terms of plot and characterization.

Unit 11 Avoiding repetition: substitution and ellipsis

Substitution

You can often substitute nouns and verbs with pronouns and possessive adjectives in order to avoid unnecessary repetition. This is equally common in writing and in speech.

Pronouns and possessive adjectives

Use pronouns such as *it, they, them, that, this* to substitute for nouns, noun phrases, and clauses:
*The castle was beautiful set against the sunset. **It** stood out clearly against the darkening sky.*
It here refers to *the castle*.

*Think about what you want to say and why you want to say **it**.*
It in this instance refers to the clause "What you want to say."

You can also use possessive adjectives to refer back to nouns and noun phrases used earlier in a text:
*Discourse markers can really help you make your writing much clearer and easier to read. But beware of **their** overuse.*
Their refers back to "discourse markers" in the previous sentence.

So

You can use *so* to substitute a verb or verb phrase:
*Do you want to improve your writing? If **so**, read these tips.*
So refers to the verb phrase "want to improve your writing."

*Many writers include anecdotes to make their writing more memorable. If you do **so** too, make sure they are short and amusing.*

So refers back to the act of including anecdotes.

Omission of words (ellipsis)

You can often drop or omit certain words in a sentence without losing the meaning of the sentence. What and how much you choose to omit depends on the context and the people you are talking or writing to. When you use ellipsis, it is important that the words you drop have either been used previously or can be understood from the context.

Main verbs

You can often avoid repeating a main verb after an auxiliary: *If you don't know what you want to say, your readers definitely won't (**know**).*
The second *know* can be dropped without losing the meaning of the sentence.

Pronouns and auxiliaries

You can drop repeated pronouns after *and* or *but*:
*Make sure you've included the right attachments and (**you**) are sending them to the right recipients.*
When the auxiliary is repeated, it too can be omitted:
*Make sure you've added a relevant subject line and (**you have**) signed off appropriately.*

Negative verb phrases

At times it is possible to omit all of the verb phrase, apart from *not*:
*I should be able to join you later. If **not**, I'll call.*
not = I can't join you later. This is understood from the context.

***To* + infinitive**

You can drop the infinitive after *to*:
*Do you do a lot of writing? I used to (**do a lot of writing**).*
*Tom asked me to go out with him tonight, but I don't want to (**go out with him tonight**).*

▶ **Now do Exercises 1 and 2.**

Unit 12 Special uses of the simple past

The simple past can sometimes be used with reference to the present or future.

In conditional sentences

You use the simple past with *if*, *I wish*, and in other conditional clauses to say that you think a present or future event is unlikely or impossible:
***If I were rich** / **If I had more time** / **I wish I could** speak Russian / **If I won** the lottery* – none of these things are true or likely to come true, therefore you use the simple past and not a present or future verb form.

In reported speech

The simple past is often used to refer to the present in reported speech.
*He said he **was** the greatest soccer player on Earth. He said he **did** it every day.*
The actions he is talking about are still true in the present, but his words are being reported in the past. In this case the present is also possible.

With *it's (about/high) time*

Use *it's (about/high) time* to say that you think something should happen now or very soon. You always use the simple past after *it's (high/about time)*:
***It's time** these kids were in bed / went to bed. / **It's about time** the politicians did something about it.*
The action is in the future, although the idea is that the action should really have happened already.

With *would rather*

Use *I'd rather* + subject + verb to explain that you don't want someone to do something, or that you're not happy with a present situation. You always use the simple past, and not a present tense, to talk about the action you don't like:
***I'd rather you didn't watch TV** when I'm eating. / **He'd rather we didn't use** his car.*
When *would rather* is not followed by a subject, you do not use the simple past. Instead you use an infinitive: *The government **would rather spend** money on health care than helping senior citizens. / **I'd rather not work** in the evenings.*

▶ **Now do Exercises 1 and 2.**

Unit 11 Exercises

1 **Look at the words in bold. Which refer to ...**

a texting?
b texting while crossing the street?

Love **(1) it** or hate **(2) it**, texting is here to stay. Some people do **(3) it** occasionally, only when **(4) it**'s completely necessary; others are totally obsessed. They **(5) do it** on the bus, as they walk down the road, even as they cross the street. **(6) This latter use** has become a hazard on the busy streets and sidewalks of some US cities, where authorities are making moves to have **(7) it** banned.

2 **Rewrite the text below avoiding the repetition of the words in bold. Use substitution and ellipsis.**

My daughter never calls her friends anymore. She prefers to text **(1) her friends**. She says that **(2) sending text messages** is quicker and easier. Not only **(3) is it quicker and easier**, she also claims that sending a text message is more efficient. She claims that there are fewer misunderstandings and arguments when she texts her friends than when she talks to **(4) her friends** on the phone. Asked why **(5) texting her friends was less problematic**, she explained that texting gave her more time to think, **(6) it gave her more time** to choose her words, and **(7) it gave her time** to change and perfect her message before she sent it. When you speak, she explained, once the words are out, you can't change **(8) the words**. You have said **(9) the words that** you have said. And you have to deal with the consequences **(10) of what you have said.**

Unit 12 Exercises

1 **Read the sentences. Change the verbs to the simple past where necessary.**

a If I have more time, I would definitely want to do voluntary work with a local charity.
b If I have enough money at the end of the month, I always give some to charity.
c The government representative explained that they have done everything in their power to ensure the early release of funds.
d A national children's charity warned that homelessness is not a problem that affects only adults.
e I think it's about time we all stop thinking about shopping as if it is some sort of sport or national pastime.
f I'd rather give money to charities than to the government; I think they'd make wiser choices about how to spend it.
g It's high time somebody does something about the growing number of homeless people on our streets.
h I'd rather the government spends money on providing homes and education than on short-term job-creation initiatives.

2 **Write five sentences explaining how you would like to see the world change in the future.**

I wish ______ .
If only ______ .
It's high time ______ .
It's about time ______ .
I'd rather ______ .

Work in small groups and exchange your ideas. Which are the most common, interesting, or unusual ideas?

Audioscript

Unit 1

1.02

Joanna

Well, I like to be able to take an active part, so it helps if there aren't some people who hog the conversation all the time, and also people need to have a sense of humor about things, I think, not to take things too seriously, and you need a conversation that flows, so that you can ... well, you don't get stuck on one point.

1.03

Mike

Um, a good conversationalist. I'd say it's somebody who has a point that they want to get across during the conversation, somebody with something to say as opposed to somebody who just talks endlessly about various subjects and doesn't engage in one particular subject. And I'd say it was somebody who listens to other people as well, that's what I'd say.

1.04

Phil

When people aren't really interested in what you're saying, that's very annoying. Also, people who interrupt you continually with grunts or opinions of their own or whatever, and also some people don't care about whose turn it is to talk, so they just, you know, butt in when you're in the middle of a thought and obviously, you know, when the topic's boring, that's very irritating. And sometimes, you know, the conversation goes nowhere, it's going nowhere, and that's also extremely irritating.

1.05

Jessica

I really hate it when I'm with somebody who just drones on and on in a conversation, and who doesn't give you a chance to speak at all. Oh, and I also really hate it when they just carry on and they don't care whether or not you are interested at all in what they're saying. They seem oblivious to how you're reacting to them. I hate that.

1.06

Brianna

It's good when you're talking about things you have in common with the person you are talking to, like you're on the same wavelength and you can share the same tastes or experiences so you know where the other person's coming from. It's also nice if you can share a joke or a personal story or an anecdote or something like that.

1.07

Rafael

I can't stand it when you have to do all the talking yourself, when the other person's not responding. Or when they are responding, but it's with monosyllabic answers, you know, they're just going "yeah," "hmm," "uh," and that's all you're getting back. And when you have to work to keep the conversation going. That's, that's really bad, when you're having to hunt around for things to say because you're just not getting anything back.

1.08

(B = Brian; S = Suzi)

B: Hello?
S: Hi, it's me!
B: Hi! How are you doing?
S: Fine, a little stressed, had a hard day at work, you know, the usual.
B: Yeah, me too.
S: So, what about the movie? I just called to check the times and it's on at seven and nine thirty. Which is best for you?
B: Listen, honey, do you mind if we go another night? I'm tired, I just feel like watching some football on TV.
S: But it's the last night. You said you really wanted to go!
B: Why don't you go with your sister? You said she wanted to see the movie ...
S: This is the third time you've pulled out. What's going on?
B: Nothing. I just don't feel like it tonight, that's all.
S: Come on, if there's something wrong, you can tell me. I'm not going to fly off the handle.
B: There's nothing wrong ...
S: Yes, there is. You've been acting funny for days. You don't talk to me, you don't want to see me.
B: That's not true.
S: Are you bored with me? Is there someone else? Have I done something wrong?
B: No, no, of course not.
S: You never used to be like this; you used to want to spend time with me. What's changed?
B: Nothing's changed. Of course I want to see you.
S: But not tonight, huh? The football game is more interesting, I guess.
B: Oh, you know that's not true. It's just that I'm tired, that's all. It's been a tough day. I just need a night at home ...
S: Alone!
B: Look, if it's that important to you, I'll come. What time did you say?
S: No, forget it! I wouldn't want you to go out of your way or anything!
B: Don't be like that. Come on, should I come and pick you up?
S: No, forget it. I don't want to go now. Let's just drop it.
B: Look, I'd love to do something tomorrow, OK?
S: Whatever. Do what you want. You always do!
B: Suzi, don't ... Suzi. Suzi?

1.10

Conversation 1
(W1 = Woman 1; W2 = Woman 2)

W1: I'd been waiting and waiting and waiting and, you know, I was beginning to think, like, you know, like, he wasn't coming or something ...
W2: Why didn't you call him ... or text, text him ... or whatever ...
W1: Yeah, well, you know, I thought he might have gotten caught up at work or something and I didn't really want to ... I didn't want him to feel ... to think ... you know, that I was like on his back, you know?
W2: So, what did you do?
W1: Well, actually, he called me! He'd been waiting for me ... but in another restaurant ... in another restaurant on the other side of town!
W2: What ...?
W1: Turns out there are two Italian restaurants named Casa Mia, and neither of us had realized! I had no idea.
W2: Me either!
W1: Yeah, and so, like, you know, neither of us had realized and we'd both, you know, thought of the other one and ...
W2: So, what happened? Did you go where he was or did he come where you were?
W1: He came to where I was. He was driving ... he had his car ... it was easier for him. He was actually really nice about it, really, really apologetic, and we ...

1.11

Conversation 2
(W = Woman)

W: OK, well ... I guess it's OK to talk to you now.
W: What? Ah, yes, well ... We've been working on it all week.
W: Yes, yes, it's almost done.
W: Yes, of course, we all understand how important it is, and we've already completed the initial plans, we're just waiting for the final details to come through ...
W: Yes, yes, of course, I'm sure we'll have finished it by then ...
W: What? Sorry? I can't hear you very well ...
W: Yes, yes, don't worry. We're working on the final details now. We'll be sending it to the printer's this evening ...
W: Yes, yes, this evening ... or tomorrow morning at the latest ...
W: Sorry, what's that? You said you were promised it by the end of last week?
W: I really don't think that's possible ... You must have been talking to the wrong person ... I mean, there must have been some kind of misunderstanding.
W: Yes, of course. I understand your concerns, and I'll make sure it gets done this evening.
W: Of course, absolutely. I'll be taking care of it personally. You can be sure of that.
W: Yes, yes, I'll bring it over later this evening. You can count on that.
W: Goodbye.

1.12

Conversation 1
(S = Sue; J = John)

S: Hey, John! Fancy meeting you here! How are things?
J: Sue? What a surprise. I wasn't expecting to see you here. You look great!
S: Thank you! You too. So, what are you doing here? On vacation? On business?
J: Yeah, on business. I'm at the conference. I forgot you lived here now. I should have gotten in touch ...

Conversation 2
(M = Man; W = Woman)

M: Excuse me. Do you know what time it is?
W: Yeah, just a sec ... it's three fifteen.
M: Shouldn't it be here by now?
W: Yeah, but it's often late ...
M: Especially when there's so much traffic.
W: Yeah, it's really busy today, there must be something going on downtown ...
M: It's that new exhibition, probably, you know, the travel fair or something ...

Conversation 3
(J = Jay; R = Ruben)

J: Hi, you must be Ruben. I've heard a lot about you.
R: All good, I hope!
J: Of course. I'm Jay, by the way. I work in accounting.
R: Hi, Jay, nice to meet you. So, how long have you been here?
J: Feels like forever! No, only joking, about three years. Before that I was ...

Conversation 4
(A = Alison; C = Claire)

A: Great party, isn't it?
C: Yeah.
A: So, how do you know Kim?
C: We work together.
A: Oh really? At the school? Are you a teacher too?
C: No, I'm the receptionist.
A: Oh, you're Claire, right?
C: Yes, how did you know?
A: Uh, well, ...

Unit 2

1.13

1

Bitter coffee in a plastic cup and milk in plastic containers. Yeah, either that or a greasy burger on a plastic tray. Looks great in the picture but tastes disgusting and is definitely overpriced.

2

Um ... watermelon maybe, or strawberries ... no, I know, big bowls of fresh salad with home-made dressing, served with cheese, bread, and a glass of chilled white wine.

3

Thanksgiving dinners, you know, huge plates of turkey served with mashed potatoes, stuffing, and tiny, sweet green peas, and on top of it all, swimming in it, the best gravy you have ever tasted.

4

Crunchy chocolate-chip cookies dipped in milk, curled up on the couch watching your favorite movie.

5

No food really, I mean, I associate it more with not being able to eat anything, well, at first at least ... and later ... maybe chocolate or fruit for some reason ... I don't know, something like strawberries, yes, succulent, sweet strawberries with ice cream.

6

I don't know, hot chocolate? Uh, no, sushi or a Chinese takeout - or some kind of microwaveable convenience food that doesn't need any cooking.

1.14

Anne

The food? Mmm, it's superb, really hot and spicy, but pretty delicate, too. Kind of like a cross between Indian and Chinese food but with its own special flavors. They use a lot of lemon grass and coconut, and a lot of fish. I really liked the soups. You can buy them from stalls on the corner of the street. You choose the meat you want in your soup and the kind of noodles - long, thin, white rice noodles, or big, fat, thick, yellowish ones, and there are these tubs of spices, too, and you choose as much or as little of whatever you want. Then you sit there on the street, or in the market or wherever you are, and eat it. I had some for breakfast one day - it was great! Really great!

1.15

Kim

The food? Actually, it took some getting used to. Although I like hot, spicy food, there wasn't really much of it. But there was plenty of rice and fish! It's kind of like the food we get in restaurants back home, but a lot better. I loved the ritual of it, going to a small, family-run restaurant where you watch your order being made up in front of you. I didn't use to like raw fish, but after tasting it freshly made, I love it, especially the salmon. I also developed a taste for *inarizushi*, little parcels of fried tofu stuffed with rice mixed with sweet vinegar.

1.16

Bill

The food? Well, to tell you the truth, I didn't really like it that much. It isn't the healthiest of diets. Everything is either fried or cooked in pig's fat and, hmm, I don't really like cabbage that much and that's a staple part of their diet, like a lot of places in Central Europe. It's usually pickled and served with sour cream - so, no, it isn't really my favorite. Having said that, there were some things I loved - the bread, for example. It's really soft and tasty, and so many different kinds, and their pastries too are really good. And some of the soups, the various kinds of goulash - that's their national dish - and the bean soups are really delicious and the paprika makes them quite spicy - great on a cold day.

1.17

Steve

The food? It isn't particularly elaborate, but it's good. The seafood in the coastal region is especially good, and there's just such a variety, so many different kinds of shellfish, I wouldn't know the names for half of them in English. Another favorite of mine is the grilled green chili peppers. They serve them by the plateful to be shared between friends over a beer or two. There's always one that's so spicy it almost blows your head off. More than anything else, I love the eating-out culture. It's pretty informal; you go to a bar and order huge platefuls of salsa or avocado dip - guacamole - with corn chips and share them, everybody eating off the same plates. It's very sociable - a really nice social eating ritual.

1.19

Conversation 1
(M = Mrs. Dersty; J = John)

M: Hello?
J: Hello. This is John from accounting. Could I speak to Mrs. Dersty?
M: Speaking.
J: I have your expense claim form here, but I'm afraid we won't be able to reimburse your dining expenses.
M: Oh, and why is that?
J: Because you could have used the company's dining facilities.
M: Yes, but it was a breakfast meeting with a client.
J: That may be, but it's company policy.
M: I think you'll find that it's only company policy if we're entertaining in-house guests.
J: I see. Well, we'll need to double-check that and get back to you.

1.20

Conversation 2
(G = Girl; M = Mother)

G: You bought strawberries?
M: Yes, what's wrong with that?
G: But they're out of season!
M: So what if they're out of season?
G: Well, apart from the fact that it doesn't help the environment, imported fruit doesn't taste as good.
M: That's garbage. These strawberries are absolutely delicious!

G: Yeah, but how much did they cost?
M: They were on sale.
G: Yeah, but they must have cost a fortune. Imported from Mexico! What about the environment?
M: OK, OK, I suppose you're right, it's not good for the environment, but I couldn't resist them.

1.21

Conversation 3
(A = Anna; B = Ben)
A: I can't believe he got her a vacuum cleaner for her birthday.
B: Oh, I don't know. It's the thought that counts.
A: No! Come on! He couldn't have given it much thought, if that's all he came up with.
B: You gave me an electric drill on my last birthday!
A: So?
B: I rest my case.

1.22

Food and eating is a universal part of being human, regardless of culture. But how and what people eat varies significantly from country to country, so it is important to be aware of what is expected and what is considered rude, in order to be as respectful as possible.

Unit 3

1.23

(S = Sandy; P = Professor Mohammed)
S: Good afternoon and welcome to the first in our series of lectures on the changing face of cities around the world. Our guest lecturer for the semester is Professor Riaz Mohammed, who is a visiting professor and researcher at the University of São Paulo. He is the Head of the Department of Urban Planning and Development at the University of Delhi where his research focuses on megacities in the developing world and population shifts from rural to urban areas. Professor Mohammed, welcome.
P: It's an honor to be here at your esteemed university and in your lovely, bustling city. As residents of one of the world's megacities, I am sure you will relate to our discussion today, both from a theoretical point of view as urban planners and researchers and from a practical point of view, having to deal with the pros and cons of living in such a large city. So let's get started.
According to figures from the United Nations, in 2016 there was 54.5% of the world's population living in urban areas. The study appears to suggest that there is a steady movement towards urban areas, which when projected, gives a figure of 60% by 2030.
My first question to you is: "What is a city? Some have described a city as "the urban agglomeration or metropolitan area it holds together," while others see it as strictly the administrative limits of an urban settlement. The varying definitions can certainly lead to confusion, making it more difficult to come to a consensus on concrete matters such as the exact physical size and population of a city. Thus, there is still some discussion as to which is the world's largest capital. If the term 'city' is taken to mean a metropolitan area, then Tokyo, with its population of more than thirty-seven million, easily tops the list as the world largest city (and capital) in terms of population. Rounding up the top five cities we have Delhi, in India, Shanghai and Beijing in China and Mumbai in fifth place. Your lovely city, São Paulo, is in the top ten at number six. The first city to have reached a population of one million was Rome, which had a population of over a million in the heyday of the Roman Empire in 133 BC. London reached this mark in 1810 and New York in 1875. Today there are over three hundred cities which boast a population in excess of one million.
Despite the problems such as urban sprawl, traffic, pollution and so on - which urban planners and even the lay man on the street love to point out - people are still fascinated by big cities. In fact, the most visited cities in the world are among the largest. It is widely recognized that Paris, with its population of over 11 million, is the most visited city in the world, with others such as London and New York in the top five.
When we think of cities, especially the big ones, one adjective which may come to mind is "modern." Cities are where things are happening, where we find the movers and the shakers, and many times where we find innovation taking place. The concept of "city" is not a new one - it goes back several thousands of years. While there is still some debate about which is the oldest city, the Syrians claim that their capital city, Damascus, is the one to crown; though other inhabitants of other Middle Eastern cities might claim the same. Sources, however, seem to suggest that the Syrians are right and that their capital is indeed the oldest in the world, having been continuously inhabited since 5000 BC.
As we mentioned earlier, cities, especially big cities and mega-cities, face many challenges. One unique challenge which we will look into in the upcoming weeks is living in cities at unusually high elevations or extremely low lands, and the problems we must face as city planners. While most capital cities in the world have some degree of elevation, there are two capitals which lie below sea level Amsterdam in the Netherlands and Baku in Azerbaijan. On the other extreme, there is no doubt whatsoever that La Paz, the capital of Bolivia, which stands at four kilometers above sea level in the Bolivian Andes, is the highest capital city in the world.
Finally, we will bring all the components together and look at cities as living organisms, in all their complexity. Cities are where people live, work, build, create, innovate, ... and have fun. Rio de Janeiro - a city not far from here - is considered one of the most exciting cities of the world; although rigorously speaking it is unclear if this information is based on popular opinion or on statistical data. Is that true? (*chuckling*) What does a city need to offer to be considered an "exciting" city?
In the coming weeks we will be exploring these and other aspects of cities and city life. I encourage you to participate, bring your ideas and questions. I am sure we can have very lively discussions ...

1.24

(S = Sharon; D = Derek)

S: Have you seen this? The article about that new survey ...

D: Yes, I was reading it earlier. It comes as no surprise ... seems pretty obvious to me. You don't need a survey to tell you that stuff.

S: Yeah, well, I don't know, I mean it's not that simple. I mean, some people like living in the countryside ...

D: Yeah, and you can see why: less stress, less traffic, less smog ... but I don't think it's just a simple question of what you like, you know ...

S: No, it's more like ... well, it seems like it's a question of work and money more than anything else, I mean ...

D: Yeah, it said that, didn't it? The main reason was that they couldn't find a job in the countryside ...

S: Well, it doesn't say that exactly, but yes, it says it's, uh, it's, you know, easier to find work in large cities and I guess that's true. Don't you?

D: Yeah, but I don't think that's the main reason. I mean, it might be the main reason for older people ... you know, no jobs, rural unemployment, whatever ...

S: Yeah, there's a lot of that ...

D: But it seems to be talking more about young people ... I mean, the statistics here are referring to people under thirty and you know, I think that even if there were plenty of jobs in the rural areas, well, they'd still go to the cities, you know?

S: Do you think so? Maybe you're right. Maybe it's more a kind of lure of the bright lights thing ...

D: Yeah, you know, nightlife, music, youth culture in general ...

S: Yeah, it says something about that, doesn't it? That part where it talks about, what is it ... "free-time activities" or something like that?

D: "Leisure facilities."

S: Yeah, that was it.

D: More like bars and night clubs!

S: Yeah, and movie theaters and exhibitions and stuff as well ...

D: Nah, dances and the chance to meet other young people ...

S: Yeah, OK, the social side of things, but it's important, isn't it?

D: Yeah, this survey seems to suggest that it's the second most important factor, in fact, after getting a job. You know, if young people decide to leave their homes in the countryside, then they say the social side of things is the second most important thing they consider. What other things do you think they mentioned?

S: Oh, I don't know. Maybe they said there were more opportunities for continuing their education, like going to college. They might be thinking about facilities for their families in the future, like being near good schools. Um, what about better living conditions ... more modern houses which need less work done to them?

D: Yeah, I guess they're all things you'd have to think about, right?

S: Yeah, the survey makes a lot of sense.

D: Hmm.

1.25

(H = Helen; R = Robert)

H: As we live in a relatively small city, I don't really think it's particularly dangerous. Just like any medium to small city, I think we are much safer than in the big cities. Of course, one has to be sensible and take the normal precautions. I mean, I wouldn't walk home alone at night and I wouldn't walk down dark alleys at night. But there isn't anywhere in town I would particularly avoid. It's a pretty safe city.

R: Yeah, on the whole I would agree, but actually there have been a couple of stories in the local papers about some thefts and muggings that's been going on lately, so you definitely shouldn't walk alone at night.

H: Oh yeah, I heard about that report. They say that things are changing and are getting a little dangerous in some parts of the city. Actually, come to think of it, I do have a friend who had her purse snatched while she was walking up one of those side streets off Main Avenue. She was completely taken by surprise and the fellow, a teenager, ran off so fast that she had no chance of catching him.

R: I'm sorry to hear that! I hope she didn't get hurt though.

H: No, she was fine. It was just her purse with some cash. Luckily she had forgotten her cell phone at home and her house keys were in her pocket.

R: Well, we really shouldn't be complacent because we live in a smaller city. We need to take care all the time - when the streets are deserted or in crowded places like the street market - both are dangerous almost in the same way. Pickpockets actually tend to target more crowded places, as it's easier to escape undetected.

H: But you don't think it's really dangerous, do you? They're not violent people ... you just have to be sensible and keep your eyes open, and ...

R: Well, I don't know. What if the thieves are carrying knives? If you resist you could get badly hurt, so that really makes you think, doesn't it?

H: Well yes, actually now you are making me think twice. Maybe it is a little more dangerous than I had realized. Did you hear about the group of tourists who were robbed last month in the city center? What do you do if you see something like that? You don't really know what's going on and you don't want to get involved in case you get hurt.

R: Yes, don't ever try to be the hero. All they want is money, so perhaps the safest thing is to give it to them. It's not worth losing your life for. Did anyone get hurt in the robbery?

H: No, they just had their wallets and purses stolen. One of the robbers had a knife, but I think it was more to scare them than to hurt them. They did lose all their cash and credit cards though, so that totally spoilt their vacation, because they had just arrived.

R: That's the problem with tourists though. They are so easy to spot. And since they are almost always carrying cash and credit cards, and sometimes don't speak the language, they are vulnerable.

H: Well again, the good thing is that nobody got hurt. And I guess you're right. It wouldn't hurt for us all to be a little more careful.

R: Yes, and if we had some more police patrols, even just on the main streets, it would scare off any potential robber and give the rest of us more peace of mind.

H: That's true. We should find out what the city plans to do. That would actually help a lot.

1.28

Stella

Hi. I am Stella. I am from Jamaica, but I have been living in Toronto for ten years. I love it here for several reasons - it's safe, clean, and you have easy access to many services. It is a bit expensive though, so in a way it proves that there is always a down side to everything. However, for me, one of the best things about Toronto is how multicultural it is. In the space of one day I probably interact with twenty different nationalities. It sounds like a lot, but it's true. From the moment I step out my door, I say hello to my neighbor from Russia, another one from the United States, and the building superintendent from the Philippines. I get my coffee near the office from a Portuguese place where the Polish attendant is very friendly. Then I get to the office and I greet my co-worker from Brazil, ... and it's not even nine o'clock yet! It is so interesting to walk down the street or ride the subway and hear all the different languages and accents. What is so cool is that when people move to a different country, they take their food, their language, and their culture with them. One thing that I have noticed about living in such a city is that people are very tolerant, polite, and accepting of others. Part of that is the Canadian politeness that rubs off on everyone. Knowing people from different countries, as opposed to knowing about them, is the best way to smash stereotypes. In the end, we learn that people are people, with similar hopes, dreams, and fears. So I am happy to be a member of many tribes.

Unit 4

1.30

Simon

This was my favorite book when I was younger. It's called *The Lord of the Rings*. It's a real epic, it's a classic - it was written for kids, but actually lots of adults read it as well. It's huge, three books in fact, but such an excellent read! It's set in a fantasy world called Middle Earth, and it has fantasy characters like elves and dwarves, and monsters and dragons, and all sorts of mythical creatures like that. And it tells the story of these creatures called hobbits, who are kind of like humans but not really humans. The main character is named Frodo and he's the one who has to get rid of the ring. Well, it's a very special ring that was crafted a long, long time ago by the Dark Lord, who is the villain of the story. And it's an extremely powerful ring, "the ring of power" you might want to call it, because anybody who puts it on becomes invisible. And, basically, this book is about their quest, the quest of the hobbits and their companions, to destroy the ring, because if the Dark Lord gets hold of it he can rule the world. Oh, and there's this other character named Gandalf who is a wizard, and he's on the side of good, and he helps Frodo and his companions to vanquish the Dark Lord. And, well, anyway, they have all sorts of, kind of, adventures, and there are lots of battles and stuff and, well, in the end Frodo throws the ring into a volcano and that's the end of the ring. Basically, it's about the battle between the forces of good and evil, and in the end, the good triumphs over evil. It's a really powerful story, a real page-turner. You get totally engrossed in the story, it's so well-written. It's really magical. I couldn't put it down. It's been made into a movie trilogy now, another epic, and very popular.

1.31

1

(T = Tammy; J = Jeremy)

T: So, have you ever been conned?

J: I'm ashamed to say I have. Um, it was years ago. I was a student and I had a car, and it had a particularly distinctive sound about it, like a rattle, and I wanted to get a different car, so I took it to a used-car dealership and the salesman conned me into believing that the sound that the engine made was something really bad and it was on its way out, and he said he would be doing me a favor by offering me a very small amount of money just to take it off my hands. I remember at the time thinking, "Is this really right?" and then I was kind of almost afraid to challenge him on it, and so I said, "OK, fine, yeah," and he gave me a very small amount of money for something that was in fact in perfect condition, and I could have gotten a lot more money for it at another time.

1.32

2

(M = Martin; J = Jennifer)

M: Do you have any experiences of being conned?

J: Yes, I do. This was at home. Somebody knocked on my door.

M: Right.

J: A really nice young woman. You know, very friendly and bright. And she said, "Can you lend me $5 because I'm here to see my mom? She's sick and I've run out of change." Really, honestly I thought, gut feeling, yeah, she seems plausible. She said, "I'll come back, I'll come back in twenty minutes and I'll pay you back." And so, yeah, I gave her the money. And I'm usually pretty, you know, you can see when somebody's lying but this, this girl was really nice. Very well-dressed and ...

M: How old was she?

J: Oh, she must have been in her early twenties and she ran off with my money and never came back. Absolutely unbelievable. I mean I guess I was pretty dumb to do that, but she just completely conned me.

1.33

3

(D = Doug; A = Anne)

D: Do you have any experiences of being conned?

A: Yeah. This is really embarrassing. You know those phone calls you get and they say oh, you've won a vacation and all you need to do is answer a few questions?

D: Yeah.

A: So I answered a few questions about, you know, my ideal place to go and how much money I'd need and how much ... you know, all that kind of stuff, and maybe have some extra money for ... to buy some clothes and things like that, and they kept me on the phone for a really long time and I was really excited and I hung up thinking I'd actually won a vacation and then I didn't hear anything and then I got the phone bill and it cost me $30 for that phone call, so I didn't get the vacation.

D: How did you feel?

A: I felt like an idiot.

1.34

4

Georgina

This is something that happened to me when I was living abroad and I was living in an apartment and my toilet broke, so I got my boyfriend to get a plumber. So the next day there was a knock on the door. This guy arrives and said, "I'm a plumber." So I said, "OK, come in, take a look, there it is," and he had a look at it and said, "Oh, yes, you'll need a new something" - I don't know what it was - "but it'll cost you $40, um, so I can go off and get it now if you want." And so I gave him the $40 and, of course, never saw him again. And then that evening I said to my boyfriend, "I don't think much of the plumber you found." And he said, "What plumber? I never found a plumber." So what had happened, obviously, was that this guy was just going around, knocking on doors and hoping to find someone gullible like me who'd hand over some money.

1.37

So there was this old guy, right, and he was driving along the highway, right, and he gets a call from his wife. Now of course he shouldn't pick up the phone, but he does. "Be careful," she says, "I've just heard on the radio that some idiot is driving down the highway the wrong way." So he says, "One idiot? I can see hundreds of them."

1.38

So there's this businessman riding on the train after a hard day at the office, and this young guy sits next to him and says, "Call me a doctor, call me a doctor." And the businessman says, "Well, what's the matter, are you sick?" And the guy, the young guy, says, "No, no, I've just graduated from medical school."

1.39

A sandwich walks into a bar and orders a beer, and the bartender says, "Sorry, we don't serve food."

1.40

A: I've got one. A mouse goes into a bar and goes up to the bartender and says, "Got any cheese?" and the bartender says, "No, it's a bar, we don't sell cheese." So the mouse goes, "Oh!" and scampers out. The next day the same mouse comes into the same bar, goes up to the bartender, "Got any cheese?" And the bartender says, "Look, I told you yesterday, this is a bar, we sell beer, we sell alcohol, we don't sell cheese, OK?" The mouse goes, "Oh!" and scampers out. Next day, same mouse, same bar, comes in again, goes up to the bartender and says, "Got any cheese?" and the bartender says, "Look, I told you yesterday. If you come in here again, I'm going to nail you to the bar," and the mouse goes, "Oh!" and scampers out. Next day, same mouse comes into the bar again, goes up to the bartender, "Got any nails?" The bartender says no. "Got any cheese?"

B: I didn't get that at all.

1.41

(W1 = Woman 1; W2 = Woman 2)

W1: I had a really scary experience when I went camping with my friend by the ocean. Actually, it was the first time either of us had been camping.

W2: Really?

W1: We pitched our tent near the edge of a cliff, so we had a beautiful view over the bay.

W2: Oh, wow!

W1: But then during the night, the wind started blowing harder and harder.

W2: Oh, no!

W1: At first I thought we could just sleep through it, but eventually I realized that the tent was going to blow away if we didn't act fast.

W2: Oh, how scary! You must have been terrified!

W1: So, anyway, we got up and started to pack our things up ...

W2: Right.

W1: ... and we were just about to start taking the tent down to pack it away in the car when I realized I couldn't find my car keys.

W2: Oh, what a nightmare! That must have been awful!

W1: So, I hunted high and low, and anyway, to cut a long story short, eventually found them lying on the grass outside the tent.

W2: What a relief! I bet you were happy!

W1: Yeah, and fortunately we were able to get everything in the car before the rain started.

W2: Oh, good!

W1: But, all in all, it was a pretty horrific night, and I don't think either of us are in a hurry to go camping again!

W2: I'm not surprised!

1.43

1

So, anyway, I finished eating and called the waiter over to pay my check. And I looked down and, guess what? My purse wasn't there.

...

But you'll never guess what happened. This man at the next table leaned over and offered to lend me the money.

...

Obviously I said no. I mean, I didn't know him, and it just would have been too embarrassing.

1.44

2

We'd been traveling for two days, but we'd run out of money. So I hadn't eaten for two days! I was absolutely starving!

...

It was the last bus home and there was a long, long line. I was thinking, what if we don't get on? We'll have to spend the night in the bus station.

...

But, anyway, we were lucky enough to get the last two seats on the bus.

1.45

3

I'd known about the concert for a long time; it was one of my favorite groups playing. But for some reason, I hadn't gotten around to getting tickets. And when I did eventually call, all the tickets had sold out.

...

But then, the next time they were playing, I called way ahead of the concert date. And so this time we got seats right in the front row.

1.46

4

I was at a party with my girlfriend, and I saw this guy I went to high school with. I was just about to introduce him to my girlfriend when I realized I'd completely forgotten his name.

...

Luckily I didn't have to introduce him though, because he introduced himself.

...

Or maybe it wasn't so lucky ... He spent the rest of the evening talking to my girlfriend!

1.47

5

I was sitting at the table, having breakfast, and suddenly there was a loud knock on the door.

...

It was the mailman. He handed me an envelope which I had to sign for, because it was Registered Mail. And so I opened it and you'll never guess what was inside ... a check for $5,000!

Unit 5

1.48

1

Ah, well, strangely enough it's a discount superstore. I just love the ease of being able to go in, do your grocery shopping, buy electronic goods, maybe buy some clothes ... and then I normally end up in the book section, and I'll buy some books that I probably don't need, but it's all under one roof, so it's absolutely perfect.

2

Oh, actually that's my responsibility. I don't like other people doing that for me, to tell the truth. I like to look around and pick out the produce that I really, really like the look of and the smell of and everything, so yes, I really enjoy that. That's not one of my most painful chores.

3

It's going to be a house, which is a pretty big necessity. It will be great to unpack and spread my stuff around a few rooms. I know that it's going to cost a lot, and organizing finance is tricky, but a house is something I've always dreamed of having.

4

I have to say I'm really not. I like to consider everything I buy. What I tend to do is I visit all the stores and I'll assess all the different prices, and in some stores you might get additional things thrown in, for example. Inevitably, I end up going back to the first store, probably because that's where I've asked all the questions and I feel a certain sense of customer loyalty, you could say ... but I might check prices online, for example, and certainly do the rounds, but I like to put a lot of work in before I actually purchase anything.

5

Well, when I was much younger I was shopping right before Christmas with my parents and I got separated from them, which was really scary at the time, and, fortunately, I guess I knew to ask somebody at the counter, and they put an announcement over the PA and, um, I waited there and eventually was reunited with my parents, but I remember it being really traumatic and really, really scary.

6

Oh, my God – I love it. I mean anything and everything to do with shopping – I'm there. I mean, they call me the plastic bag lady because I'm constantly carrying bags, you know – down at the mall. I mean retail therapy, it's got to be the best thing for everybody.

1.49

Good evening and welcome to *The Money Show*, the show that helps you navigate the world of spending and saving, and manage your personal finances. Today we've asked you, the listeners, to write, email, or call in with your tips for saving money or making it go further. The lines are open now at 676-7888, that's 676-7888, if you'd like to share your ideas.

First of all, we've had an email from Tony Mendez, who says: "I've made huge savings by canceling my gym membership. I found I was only going once or twice a week, which was not only making me feel guilty for not going more often, but was also costing me a fortune in monthly membership fees. With all the money I've saved, I've bought a bicycle, and now I get my exercise for free. And on top of that, now that I'm cycling to work, I'm saving on gas, too!"

Thank you very much, Tony, for that idea. How to save money and get in shape at the same time – great thinking! And here's another idea from Riley Tucker. Riley writes: "It really makes sense to buy things that are on sale whenever you can. Why overpay when, if you wait for a sale, you can get it for half the price? And if you buy in bulk, you can also stock up on gifts so you're never at a loss if you need a birthday gift for somebody."

I agree, Riley. In fact, I can't honestly understand why anybody buys things at any other time. And talking about purchases, here's a tip from Isabel Costa, who writes: "My tip for saving money is to stop buying designer clothes. My closet used to be stuffed with pricey clothes and accessories I hardly ever wore. Then a friend said to me, 'Face it, Isabel – celebrities are given expensive clothes to wear – they don't actually go out and buy them. You're not a celebrity and never will be.' How can you justify overpaying just because a top designer has had his or her name sewn into the label? And can you honestly tell the difference between an exorbitantly priced designer bag and one bought at a fraction of the price? Get your clothes at a thrift store or in discount stores and you'll save a fortune."

Thank you, Isabel. So, those of you with a penchant for upscale clothes, take note – not sure I come into that category myself, though. And here's another money-saving idea from Paul Moore, who's emailed us with the following suggestion: "If you're an impulse buyer like me, my suggestion is when you're waiting at the checkout with your new purchase, count to ten and ask yourself, 'Do I really need this?' The chances are the answer is no. Even if it's half price, if you don't need it, you're not saving money. So, put it down, walk away, and believe me, you'll feel a lot happier, and a lot richer, when you get home. Plus the fact that your house won't be cluttered with stuff you're only going to give away or get rid of in a few months' time."

I like that suggestion, Paul. I'm sure we'd all be a lot happier if we could just be content with the bare necessities of life. And talking of bare necessities, here's a tip from Sally Weiss ...

1.50

(B = Barney; M = Maiara)

B: So, do you have any experience bargaining?

M: Yeah, yeah, I do, as a matter of fact. I was in Turkey and I have a real passion for rugs, and I saw a kilim, and I really liked it but it was way overpriced, and so I got into this whole bargaining thing with this guy and because I, in a way, I kind of liked it – I mean it was beautiful, but I also didn't really want it, and so because I didn't really want it, I just made up a price, you know, and really low. I started really low.

B: Well, don't they say, go like a fifth of the price or something? (Yeah, that's right.) I mean, I know it's probably different in different countries, but I know in North Africa they kind of literally go a fifth of the price, you know, and you think that you're kind of insulting them, but ...

M: But anyway, and so, because I didn't really care about it that much, there wasn't a huge emotional investment. I just, you know, I just made up a figure and, basically, we got it just above the figure that I had quoted.

B: It's fun though, don't you think?

M: Yes and no. What about you?

B: No, I really enjoy it. I think because they are so used to doing it, you know, in Turkey and North Africa and, you know, a lot of places other than the United States, I think they enjoy it. You know, they get a kick out of it and they know that they've got a margin that they can sell it at and they try and get the most out of you and I think it is a challenge for them, you know, and I've never left a bargaining situation not feeling happy and the seller not feeling happy. And that's always a good thing. You know, you go into a store in this country and you know you've been ripped off, but you still buy it because you want it or you need it.

M: But, you know, I think right now you can do some bargaining here, too.

B: Do you think?

M: Yeah, sure, definitely.

1.52

(C = Customer; M = Market trader)

C: Excuse me, how much is this vase?

M: This one? It's 50 dollars. Solid marble.

C: Hmm. Yes, it's beautiful, but it's a little bit more than I was prepared to pay. Could you give me a discount, do you think?

M: Well, I suppose I could give you ten percent off. So, that would make it 45.

C: Hmm. The thing is, it's a little chipped, here at the top, and I wanted to give it to somebody as a gift.

M: Well, I suppose I could knock off another 5 dollars. But that's as low as I'm prepared to go. It's solid marble. Hand carved. You won't get another one like it.

C: Yes, yes, I can see that, but I'm afraid it's still above my price range. I think I'll pass, thanks.

M: Tell you what, you can have it for 35, and I'll throw in this little box as well.

C: Oh, OK. Is that your best price?

M: Yes, I can't go any lower than that or I'll be giving it away.

C: OK, I'll take it. Thanks very much.

M: Thank you. That's 35 dollars, please. You've got yourself a bargain.

1.56

(I = Interviewer; A = Amanda)

I: Welcome to the show, Amanda.

A: Thank you for inviting me.

I: So, Amanda, we understand that your school has won the Sustainable High School of the Year Award for the second year in a row. Can you tell us how you achieved this?

A: It was truly an effort on the part of all the students, teachers and staff to make our school more sustainable and reduce our environmental footprint. It all started when I learnt about the United Nations Sustainable Development Goals in 2015 in my civics class. I started thinking about how we could implement these in our school. A group of friends and I formed a committee and we came up with some initial ideas such as reducing plastic waste to a minimum, recycling, and reducing water consumption.

I: How did you put these ideas into action?

A: To reduce plastic waste, we petitioned the school to stop serving plastic straws with drinks. Did you know that we throw away over 500 million straws a day, just in the United States? Since straws are not recyclable, they end up in landfill and in the oceans, where they harm animals. We also had more water filters installed around the school and petitioned the school to stop selling and serving drinks in plastic bottles. It was a long battle and it took us nine months, but we finally succeeded. Today, the cafeteria and vending machine do not sell anything with disposable plastic. We also raised money to put recycling bins in each classroom and along the hallways. And we started an education drive, teaching students and staff how to recycle. Today, we recycle 90% of our waste.

I: That is absolutely amazing. I guess small actions can make a big difference.

A: Yes, they can.

I: Amanda, I want to thank you for sharing what you and your school are doing. You have certainly been an inspiration to me and I hope to our listeners out there.

A: It was a pleasure, thanks for having me.

Unit 6

1.57

1

Hmm, that's a difficult one. I think a crossword. Um, I don't think I've ever completed one by myself, though. And I'm a college graduate! Yeah, I mean, I've spent hours and hours ... I always need help. But, um, you know, we get there in the end!

2
Oh, I have really wonderful and clear memories of playing chess with my dad. I mean, we used to spend hours playing and, um, he taught me practically everything I know and, you know, I've continued playing throughout my life and I find it a wonderful thing to pass on to my kids.

3
I'm absolutely obsessed with Sudoku. I play it all the time, if I'm on a train or a bus, or I can actually spend hours at home doing it, it's pathetic!

4
Well, I think those hand-held game things are just pointless. I mean, I don't see, I really don't see the point in them. People say, you know, it improves hand-eye coordination and all that kind of thing, but I don't get it, I don't like them, and I don't see how people can spend hours and hours playing them.

1.58

Mike
Hmm ... sight, I suppose. Yes, the most important one is sight, I guess ... I mean, if you're blind, if you can't see, then although you can lead a full life and all that, I think it does make you more vulnerable, more dependent on other people, I don't know, for silly little things like, for instance, like grocery shopping or whatever, and I would really hate it if I couldn't see what things or people looked like ... or the expression on a person's face when they're talking to you. I mean, you wouldn't even know if they were looking at you or whether they looked interested in what you were saying.

1.59

Maria
No, I haven't, but I read an article about a man who went deaf and then his hearing was restored to him, and he talked about how isolating it can be if you can't hear. He said that you miss out on a lot of things, that although you can communicate fine when you need to, you miss out on the subtleties of a conversation, and the thing he missed most was humor ... the humor in spontaneous conversation ... because it all gets slowed down when you're signing. And he really missed listening to music; that was the worst part, he said. That, and not being able to hear his wife's voice. And he said that it was really strange to start with when he regained his hearing. Everything sounded much louder. He said he actually misses total silence sometimes, just not hearing anything, and that it can be really relaxing.

1.60

Helen
Um, I don't know ... but maybe smell, I guess ... like somebody can just walk past you on the street and you can catch the smell of their perfume and it reminds you really strongly of somebody ... or food ... I can't remember where I was the other day, but I suddenly smelled the most wonderful cooking smells: coconut oil and spices, and it reminded me so strongly of my vacation in the Caribbean ... I could see the palm trees, taste the food, feel the sun on my skin ... yes, I think smell triggers the strongest, most vivid memories.

1.61

Nick
This may seem like a strange answer, but maybe touch ... you know, the sense of touch ... I think it's probably the one we take the most for granted, being able to feel things, and it's not ... it's not, you know, a sense that's limited to one part of your body, either – it's everything, every single pore, every single bit of your skin. I remember seeing a documentary about a man who was born deaf and mute and had later lost his sight in an accident – he lived a full life – he was eighty-something and he still worked and even traveled. He just lived his life totally through his sense of touch. In this program, they showed him visiting other people like him in Japan. It was amazing – they used an international signing language which was based on touch – they would touch each other and sign on each other's palms, and they could feel each other talking – and it showed them going to a drum concert too – like a traditional Japanese drum concert – and they could feel the music, I mean they could feel the vibrations of the drums, even though they couldn't hear them. It was just totally amazing.

1.62

Petra
Well, usually I'm renowned for my sense of taste! Sometimes I can taste things that nobody else even notices. For example, when someone cooks for me, I can tell which spices were used. Sometimes my mom will try to fool me by putting something I've never eaten before in the food, but in that case I can always identify that there is something strange in the food. I love tasting something I've never tasted before! If food is spoiled, I know it right away. Recently I had some really hot soup and burned my tongue. It was strange not being able to taste things as strongly, everything tasted so bland, but I was back to normal after a couple of days.

1.64

(A = Adam; B = Brad; D = Dylan)
A: Do you mind scooting over a little?
B: No, of course not.
A: Thanks. Dylan, would you mind not sitting there?
D: Why?
A: You're leaning on my jacket.
D: Sorry!
A: So, Brad, have you decided?
D: Decided what?
A: Mind your own business!
D: Oh, come on!
B: Dylan, would you mind getting us some drinks?
D: Yes, I would.
B: Oh, come on! It's just boring work stuff.
D: Oh, OK. I don't believe it for a second.
B: No, I haven't made up my mind yet.
A: You know, I'll cover for you while you're gone.
B: Would you?
A: Yeah, really, no problem.
B: Hmm, but what about Peter? Do you think he'll mind?
A: No, of course not. Of course, Nick will.
B: Really, why?

Unit 7

2.02

You thought smart glasses were a flop? We did too! But it could be time to reconsider. In this episode of *Smart Tech* we're looking into the future of hands-free technology. This version of the glasses is less obtrusive than the first iteration. The glasses look like, well, glasses! With an almost invisible earpiece and texts transmitted directly onto your retina, there's almost no telling that you're answering an email or making dinner reservations. The keyboard and touch screen have been replaced with voice commands and eye gestures. The glasses link up with all your other tech seamlessly, so you can access data from your smart watch, or make a phone call just by swiping with your eyes. How much will it run you? Ay, there's the rub! This retooled version should be retailing in the range three to four times the price of a top of the line smartphone, which prices out all but the most passionate tech consumers. However, the next version should see more accessible pricing and fewer bugs. Our verdict: a huge improvement over the first version, but it might be better to wait for prices to come down out of the stratosphere.

2.04

(J = John; S = Sue)

J: So, what cool new gadget are you going to wow us with today, Sue?

S: Not so new, John: it's an e-reader - or an electronic reading device.

J: Thanks, but no thanks. I love the feel of a book in my hands. There's no replacing it.

S: But this is so much more than a book. It's a thousand books, all stored in one small device. No more hunting around in bookstores, no more dusty bookshelves ... books have gone digital. It fits in your pocket or purse and you can take it with you anywhere, with more books than you could possibly read.

J: You've been reading too much hype! Plus, I love my dusty old bookshelves - my house would look bare without them ...

S: Yes, but think of this, you're going on vacation, you're packing your bags, and you've got to decide which books to take with you. How many can you fit in your suitcase? Which one are you going to take on board with you? What if you don't like it? What if you finish it halfway through the trip and have nothing left to read except the in-flight magazine ...

J: Horrors ...

S: Problem solved. You can take them all with you ... and if you need a local guidebook while you're there, just connect to the internet and you can download anything you need.

J: Yes, but looking at a small screen like that for hours on end can't possibly be good for your eyes ... I mean, it's like sitting in front of a computer for hours on end ...

S: Oh, but it isn't ... the screen doesn't emit light, so no glare and very little eye strain, no more than reading a normal paper book ... you can even read it in strong sunlight. I'd say it's even easier on the eyes than a real book.

J: Yes, but it isn't a book. I'm sorry, but I really don't think any device, no matter how slick and quick and easy to use, can possibly replace a much-loved book.

S: Sure and when the first trains were built, nobody wanted to go on them because they thought the human body would be sure to explode if it traveled at over 40 miles an hour ...

J: I know, I know, and nobody thought there'd be a market for personal computers back in the 1960s ...

S: Also, think about the environmental impact - what about the costs of making the paper, printing the books, and then shipping them all over the world? Not to speak of the mountains and mountains of newspapers trashed every single day ... You know, it may not save the planet, but it'd be a step in the right direction if we gave up paper publications and turned to e-reading instead ...

J: Hmm ... I can see you're definitely sold on the idea.

S: Why not try it? Borrow this one for a week and we can talk about it again on the next show ... I'm sure it'll give you plenty to write about on your blog, which, by the way, you'll be able to read on your new e-reader!

2.05

1

(C = Carla; B = Bette)

C: I don't know if I want to do it ... I mean, I do, but then ...

B: Oh, come on, it's not such a big deal, is it? I mean, everybody does it ... even my mom has one.

C: Yeah, but the thing is, once you get one, there's no going back ... You know, what's done is done and all that ...

B: Ah, yes, sorry, I obviously hadn't thought through all the possible consequences. I mean this could have a truly life-changing effect, couldn't it?

C: Oh, stop! It's just that, you know, once it's there, I can't get rid of it, you know? And what if I decide I don't like it anymore?

B: Well, you'll just have to live with the consequences, I guess! But no, seriously, I think it'll look really good. Go for it. Go ahead. You know you want to.

2.06

2

(M = Mrs. Taylor; A = Austin)

M: So, have you had a chance to think about it?

A: Yeah, but the thing is, I keep going around and around in circles ... I mean, you know, it's a big decision.

M: It certainly is. I mean, you know, it's the next four years of your life ... and not only that ... it will effect what choices you have afterwards as well ... but remember, it isn't the end of the world if you choose one and then decide it isn't for you ... Lots of people change their minds, you know. I think you have to go for the choice that you feel happiest with now - what feels best for you right now.

A: Yes, I suppose you're right ...

2.07

3

(A = Anna; R = Rachel)

A: I've been thinking about what you said ... you know ... how I should stop dithering all the time ... how I should learn to be more assertive ... stand up for myself and all that ...

R: ... and?

A: Well, I've made up my mind ... I'm going to tell them tomorrow!
R: You mean, you're actually going to resign?
A: Yep, that's right! At long last!

2.08

4

(P = Peter; S = Stuart)
P: It's a great honor ... I'm very flattered that you think I'm capable ... but I need time to think about it ...
S: Look, why don't you sleep on it? Talk to your wife about it. You can let us know tomorrow ...
P: OK, thanks. I will. I'll call you first thing in the morning. Once I've had a chance to think things over ... I mean, it really is a great honor ... but, you're right, I need to talk to my wife about it.
S: That's fine ... we understand. It's a big decision.
P: OK, thank you. I'll call you in the morning.

Unit 8

2.09

1

(D = David; M = Margaret)
D: So, did you talk to Tom?
M: Yes.
D: And does he think you have a case?
M: Well, he says I certainly have a case, but it'll probably cost me more than it's worth to take them to court. So, I'm not sure what to do.
D: Well, I think you should sue, even if you only get minimal compensation. It's the principle that counts. People just can't go around spreading lies and rumors like that. What I mean is, you have to stand up for yourself, you know, show that it's important to you.
M: Yes, I agree. The only reason I'm hesitating is because I don't want any more bad publicity.
D: Well, it might not all be bad, and you know what they say, there's no such thing as bad publicity. But, if you want a second opinion, the best person to ask is Mike Zurack.
M: But, surely it's too late now, anyway? I mean, it's been almost three weeks since they published the article ...

2.10

2

(D = Daniel; R = Rani)
D: Well, I guess what I should have said is, "Yes, officer. I'm sorry, but I was in a terrible hurry."
R: But you didn't.
D: No, I tried to deny it, you know, make out that I couldn't possibly have been doing 100 miles an hour.
R: And?
D: And, he gave me a ticket and said that if it happened again I'd lose my driver's license.
R: Uh-oh. How much was the ticket?
D: Eighty dollars.
R: Ooh!
D: That's a lesson I won't forget in a hurry!
R: What, don't lie to a police officer?
D: No, it's better to be late than lose eighty dollars!

2.11

3

(R = Rachel; D = Doug)
R: Yeah, being on the jury was a really weird experience.
D: How long did it last?
R: Oh, a couple of weeks. It was fascinating, seeing how a court works, you know, how formal it all is and everything. We had to stay in a hotel overnight because we couldn't reach a verdict in one day. That was exciting.
D: Really? What was the case? Murder?
R: No, nothing that serious! It was your usual story of a guy setting up a company, borrowing money from banks, getting things on credit, and then using the company money to buy himself and his girlfriend some nice treats, you know, a Ferrari®, a Rolex™ ...
D: A couple of diamond rings!
R: Exactly. But the main issue was that the accused used to be a local politician. Didn't you read about it in the papers? It was big news at the time.
D: Yeah, now that you mention it, I do remember something ... John Gomez or something like that?
R: Yeah, John Ramirez.
D: And what did you decide?
R: Well, in the end, the verdict we returned was unanimous: guilty!

2.12

1

Well, I suppose it's not really an offense, not a serious offense at least. I just think people do it without thinking. They see other people do it, so they do it, too, and then you end up with a really filthy street. People should think more about the environment, about their surroundings, and perhaps rather than punishing them, they should have a deterrent fine or, or, you know, enough of a fine to make them think twice about doing it again, frankly.

2.13

2

Well, first of all, I think the damage these things do should not be underestimated. This is in no way a misdemeanor. It is extremely, extremely serious. It can have worldwide effects. It can lose businesses and individuals millions of dollars, and I think the punishment should reflect this. It's a difficult problem, because I think jail might be too harsh, but maybe we should consider community service. I mean, a lot of these people that commit this kind of crime are obviously extremely talented and have a lot of knowledge, and maybe that could be put to better use.

2.14

3

That's a tough call, because some people do it out of necessity. You know, a mom might do it for her children because she doesn't have a choice, but then some people just do it because they see other people doing it. You know, they're copying their friends. No ... nobody really gets hurt, unless it's a, you know, very small company, but, you know, nobody really gets hurt. So, I think it's one of those things where if you are going to punish them – something a bit softer - you know, therapy, counseling, to try and find out why they did it in the first place.

2.15

4

F: Well, I ... my main concern is that, you know, it's usually the super-rich who get away with this, and because they are so wealthy they can employ, you know, excellent lawyers, and they just wriggle out of it. Now I think the crime, I think it's an enormous crime, and I think it needs to be punished accordingly ...

M: In what way?

F: Well, I think a minimum of five years in jail, um ... because they are depriving people, you know, they're depriving the country of huge amounts of money by siphoning all this - you know, they're siphoning off their own wealth and I just don't think it's ... I think it's a really serious crime.

M: Right.

2.16

5

M: I think these guys are really evil, I mean, I think they're preying on innocent people and they're getting other people to do their dirty work by using the power of the word. I think they're very low. I really think they need to be punished severely, myself.

F: And how? How would you do that?

M: Well, I mean, you know, a long jail sentence I think is the only way. Get them off the streets and then they can't continue to do it anymore!

2.17

6

M: I actually don't think it's a crime at all. To be completely honest with you, I ... I love seeing it, I love seeing it, I've, you know, seen it all over the world. There's this place in New York where it's just everywhere and it's beautiful.

F: Really?

M: Yeah, and it brings the tourists in to look at it. You know, the locals love it, they add to it all the time. I mean, let's face it ... it's artwork, it really is. It's street art, and it's just beautiful, and I mean, I don't think there should be any punishment. If anything, these people should be paid for decorating and making our streets look brighter and, yeah, a more interesting place.

F: Wow.

2.18

(T = Tim; A = Anna)

T: Have you ever had anything stolen?

A: Yeah, I have, a brand-new car! I'd had it for less than a month.

T: You're kidding!

A: No!

T: You were insured, I hope?

A: Of course, but the insurance company wouldn't pay up.

T: What do you mean, wouldn't pay up? I mean, a brand-new car and you didn't insure it against theft?

A: Of course I did, and I was insured against theft ... but they just didn't want to pay up. It was a kind of complicated case ... Fortunately, my boyfriend at the time was a lawyer, so everything was fine, eventually.

T: How did it happen?

A: Well, you see, these three teenagers broke into my car ... they'd broken out of this special school for young offenders, and well, it seems they wanted to run away, so they decided to steal a car - my car! Anyway, while they were driving away they started arguing and drove the car straight into a tree.

T: Oh, no!

A: The car was totaled, completely totaled. I couldn't believe it when I saw it!

T: What about the kids?

A: Well, they weren't seriously hurt or anything, miraculously ... but they got arrested of course and sent back to the school. I was just relieved I'd taken out insurance, and I was already thinking I'd get another car with the insurance money ... maybe buy a used one this time and make a little money on the deal!

T: Sounds like a good idea ... but they wouldn't pay up, you said?

A: Yeah, when I explained to the insurance company what had happened, they told me they would need to see my insurance documents. So, I went down to the garage where my car had been towed, only to find that all my documents had mysteriously disappeared from the glove compartment.

T: So, what did you do?

A: Well, I went back to the insurance people and explained the situation, and they said it didn't matter because they had their own copy of the original contract and that, anyway, I wasn't covered.

T: But didn't you say ...?

A: Well, I thought I was covered, but they said I was insured against theft, but that the car had been found, so technically it was no longer stolen. The problem was that I wasn't covered for any damage incurred in the event of theft.

T: Surely they can't include such a ridiculous clause?

A: Well, apparently they can, and they did. The box with this condition had been checked. I hadn't read all the small print in the contract.

T: But why not? You really should have read it before signing it, you know. You were almost asking for trouble.

A: Thanks! Yeah, I suppose with the benefit of hindsight I should have, but I didn't bother at the time.

T: But couldn't you have asked your boyfriend to check it over for you? He was a lawyer, wasn't he? Or you could have asked a friend.

A: Well, I suppose I could have, but you know how these things are, they're standard forms, so I thought it would be fine. Anyway, I have no idea if I had actually checked the box or not. I might have, but I didn't have my copy, and so they might have just checked the box themselves so they didn't have to pay the equivalent of $8,000.

T: They wouldn't have done that, would they? That's a very serious accusation ...

A: I don't know. They certainly could have done it if they wanted to.

T: It would have been far too risky, I mean, you might have found your copy of the contract.

A: Not if they had it.
T: What do you mean?
A: Well, the man who ran the insurance-company office was the brother of the man who owned the garage where my car was towed. I believe they must have taken it from the car, along with all the other documents.
T: That sounds too far-fetched. There's no way they would do something like that, surely? I mean, I know you must have been upset at the time, and of course, you may be right ... but they couldn't have just stolen the documents like that!
A: I know it all sounds very unlikely, but it all seemed so suspicious at the time.
T: So, how did you finally resolve it?
A: Well, my boyfriend decided the best way to get the money back would be to sue the boys' school, which he did, and four years later we got the money back. Not that I saw much of it.
T: What, all swallowed up by the lawyers?
A: Yeah, my husband.
T: Oh, you married your boyfriend!
A: Yeah, to avoid the legal fees!

2.21

1
A: Have you heard? Robyn and Steve are getting married.
B: Really? No kidding? That's great news.

2
A: So, what do you think of the news?
B: What news?
A: Jeff is quitting the team.
B: What? But that can't be right! I mean, they just made him captain.

3
A: Katy says she's going to pay for the damages.
B: Yeah, right!
A: No, honestly, she is. She told me so herself.
B: Yeah? Well, I'll believe that when I see it.

4
A: So, anyway, Rick thinks the boss is going to give us an extra bonus this year.
B: Yeah, and pigs might fly!
A: No, really, that's what everybody's saying. He's really happy with the way business is going, and he wants to thank everybody for their hard work.
B: OK, I'll take your word for it, but I won't be convinced until I've got the money in my hand.

Unit 9

2.22

(A = Anne Kramer; D = Dr. Holmes)
A: Well, a very good morning to you and welcome to this week's edition of *Science Matters* with me, Anne Kramer. Today we have in our studio Dr. Simon Holmes, who is an expert on body clocks, circadian rhythms, and all things sleep-related, and who's going to tell us a little more about what it all means. Dr. Holmes, a very warm welcome to the show.
D: Thank you.
A: So, first of all, tell us, what exactly are circadian rhythms?
D: Well, Anne, circadian rhythms are essentially the changes that occur in our brain and in our body over the course of a day – our daily cycle of sleeping and waking, as it were. In fact "circadian" is a Latin word meaning "around a day." In other words, we operate in cycles of just over twenty-four hours, broadly in tune with the cycles of nature. And all animals and most plants live according to these rhythms. But in the animal kingdom, the rhythms vary according to whether an animal is a diurnal or nocturnal creature.
A: Diurnal or nocturnal? What's that exactly?
D: Well, basically that refers to whether the animal is awake during the day or during the night. As you know, we humans are diurnal, not nocturnal, creatures. That means that we are active during the day and sleep during the night. Whereas some animals, such as bats or owls or foxes, are largely nocturnal – they sleep by day and hunt by night.
A: I see. And how exactly does that tie in with our body clock? And what *is* a body clock, in fact?
D: Well, a body clock is actually just what it sounds like: it's a mechanism in the body that works like a clock and that regulates our circadian rhythms. Nobody knows exactly how it does this, but what we do know is that it interacts with signals, such as variations in sunlight and environmental activity, noise, and so on, and then it, as it were, fine-tunes our feelings of sleepiness and wakefulness to keep them in sync with the external cycle of dark and light.
A: I see. So, is that why we tend to wake up earlier in the summer and need more sleep in the winter, for example?
D: Exactly. But research has shown that the normal circadian rhythm for most people is, like I said, roughly twenty-four hours – twenty-four hours and eleven to fifteen minutes, to be precise; that's according to some research, although other scientists have put it slightly higher, at more like twenty-five hours.
A: Hmm, that's interesting, because you say that humans are diurnal, not nocturnal, creatures, but that's not true of everyone, is it? Is it not the case that some people are night owls and other people are early birds – by nature, maybe? What does science have to say about that?
D: Well, you're right, and it's important to stress that there is actually a lot of individual genetic variation in the pattern of circadian rhythms. It does seem that some people are genetically early risers and others genetically night-owlish, as it were. And these rhythms also fluctuate with age. Young children tend to get up very early and then, sometime around the onset of puberty, it all changes. Adolescents start needing a lot more sleep, and shift to waking and performing better later in the day. And then, around the age of twenty or so, it all changes again. And then, in later stages of life, it shifts *again*, and elderly people tend to get up earlier and earlier.
A: So, does that explain why most teenagers seem to be physically incapable of getting out of bed at a reasonable

time in the morning? Like my nephew, for example, who never surfaces until it's time for lunch?

D: Well, you could be right!

A: So, I can tell my sister that my nephew will just grow out of it, in due course?

D: Well, yes, he might! Or he might just be one of nature's night owls, I suppose.

A: And what happens when these circadian rhythms get disrupted? Say, if we cross over to a different time zone, or have to work night shifts? How does our body clock adapt?

D: Well, obviously, if we cross over several time zones all at once, as on a long international flight, for example, our body struggles to adapt to the change, and that's when we suffer from what's known as jet lag.

A: Right.

D: Now, jet lag is a condition that affects us when our body clock is out of sync with our destination time, and the body's natural rhythms are upset. And it manifests itself in all sorts of symptoms, such as fatigue, insomnia, irritability, nausea, loss of appetite, and even mild depression.

A: And what about night workers?

D: Yes, night workers, people who work on a night shift are also prone to all sorts of physical and psychological problems, especially if they aren't able to catch up with their sleep during the day.

A: And moving on now to sleep patterns, there are a number of interesting questions ...

2.23

James

(M = Mark; J = James)

M: You've been to the Himalayas, haven't you?

J: Yeah, I had this one unforgettable night up in the mountains, in Nepal. There was a full moon and we were up in the mountains. So we were in the jungle, below the snow line - we could see the snow line up in the mountains up ahead. But as the moon rose - because it was a very big, low, pale moon and we watched it come up through the mountains - we just couldn't take our eyes off it and the hours just passed, you know, just talking about the sky, basically, as you watched the moon rise and change color. It lit up the whole valley of the Himalayas and the snow and it was just beautiful, and of course then you'd choose a little area of the sky - we had binoculars and a telescope - and we just concentrated on a square and watched the shooting stars as they would fly past. And you could be guaranteed, within about five minutes, to see a shooting star.

M: Amazing.

J: And it just took all night. We had a little fire dug in the ground keeping us warm and some food and the next minute the sun was coming up.

M: Wow.

2.24

Rosie

(R = Rosie; M = Mark)

R: I went to the Country Thunder music festival and it's great. It's just completely wild. The whole experience is crazy, but I was really lucky because I was there when it was sunny and so there was no rain, and I think it's crucial when you're at a music festival to have at least one morning when you see the sun come up, so there's clearly no point in going to bed because everybody's up anyway and it's really noisy. So we just went out and went dancing and stuff and then sort of just hung out and sat on top of this hill and watched the sun come up and it was amazing, and it was really hard to stay awake all that time, but it was definitely worth it.

M: And how was the next day?

R: The next day was ... A lot of sleeping was involved in the next day, which is a difficult thing to achieve during Country Thunder!

2.25

Phillip

(P = Phillip; M = Mark)

P: A few years ago there was a talk-show host that came to do one show in Iowa and my friends and I are huge fans, so we really wanted to see the show. So, we went to the studio where they were filming the night before and camped out to try and get tickets and, unbelievably, there were about, I think, twenty people there in front of us, but we thought, oh, that's fine, we'll camp out, this'll be great, and we spent the whole night on the sidewalk and obviously just didn't sleep. It was a total nightmare. It was so cold, and we felt terrible the next day, but the thing that kept us going was that we were going to see this show - literally our hero, and go and see this talk-show host. The next day when they were about to film the show, they called the people in and had a line and we didn't realize we were the standby line, and they had twenty tickets and there were twenty people in front of us, and so we slept out the whole night and spent the whole night there and didn't even get to see the show, unfortunately. We were really upset.

M: That's awful. Did you see it on the TV when they showed it?

P: Yeah, we did, but it wasn't the same.

2.28

(K = Ken; C = Cathy)

K: Have I ever told you about my trip to Peru?

C: No, I don't think so. Where did you go?

K: I went to Machu Picchu, which was somewhere I'd always wanted to go.

C: Oh, wow, that must have been awesome.

K: Yes, it was great in a lot of ways - seeing the ruins is really awe-inspiring, and the setting is magical, right in the middle of the jungle - but in other ways it was kind of disappointing.

C: Oh, what do you mean?

K: Well, to begin with, it was packed with tourists, which meant that you couldn't really get a feel for the atmosphere of the place. I'd have liked to have gone there in the low season, when there are fewer visitors, but unfortunately I couldn't get time off work then.

C: Oh, right, that's too bad.

K: And another problem was the altitude. I started suffering from altitude sickness as soon as I arrived so I just went straight to bed. I think if I'd taken those altitude pills I would have been OK.

C. Yeah, I've heard about that. They say it takes a couple of days to acclimat ...

K: That's right, yeah ... I'd also been planning to get up early the next day to see the sun rise over the ruins, but, unfortunately, I was just too exhausted – I slept right through the alarm. Then the next day it was pouring rain so obviously there was no sunrise. And then it was time to leave, which was a shame. I only had two days there. It's too bad I couldn't have gone for longer.

C: Oh, well, at least you got some good pictures, hopefully?

K: No, that was another problem. It was raining so hard that my camera got soaked, and I couldn't take any pictures.

C: Oh, no! Still, at least you have your memories?

K: Yeah. I don't regret going, not in the least. But I think I'd like to go again with more time and maybe read more about the history beforehand so I could understand more about what I was seeing, and it would all be more meaningful. And maybe not go by myself next time, either. Maybe you'd like to come with me?

C: Uh, we'll see ...

Unit 10

2.32

(C = Chloe; B = Barbara)

C: Mom! You left the lights on again.

B: Excuse me?

C: You left the lights on again. When I came downstairs this morning, all the lights were on. And the computer and the printer were plugged in, and the TV was still on standby. Just think how much energy that was consuming.

B: Oh, this isn't going to turn into another carbon-footprint lecture, is it? It was bad enough you coming into the bathroom this morning and turning off the faucet while I was still brushing my teeth ...

C: Well, somebody has to think about our carbon footprint! You'd already been in the shower for five minutes before that. You could easily have a shower in two minutes instead of five.

B: Chloe, I hardly think that one person cutting down their shower by three minutes a day is going to have a huge effect on reducing our carbon footprint.

C: Yes, Mom, but if everybody said that, nothing would change. We all have to do our part to combat climate change. If you spent two minutes in the shower instead of five, you'd save 7,000 liters of water a year. And you'd have three extra minutes a day as well, that's 18 more hours per year you'd gain. Just imagine what you could do with all that extra time!

B: Chloe, I'm all for doing my part. I put out my paper and glass to be recycled. I get biodegradable plastic bags when I go grocery shopping. And I even reuse them sometimes.

C: Yes, Mom, but that's all you do. That's just a drop in the ocean. You're not going to save the planet unless you make some major changes in your lifestyle.

B: Like what, for example?

C: Like cycling to work instead of taking the car. Did you know that the average car produces three tons of CO_2 a year? If everybody in this country went to work by bike instead of taking the car, that's a million tons of CO_2 a year we'd save.

B: I hate to mention this, Chloe, but I don't remember you refusing any rides lately. And I also seem to recall that you were overjoyed when I showed up in the car to pick you up from Sam's the other night when it was pouring rain ...

C: Yeah ... well ... but when are you going to stop flying everywhere? You do know, don't you, that planes are *the* major contributor to climate change? If you go by bus, you cut back on emissions by ninety percent on every trip.

B: Oh, so planes are the bad guys, huh? I seem to remember parting with a considerable amount of money to pay for a certain ticket to Europe for a certain person's school trip. And to tell the truth, I can't see the point in giving up flying when the rest of the population are happily going everywhere by plane. Why be so eco-friendly that you make yourself miserable?

C: Honestly! You are so selfish. The ice caps are melting and the polar bears are dying and all you can think about is your own comfort.

B: Well, I'm not going to spend a week getting somewhere I could be in a few hours, just to make a couple of polar bears happy. Now, if the lecture's over, I'm going to make myself a cup of coffee and have my breakfast. I have a busy day ahead of me.

C: Mom! Those aren't even fair-trade coffee beans! Don't you realize how many people are being exploited ...?

2.33

I was a walker. Weather permitting, I would walk almost every day – two miles, sometimes three – determined that the knee injury and subsequent surgery that had derailed my running career two years prior would not affect my personal fitness or enjoyment of the outdoors. Although I missed the thrill and intensity of training for and participating in half-marathons, I had surprisingly come to enjoy walking a great deal. It had even become for me a form of daily meditation. There was something quite therapeutic about rising at dawn and going out into the still, cool early morning before the sun's warmth had evaporated the dew from the grass and the sounds of domestic activity had yet to make their way around the neighborhood. More often than not I would be accompanied by my dear friend Max. His silent companionship was just what I needed. Besides, he was probably the only friend who didn't need much convincing to get out of bed in the wee hours all in the name of exercise. Golden Retrievers are like that. I did some of my clearest thinking and got my best ideas while on these walks. It's true what they say that "the single best way to still one's mind is to put the body in motion."

Then Jessica came to visit. I hadn't seen my sister in years so when she showed up looking the picture of health and gushing about her newfound love of hiking my curiosity got the better of me and we decided to explore the hiking trails just outside of town together. I thought a temporary change in my routine would do me good and it wouldn't hurt to try something different. I certainly didn't expect to fall in love with hiking. Walking is to hiking what trampolining is to hang gliding. For starters there was more to think about including the level of difficulty, the terrain, and the gear. My fitness level was important in determining which trail we would attempt since steepness and elevation would be an issue. I fancied myself to be quite the walker, averaging fifteen miles a week, so we decided on a trail that was of moderate difficulty. This would soon prove to be an illustration of the saying that 'everything is relative.'

My usual walking shoes wouldn't suffice since the terrain was expected to be considerably more rugged than the suburban streets I was used to, so we went shopping for hiking boots and a pair of trekking poles to provide stability and lessen the stress on my knees. A few protein bars and a hydration pack completed my ensemble and we were ready.

During the hike there were several things that I was unprepared for. In spite of the seemingly gradual slope of the trail I was unprepared for the intensity of the workout. I was walking much slower but my heart rate was higher than it was when I walked on flat roads at twice the speed. Not only that, but my muscles and my lungs were responding in a way that I found to be, in a word, exhilarating. Even with the poles I felt like I was getting a full body workout. I had to engage my core muscles to navigate the uneven terrain. On the other hand, the scenery, the fresh mountain air, the smells and sounds of nature were an absolute delight to my senses. But what was most surprising of all was that I thoroughly enjoyed not just the companionship but the conversation, that is, when I could find enough breath to have one. And the sense of accomplishment we felt when we got to the summit and surveyed the breathtaking view of the valley below was unparalleled.

2.36

1

I wear these shoes mainly for work. I'm on my feet all day, so I really need practical, low-heeled shoes that are going to be long-lasting. They're a little scuffed and they could use some polish, but I don't think anybody looks at my feet, so I can probably get away with it.

2

I've had these sneakers for about three years now, and to tell you the truth, I wear them day in, day out. They're probably not the trendiest style out there, but I tried on lots of different pairs, and the others were nowhere near as comfortable as these. They're a little worn out now, but I hate buying shoes, so I always make mine last longer than they probably should.

3

I saw these shoes on sale and I couldn't resist buying them. I wear size 14 and I need a wide fitting too, so sometimes it's hard to get shoes that fit right and look good too. I mean, they're just classic shoes, but I think they're reasonably stylish, and they're good for wearing on occasions when I need to dress up.

4

I got these shoes for my sister's wedding, to go with a red outfit. There's a matching purse too. They're designer shoes, and they're by far the most extravagant ones I've ever bought; they cost an arm and a leg. And they're not the most comfortable of shoes, either – I had to take them off after the ceremony and again after all the pictures were taken because my feet were killing me, and to be honest with you, I haven't worn them since. But I love the little pointy toes, and I think they make me look elegant, even though I tend to wobble on the high heels.

2.37

(P = Poppy; M = Margaret Banks)

P: Welcome back. Now, as promised, I'm joined in the studio by psychologist Margaret Banks, who has written a fascinating book called *Let Your Shoes Do The Talking*, which promises to help us discover what people's shoes really say about them. Margaret, welcome.

M: Hello, Poppy.

P: Now, we asked some of our audience today to bring in their favorite pair of shoes. Margaret, would you care to look them over? What kind of person do you think would wear these, for example?

M: Hmm, well, I'd say that these shoes certainly suggest someone who is creative and idealistic, who perhaps has an alternative, slightly hippy lifestyle. The shoes are designed to be comfortable and good for your feet. And the vibrant color indicates to me somebody who is pretty self-assured and comfortable with herself.

P: Great! Well, we'll be finding out soon if your predictions about the wearer are correct. In the meantime, would you mind taking a look at these shoes?

M: Oh, yes. These shoes tell me that their owner is fashion-conscious and glamorous. She's certainly no shrinking violet, but probably a little more flirtatious and feminine, and less domineering than somebody who might wear boots, for instance. They're really for a woman who's looking to make a red-carpet entrance.

P: I see. Very interesting ... And how about these?

M: Well, these shoes look like they belong to a man, is that correct?

P: Um, no ...

M: OK, well, they're actually men's shoes, so they probably belong to somebody who is somewhat older than the other women, who is likely to be quiet, conservative, and conventional. She is a follower rather than a leader, and possibly not very dynamic. She is trying hard to fit into what she feels is a man's world.

P: Oh. I see. Um ... OK, finally, what about these?

M: OK, well, clearly the owner is young and trendy, and someone with a carefree and fairly casual approach to life. The shoes give off a playful, fun vibe. They say, "I don't care about expensive designer fashions, there are so many other things that are far more interesting."

P: Fantastic! Margaret, thank you so much for your assessments. Now it's time to reveal how accurate your predictions were ...

2.38

1

(Y = Yvonne; M = Man)

Y: Excuse me, sir. Can you sign this petition to save the rainforests?

M: Well, it's a good cause, but I don't really see the point in signing a petition. Nobody's ever going to pay attention to a few signatures.
Y: Oh, I disagree. I think it's definitely worth making our voices heard. If we got several thousand signatures, I think people will sit up and listen, and then our message will start to hit home.
M: Well, OK then, but I still don't think it'll make any difference.

2.39

2

(K = Kathy; S = Sally)
K: Oh, Sally, they look gorgeous! You should get them.
S: Yes, but they're so expensive. What's the point of spending so much money on shoes you're only going to wear once?
K: Oh, go ahead! It's your sister's wedding, it's once in a lifetime. Treat yourself! You'll regret it if you don't buy them.
S: Well, it's a lot of money, but ... OK. If you really think so.

2.40

3

(M = Matt; T = Tom)
M: Hey, Tom, have you seen this ad for a fitness trainer at the Carlton Health Center? You should apply.
T: What's the use of applying? They're bound to get tons of applications, from people far more experienced than me.
M: Oh, come on, nothing ventured, nothing gained. You might as well try. You never know, you could get shortlisted for an interview.
T: Yeah, but even if I got an interview, I wouldn't get the job. I'm terrible at interviews.
M: Oh, come on, don't be defeatist! You're a qualified trainer. Just send in an application! It's worth giving it a try.
T: Well, OK then, if it'll make you happy. But I think it's a waste of time, frankly.

2.41

4

(J = Jess; M = Maria)
J: Hey, guess what? Sarah and Ruth are going sailing next summer, and they want me to go with them.
M: Jess, what a fantastic opportunity! You have to go.
J: Hmm, I'm not sure. I've never done any sailing before. What if I get seasick? And what if I don't like sailing?
M: Well, you should cross that bridge when you come to it. I think you should go for it. You'll really enjoy it.
J: Well, maybe you're right. Maybe I should give it a try.

2.42

(S = Stephanie; P = Pam)
S: Come on, you know you want to!
P: No, absolutely not! It's out of the question! I'll freeze!
S: No, you won't. You'll love it. Come on, just for me! Mary went last week, you know. She loved it.
P: Honestly, I'm not in the mood and I don't have a swimsuit anyway.
S: I told you, I have an extra one. You can borrow it. Look.
P: Hah, you must be joking! That's awful! I'm not wearing that.
S: OK, OK, you can have this one. It's brand-new!
P: Hmm, well ... I'm still not sure I feel like it.
S: Come on, it'll do you good. Just think how much better you'll feel when you get out!
P: Hmm ... Oh, all right. You've twisted my arm. But I get to use the towel first when we get out!
S: I can live with that! Let's go.

Unit 11

2.43

1

(G = Gina; K = Kevin)
G: Gosh, there are lots! Like "blogging."
K: Oh, yeah.
G: Anything to do with ...
K: Anything internet-wise, yeah.
G: Yeah, absolutely. "World Wide Web."
K: Even "online." I mean, it's two words that already existed, but put them together and suddenly it's a whole new ...
G: Yeah, completely, I think, you know ...
K: "Surfing."
G: Web surfing.
K: Surfing, which again already existed but is different now. It's amazing.

2.44

2

(T = Trudy; J = Jason)
T: "Mellifluous." Such a nice-sounding word. It was used to describe an actor's voice: mellow, flowing - I just thought it was beautiful. How about you?
J: I heard this thing called "impostor syndrome," which is something that apparently we, well, a lot of us feel, which is that we don't really have the skills that we say we do, or we feel inadequate about those - you know, about a certain job we're doing, which I thought was really interesting.

2.45

3

(Carolina)
Well, I think there's a lot of words in English that are currently in Spanish. A lot to do with technology - for instance, we say "download," which is not a Spanish word, it's English. We also - we say "lunch" - it's very bad because of course it's *comida* in Spanish, but now we've inherited this word - lunch.

2.46

4

(C = Carla; M = Marco)
C: It was, I think, "sidewalk."
M: Really?
C: Yes, it's very strange for me, you know, because I didn't know the word for the thing that you walk on when you are off the road.
M: And how did you learn that?
C: I was in New York and they said to me, "You have to cross onto the other sidewalk." I didn't know what they said,

what are you talking about, you know, but yes, so that was when I figured it out. It was great.

2.51

(M = Matt; S = Sue)

M: So, are you saying that people who socialize online are all freaks and weirdos?

S: No, you know I didn't say that! You're deliberately misconstruing my words! My point was that it can be a problem, you know, you don't know who you're talking to ... and they could be ... yes, I guess, they could be weirdos or something ... I mean, you never know ...

M: So, what are you implying? That we should all stop using chat rooms and networking sites and whatever?

S: No, that's not my point ... and you know it ... what I want to say is that we need to be careful, that's all ... you know, don't give away too many personal details ... don't make yourself vulnerable ...

M: But surely it's much safer to talk to somebody at a distance than to talk to a stranger in a nightclub or a bar ...

S: You just don't understand ... I'm not saying that it's dangerous to chat with people online ... my point is that you have to be really careful when it comes to arranging to meet them in real life ... you just don't know who they are, or what they want ...

Unit 12

2.54

1

Well, I don't think it's such a good idea to give money because, um, well, I'd be really worried that somebody would spend it on alcohol instead of food, or, you know, because they always say, like, "Can you spare some change?" or whatever. So what I think I might do is, buy a sandwich or a hot drink or something in the winter and give it to them there, or maybe, find some old clothes.

2.55

2

Yes, I usually put a few coins in the donation bucket, um, I mean, obviously if it's, if I'm not in a hurry and if it's easy to get to my change. Um, the thing I don't do is, I don't believe in giving money to beggars.

2.56

3

Well, I never give money to anybody. As far as I'm concerned, it just encourages them. You know, I pay my taxes and I don't see *why* I should help these people. Frankly, I just think it's sheer laziness. I mean, I think they could get up off their butts and get a job if they really wanted to. It's just that they don't want to work.

2.57

4

Well, I don't mind giving money to people who are doing something to earn it, I mean, you know, I'd rather they actually did something to earn the money, you know, like street artists or musicians. I mean, I think somebody who is actually playing music, it puts people in a good mood on the way to work, so, you know, I usually give those people something. A few cents.

2.58

5

Yeah, I never give money on the street anymore. I do give money through my company's matching gift program, um, to non-profit organizations that, um, I'm particularly concerned about. And that way I know where it's going and it also means that you're giving extra money if your employers do a matching gift.

2.59

6

Oh, it really annoys me. These people trying to wash your windows. I don't see why I should give money for cleaning my windshield. I haven't, I haven't asked them to do it. I think it's about time the government did something about it, because it really is annoying. No, I never give them anything.

2.61

(K = Kiera; J = Jade)

K: Hey, Jade, how you doing'?

J: Fine, you?

K: Fine. Hey, we're going to Tom's grandparents' cabin in the mountains this weekend. Want to come?

J: Oh, I'd love to ... But I can't ...

K: Why?

J: I promised I'd take care of my neighbor's cat. She's on vacation. I have to go over and feed it every day - and I promised I'd water the plants and ...

K: Hey, the plants'll survive for a weekend without water, won't they?

J: Yeah, I guess so ...

K: And you can put some food out for the cat ... I mean, it's not like a dog, you don't have to take it for walks or anything, right?

J: No, but ... well, you know, I promised ... and, well ...

K: I know, you hate letting people down! You and your guilty conscience. You need to lighten up a little! Hey - I've got an idea!

J: What?

K: You know my cousin Beth?

J: Yeah ...

K: Well, she doesn't live very far from you ... and she'd do anything, absolutely anything, for a little extra money ... why don't you ask her to do it for you? Give her a few dollars, you know ... you'll be doing both of you a favor ...

J: Well, I don't know ... I mean, she's only fifteen ... what if something happened? What if she lost the key? Or ... or ...

K: Or what? Oh, you're such a worrier! What can possibly go wrong? Look, if it makes you feel better, give her your cell phone number - then, if anything does go wrong, she can call you ... and if you really feel you need to, you can make an extra copy of the key and leave it with my mom or something ...

J: Yeah, I guess ...

K: And you can go with a clear conscience ...

J: Yeah, but ...

K: No buts ... oh, and almost forgot to tell you ... Paul's coming ...

2.62

Conversation 1

A: Did you call the restaurant?

B: Oh, I'm sorry, it totally slipped my mind! I'll do it right now.

A: Yeah, well, don't waste any time – there might not be any tables left!

2.63

Conversation 2

A: Oh, hi there.

B: Hello.

A: Look. I've been wanting to talk to you about the other night.

B: Oh.

A: Yeah, well, the thing is, I've been thinking about what you said and how I reacted and I think I owe you an apology. I overdid it.

B: You certainly did. You were completely out of line! All I said was that you played better before you started spending half your life in front of a computer screen.

A: Yeah, yeah, I know. I'm sorry. I completely overreacted. Friends?

B: Yes – this time! You owe me dinner, though.

A: OK, OK.

2.64

Conversation 3

A: Listen, I'd rather not talk about it, if you don't mind.

B: Sorry! I had no idea you were so touchy today!

A: Can we just drop it, please? I'm not in the mood.

2.65

Conversation 4

A: Excuse me ... but I think that's my bag.

B: Sorry? What did you say?

A: I think you have my bag.

B: What? Oh. Oh, yes, oh, dear. I'm so sorry. I thought it was mine.

A: That's all right. Don't worry about it. It's an easy mistake to make.

2.66

Conversation 5

A: How did the meeting go yesterday? Sorry I wasn't there, by the way.

B: Sorry! Is that all you can say? I had to deal with all those people by myself and all you can say is sorry? It's just not good enough. You think you can apologize and everything's going to be OK? Well, it doesn't work that way.

A: Look, I really, really am very sorry. I know I left you in the lurch. But it won't happen again. I promise.

B: Yeah, well, it better not!

2.67

Conversation 6

We regret to inform you that tonight's concert has been canceled due to circumstances beyond our control. We apologize for any inconvenience caused. All tickets will be refunded at the box office.

2.69

(K = Kelly; L = Laura)

K: You know, I was thinking, I'd really like to get involved a bit more in the community, maybe do some sort of volunteer work.

L: Oh yeah? Why?

K: Well, you know, ever since Maddie started kindergarten, I've had a bit more time on my hands, and ...

L: Must be nice!

K: Ha, yeah, I can't say I mind all that much, but I sometimes feel like I could be doing more to make the most of my time. I remember when I was pregnant, I had so much help from my friends, my family ...

L: I remember that – I took care of both your dogs for a couple of weeks!

K: Exactly! And I'm truly grateful, which is why I'd like to pass on that kindness.

L: What about doing the same thing for others? There are a lot of dogs that could use your assistance.

K: What a great idea, but I don't know where I'd begin.

L: I'm pretty sure that there's an organization near my place that works with dogs – walking them, getting homeless dogs adopted, stuff like that. I think they're called the Greenfield Animal Shelter – why not look them up online and shoot them an email?

K: I definitely will – hopefully I can lend a hand. Now, I just need to figure out what to say to them ...

Phonetic symbols

Single vowels

/ɪ/	ship	/ʃɪp/	(build, business, gym, spinach, women)
/i/	need	/nid/	(bean, he, key, niece, people, sardine)
/ʊ/	put	/pʊt/	(could, foot, woman)
/u/	pool	/pul/	(flew, fruit, lose, rule, shoe, through, two)
/e/	egg	/eg/	(breakfast, friend, many, said)
/ə/	about	/əˈbaʊt/	(arrive, husband, lemon, nervous, police)
/ɔ/	saw	/sɔ/	(abroad, caught, talk, thought, water)
/æ/	back	/bæk/	(bag, fast, laugh)
/ʌ/	bus	/bʌs/	(blood, does, enough, onion)
/ɑ/	father	/ˈfɑðər/	(car, heart, pasta)

Diphthongs

/ɜr/	verb	/vɜrb/	(learn, curly, skirt, word)
/eɪ/	face	/feɪs/	(break, eight, fail, say, they)
/ɔɪ/	boy	/bɔɪ/	(noise)
/oʊ/	nose	/noʊz/	(although, coat, know, shoulder)
/aɪ/	white	/waɪt/	(buy, die, eye, height, high, my)
/aʊ/	mouth	/maʊθ/	(town)
/ɪr/	hear	/hɪr/	(near)

Consonants

/p/	pen	/pen/	(happy)
/b/	bag	/bæg/	(rabbit)
/t/	tea	/ti/	(ate, fatter, worked)
/d/	dog	/dɔg/	(address, played)
/ʧ/	chip	/ʧɪp/	(natural, watch)
/ʤ/	jazz	/ʤæz/	(age, bridge, generous)
/k/	cake	/keɪk/	(chemistry, kitchen, knock, toothache)
/g/	girl	/gɜrl/	(foggy)
/f/	fat	/fæt/	(different, laugh, photographer)
/v/	very	/ˈveri/	(of)
/θ/	thin	/θɪn/	(think)
/ð/	these	/ðiz/	(they)
/s/	snake	/sneɪk/	(city, message, race)
/z/	zoo	/zu/	(has)
/ʃ/	sugar	/ˈʃʊgər/	(description, machine)
/ʒ/	measure	/ˈmeʒər/	(garage, usual)
/m/	map	/mæp/	(summer)
/n/	name	/neɪm/	(sunny, knife)
/ŋ/	ring	/rɪŋ/	(thanks, tongue)
/h/	house	/haʊs/	(who)
/l/	leg	/leg/	(hill, possible)
/r/	road	/roʊd/	(carry, write)
/w/	wine	/waɪn/	(one, why)
/j/	yes	/jes/	(used, usual)

Stress

Word stress is shown by underlining the stressed syllable: *water, amazing, Japanese*.

Letters of the alphabet

/eɪ/	/i/	/e/	/aɪ/	/oʊ/	/u/	/ɑr/
Aa	Bb	Ff	Ii	Oo	Qq	Rr
Hh	Cc	Ll	Yy		Uu	
Jj	Dd	Mm			Ww	
Kk	Ee	Nn				
	Gg	Ss				
	Pp	Xx				
	Tt					
	Vv					
	Zz					

Irregular verbs

Infinitive	Simple past	Past participle
beat	beat	beaten
become	became	become
begin	began	begun
bend	bent	bent
bet	bet	bet
bite	bit	bitten
blow	blew	blown
break	broke	broken
bring	brought /brɔt/	brought /brɔt/
build /bɪld/	built /bɪlt/	built /bɪlt/
burn	burned/burnt	burned/burnt
burst	burst	burst
buy /baɪ/	bought /bɔt/	bought /bɔt/
catch	caught /kɔt/	caught /kɔt/
choose	chose	chosen
come	came	come
cost	cost	cost
cut	cut	cut
deal /dil/	dealt /delt/	dealt /delt/
dig	dug	dug
draw	drew	drawn
drink	drank	drunk
drive	drove	driven
eat	ate	eaten
fall	fell	fallen
feed	fed	fed
feel	felt	felt
fight	fought /fɔt/	fought /fɔt/
find	found	found
fly	flew	flown
forget	forgot	forgotten
forgive	forgave	forgiven
freeze	froze	frozen
get	got	gotten
give	gave	given
go	went	gone/been
grow	grew	grown
hang	hung/hanged	hung/hanged
have	had	had
hear	heard /hɜrd/	heard /hɜrd/
hide	hid	hidden
hit	hit	hit
hold	held	held
hurt /hɜrt/	hurt /hɜrt/	hurt /hɜrt/
keep	kept	kept
kneel	kneeled/knelt	kneeled/knelt
know	knew /nju/	known
lay	laid	laid
lead	led	led
leave	left	left
lend	lent	lent
let	let	let

Infinitive	Simple past	Past participle
lie	lay/lied	lied/lain
light	lit	lit
lose	lost	lost
make	made	made
mean	meant /ment/	meant /ment/
meet	met	met
must	had to	had to
pay	paid	paid
put	put	put
read /rid/	read /red/	read /red/
ride	rode	ridden
ring	rang	rung
rise	rose	risen
run	ran	run
say	said /sed/	said /sed/
see	saw /sɔ/	seen
sell	sold	sold
send	sent	sent
set	set	set
shake	shook	shaken
shine	shone	shone
shoot	shot	shot
show	showed	shown
shrink	shrank	shrunk
shut	shut	shut
sing	sang	sung
sink	sank	sunk
sit	sat	sat
sleep	slept	slept
slide	slid	slid
speak	spoke	spoken
spend	spent	spent
split	split	split
spoil	spoiled/spoilt	spoiled/spoilt
spread	spread	spread
stand	stood	stood
steal	stole	stolen
stick	stuck	stuck
swear	swore	sworn
swell	swelled	swollen/swelled
swim	swam	swum
take	took /tʊk/	taken
teach	taught /tɔt/	taught /tɔt/
tear	tore	torn
tell	told	told
think	thought /θɔt/	thought /θɔt/
throw	threw	thrown
understand	understood	understood
wake	woke	woken
wear	wore /wɔr/	worn
win	won /wʌn/	won /wʌn/
write	wrote	written

Macmillan Education
Companies and representatives throughout the world
American Inside Out Evolution. Student's Book Advanced

Adapted by Petter Maggs and Catherine Smith
Content Writers: Ben Naismith, James Michael Ubriaco and Lavaughn John
Macmillan is a registered trademark.
First edition published 2018

ISBN: 978-607-473-626-7

Based on New American Inside Out Student's Book Advanced
D.R. © Macmillan Publishers, S.A. de C.V. 2010
Published under license from Macmillan Publishers Ltd.

Director of Languages Brazil: Patrícia Souza
Editorial Manager: Patricia Muradas
Art Editor: Jean Aranha
Content Editors: Cintia Zaitune and Larissa Vannucci
Digital Editor: Ana Paula Girardi
Concept design: Martha Tadaieski
Page make-up: Figurattiva Editorial
Illustrations: Gustavo Gialuca
Graphic Production: Kelly Gobbo and Tatiane Romano
Proofreaders: Edward Willson and Larissa Vazquez
Photographic research: Cintia Zaitune, Denis Araujo, Jean Aranha and Marcia Sato
Image Processing: Denis Araujo and Jean Aranha
Cover concept and design: Jean Aranha
Cover photo: Steve Keller | Dreamstime.com

The authors and publishers would like to thank the following for permission to reproduce their photographs:
iStock / jacoblund p8; iStock / Steve Debenport p8; iStock / michaeljung p8; iStock / martin-dm p9; iStock / BartekSzewczyk p10; iStock / Tinpixels p10; iStock / Poike p11; iStock / Dusan Ilic p12; iStock / zoff-photo p12; iStock / AntonioGuillem p12; iStock / DGLimages p13; iStock / Halfpoint p14; iStock / Willowpix p14; iStock / AntonioGuillem p16; iStock / AdShooter p18; iStock / Piotr Krzeslak p18; iStock / Aksenovko p18; iStock / ValentynVolkov p18; iStock / Merlas p18; iStock / EMPPhotography p18; iStock / mbbirdy p18; iStock / PeopleImages p18; iStock / Aleksej p19; iStock / MaboHH p20; iStock / LarisaBlinova p20; iStock / robynmac p20; iStock / Nikada p21; iStock / travnikovstudio p22; iStock / xijian p23; iStock / duckycards p23; iStock / benedek p23; iStock / MARCELOKRELLING p24; iStock / Fudio p24; iStock / Tatiana Volgutova p24; iStock / filadendron p26; iStock / DavidCallan p27; iStock / McIninch p27; iStock / pawel.gaul p28; iStock / sanjeri p29; iStock / Torsakarin p30; iStock / Ababsolutum p31; iStock / RudyBalasko p32; iStock / heyengel p33; iStock / extravagantni p33; iStock / AndreyKrav p34; iStock / DMEPhotography p35; iStock / filadendron p35; iStock / DenisTangneyJr p35; iStock / MarioGuti p36; iStock / Terraxplorer p36; iStock / JohnnyGreig p36; iStock / onlyyouqj p37; iStock / RelaxFoto.de p37; iStock / olli0815 p39; iStock / Martyn Hayes p41; iStock / georgeclerk p41; iStock / bernardbodo p42; iStock / vadimguzhva p43; iStock / Svitlana Unuchko p43; iStock / ElenaNichizhenova p45; iStock / ferrantraite p46; iStock / monkeybusinessimages p48; iStock / snedorez p49; iStock / gilaxia p50; iStock / andresr p51; iStock / LuckyBusiness p52; iStock / StockRocket p53; iStock / teekid p53; iStock / saiko3p p54; iStock / Lordn p54; iStock / v_zaitsev p55; iStock / PeopleImages p55; iStock / JulNichols p56; iStock / Makidotvn p56; iStock / g-stockstudio p57; iStock / bowie15 p57; iStock / pixologicstudio p60; iStock / CTRPhotos p60; iStock / Popartic p60; iStock / GA161076 p60; iStock / calvinng p60; iStock / domin_domin p60; Alamy / Fotoarena p62; Warren Medical Museum p62; iStock / max-kegfire p 62; iStock / youngoggo p63; iStock / wundervisuals p64; iStock / andresr p65; iStock / ClarkandCompany p65; iStock / deimagine p66; iStock / macniak p67; iStock / FatCamera p70; iStock / YakobchukOlena p70; iStock / baona p70; iStock / tzara p72; iStock / hkuchera p72; iStock / artisteer p72; iStcok / gece33 p72; iStock / BongkarnThanyakij p72; iStock / metamorworks p73; iStock / Wavebreak p74; iStock / wonry p76; iStock / PhonlamaiPhoto p77; iStock / vchal p77; iStock / farakos p77; iStock / da-kuk p78; iStock / BahadirTanriover p78; iStock / hocus-focus p79; iStock / bowie15 p80; iStock / kupicoo p80; iStock / anyaberkut p80; iStock / Dangubic p81; iStock / MarianVejcik p82; iStock / tommaso79 p85; iStock / AndreyPopov p85; iStock / vm p85; iStock / Wavebreakmedia p85; iStock / CathyKaplan p86; iStock / labsas p86; iStock / biffspandex p86; iStock / bmcent1 p87; iStock / LaraBelova p87; iStock / Juan Jose Napuri p88; iStock / AndreyPopov p89; iStock / Sezeryadigar p89; iStock / gbh007 p91; iStock / solidcolours p91; iStock / leaf p92; iStock / ljubaphoto p92; iStock / shaunl p93; iStock / Smileus p93; iStock / izusek p93; iStock / AndreyPopov p94; iStock / jeffbergen p96; iStock / uschools p96; iStock / santypan p96; iStock / franckreporter p96; iStock / pixelparticle p97; iStock / DragonImages p97; iStock / Pedal-Power-Photos p98; iStock / fotografixx p99; iStock / PytyCzech p99; iStock / LauriPatterson p101; iStock / DNY59 p104; iStock / zhaojiankang p104; iStock / chokkicx p104; iStock / ljubaphoto p105; iStock / laflor p105; iStock / sculpies p106; iStock / peffan p106; Alamy / Fotoarena p106; iStock / NicolasMcComber p107; iStock / Tom Merton p108; iStock / Tom Merton p108; iStock / Solovyova p109; iStock / captainsecret p110; iStock / BeylaBalla p1 10; iStock / Sashkinw p110; iStock / Jillwt p110; iStock / aldomurillo p110; iStock / yavdat p110; iStock / Igor Alecsander p111; iStock / max-kegfire p111; iStock / fotostorm p111; iStock / GlobalStock p111; iStock / DorianGray p111; iStock / Riccardo_Mojana p111; iStock / Bill-Livingstone p111; iStock / clubfoto p111; iStock / T_Bailey p111; iStock / popovaphoto p111; iStock / sanjeri p112; iStock / apichon_tee p114; iStock / csy302 p114; iStock / shapecharge p114; iStock / Phaelnogueira p114; iStock / Geber86 p115; iStock / Daviles p116; iStock / Krakozawr p116; iStock / filadendron p116; iStock / StationaryTraveller p116; iStock / Gal_Istvan p117; iStock / PRImageFactory p117; iStock / monkeybusinessimages p117; iStock / Tinpixels p118; iStock / ra2studio p119; iStock / hh5800 p119; iStock / ilbusca p121; iStock / aldra p123; iStock / Paul Bradbury p123; iStock / fightbegin p124; iStock / monkeybusinessimages p124; iStock / robyvannucci p124; iStock / Quanthem p124; iStock / Hung_Chung_Chih p126; iStock / LightFieldStudios p126; iStock / coldsnowstorm p126; iStock / PeopleImages p127; iStock / skynesher p128; iStock / Dean Mitchell p128; iStock / andresr p128; iStock / Blackzheep p128; iStock / Ales-A p129; iStock / UberImages p129; iStock / Kurhan p130; iStock / Wavebreakmedia p130; iStock / mihailomilovanovic p130; iStock / DmitriMaruta p130; iStock / Anatoliy Sizov p130; iStock / DMEPhotography p131; iStock / shapecharge p131; iStock / shironosov p131; iStock / ajfletch p132; iStock / Jarin13 p132; iStock / monkeybusinessimages p132; iStock / andykatz p132; iStock / gorodenkoff p133; iStock / BONNINSTUDIO p133; iStock / Alexey Bezrodny p133; iStock / Highwaystarz-Photography p133; iStock / duncan1890 p134; iStock / talevr p134; iStock / vblinov p134; iStock / Serhii Tsyhanok p134; iStock / RossHelen p147; iStock / Imgorthand p149; iStock / Halfpoint p153;

The team of publishers of the series is especially thankful to Cristina Neville and her team for all the support throughout all the stages of the editing process of this publication.

CANIEM No. 2275

Macmillan Publishers S.A. de C.V. Insurgentes Sur 1886
Col. Florida, CP 01030
Álvaro Obregón
Ciudad de México
Tel: +52 (55) 5482 2200
elt@grupomacmillan.com

www.grupomacmillan.com
www.macmillan.com.mx
www.macmillanenglish.com

Printed in Brazil

This book was printed in June, 2018 by: Eskenazi Indústria Gráfica Ltda, Avenida Miguel Frias Vasconcelos, 1023 - Jaguaré - São Paulo - SP.